STRAIGHTEN UP!
BOSS REGGAE FROM PAMA

The authorised illustrated story of Pama Records

John Bailey

CONTENTS

FOREWORD

HARRY PALMER

PAMA RECORDS began out of a sense of desperation. I had owned a record shop (Happy Sound) in Harlesden, London and founded a small musical group called "The Shadracks" which played at local clubs in/and around London.

I next discovered a female singer which we named Joyce Bond, releasing her first single which I wrote titled: "Do The Teasy" released on Island Records. This was a sort of instant hit playing on Pirate Radio Stations. Sadly, we never received a statement nor any payment on this from the record company. Other singers and groups clambered to us seeking stardom. One of which we named "The Mohawks."

Approaching other Record Companies, we got really tired of the frequent refusals and so my brothers, Jeff, Carl and I came to the conclusion that, why not launch our own Label - 'PAMA.' Of course, The Mohawks CHAMP became a hit and was sought after by foreign companies, like Atlantic and Phillips in Holland and other companies far and wide. PAMA became a focal point in the music industry and we backed this up by opening quite a number of record shops all over London – 'SOUNDVILLE.' We opened 11 shops in all and this helped to boost sales of our own releases.

In 1968, I visited Jamaica and signed quite a number of artistes and record producers – Bunny Lee, Lee 'Scratch' Perry, Derrick Harriott, Clancy Eccles, Lloyd Matador, etc.

A flood of great reggae productions flooded in from Jamaica and of course we started producing British Reggae and R & B Music; from here saw the beginning of "Rock Steady" flowing off SKA and Blue Beat.

By the end of 1968, we outdid Trojan which was an Island Records Label and very much all the best sellers are on the PAMA and the other labels we launched to handle productions from various producers.

I retired some years ago and now Phoenix has agreed to keep this force going with their relaunch of PAMA in a very big way.

Sure, I know that from humble begins PAMA became a legend and a musical force to be reckoned with.

Keep on rocking, keep on ska-ing and steady on the rock!

Harry Palmer

INTRODUCTION

When putting together The Story of Skinhead Reggae 1968-1972 I was told it was a work long overdue. That was almost a decade ago and at the time I could find little or no contact with the Palmer brothers and it seems that Pama was destined to remain in the mists of time, their vibrant colourful and sometime risqué album covers and iconic labels would maybe never see the light of day again.

Well all that has changed on two fronts - The entire Pama back catalogue is now being re-mastered and made available in high quality audio for the first time and the iconic images are getting a new lease of life thanks to Phoenix Music International.

Trojan will always be first on the lips of the general public when reggae in its original guise is mentioned but to the connoisseur and in that I include the original skinhead of '69 Pama is up there as well, as by the end of the swinging 60s they were the two main rivals fighting it out for their fair share of the reggae market. Trojan by this time were hitting the charts on a regular basis and began sweetening the music but the raw unpretentious sounds were coming from another company barely a mile away in Harlesden, it was of course Pama.

What a delight it was to purchase a boss reggae tune back then for around 7/- or should that be 35p, but an ever bigger bonus to find it was on the iconic Punch label or the equally desirable Camel label, or the Crab imprint. Then Pama started issuing the best of their label series, what a bargain a dozen tracks for just 15/6, many tracks had been hard or impossible to get hold of when first released as Pama didn't enjoy the distribution of their close rival.

That brings me onto the skinhead movement that emerged in the late 60s who were conceivably the most misunderstood youth subculture of all time. To the uninitiated the skinhead involvement in the rapid rise of Jamaican music is seen as curious. When the psychedelic 60s hit Britain the mods split into a wide variety of fashion and styles including hippies. This is the time when the skinhead was first defined with the hard mods, who couldn't empathise with the hippie hedonistic attitude of flowers and beads, showing a pride in the traditional English working-class look. The new movement was a coming together with newly arrived migrants from Jamaica who brought with them the vision of Kingston's street tough youth, so with a little influence from the rude boy back in Jamaica the traditional skinhead was born.

Reggae was evolving from rocksteady distinguishable by the faster beat marked out by the drummer using the hi-hat, heavy organ lines, lower mixing of the bass and electronically doubled rhythm guitar strokes. What was in no doubt by the summer of '69 the skinhead and reggae were inseparable, a phase that lasted until early 1972.

The success for Trojan with the British charts was thanks in the main to the skinhead embracing the music and adopting it as their own although Harry Palmer cited the influence of the skinhead on record shop owners could be damaging fearing the shops would be overrun with the working class youth on a Saturday, a daunting proposition to other customers. By '71 reggae was beginning to lose its charm with the skinhead due in the main to the emergence of conscious lyrics concentrating on Babylon and Africa which left many turning toward the music from Slade et al.

A point to clarify is that the original skinhead of '69 with their cropped not shaven heads had never regarded attitudes towards racism and politics as central to their subculture, unlike the later generation that took the name.

The book is set out in two main sections. The first covers each Pama imprint in alphabetical order with a brief introduction followed by a full discography. Boss Sounds looks in more detail at some of the singles issued on the label followed with details on artists, producers and albums associated with each label. The main Pama label discography includes all the soul releases during the early years highlighted appropriately in blue. The second section covers in detail the remaining albums, with a full discography, many of which were compilation budget issues. A look at the albums in detail kicks off with the iconic Straighten Up Series. Many of the albums came with informative sleeve notes and these have been reproduced in their entirety where appropriate.

A note of reference: Artists names were often miss-spelt inadvertently or otherwise and titles altered or even the artist is an alias, however to maintain the authenticity the discography retains all the information taken from the original 45s labels and album sleeves. An example being CRAB-4 issued in 1968 Reggie Hit The Town - The Eathopians AKA Reggae Hit The Town - The Ethiopians. On Nu-Beat NB-043(2) Baby Lon Gone AKA Babylon Gone, Peter Touch AKA Peter Tosh and Winston Gruvy AKA Winston Groovy.

A lasting note of sadness to remember with respect the artists and producers who have passed on, their contribution to the wonderful world of Pama and reggae will live on forever in their music and song.

ACKNOWLEDGEMENTS

There is a significant debt of gratitude we all owe to Harry, Jeff, Carl and the many producers, musicians and artistes that have bestowed on us the celebrated sounds from Pama. Boss sounds that will now live on forever.

The book would not have been possible without the assistance and support of Jessica Munro at Phoenix Music International and her colleague Curtis Lynch who has overseen the re-mastering of the Pama catalogue. I was privileged to be a part of the burgeoning boss reggae sounds and its followers in the late 60s and this has been an absolute labour of love to listen once again to tracks in high quality audio like Max Romeo's What A Cute Man and Lloyd Robinsons The Worm to name just two.

When discussing the book at an early stage with Jessica and Curtis the question was raised and unanimously answered about who should be invited to write a foreword. Who else could it have been apart from Harry Palmer and I would like to acknowledge his most valuable contribution to the book.

PAMA RECORDS

The musical journey began for the Palmer brothers when Harry bought his first record shop in Harrow Road North London in 1962 naming the business Happy Sound. The brothers had emigrated from Jamaica at various times during the 50s and 60s with Jeff the eldest brother arriving first to escape the toil of farming for little return, planning for a more rewarding future. Harry followed starting his new life as a factory worker but was ambitious and took business studies. Carl was the last to arrive. The record shop was successful for a while but fire destroyed the premises. Undeterred they set up an estate agency which proved so successful they relocated to Harrow-On-The-Hill with the estate agents now run from 16, Peterborough Road.

Jeff digressed into night club management, eventually taking a lease on the Apollo Club on Willesden High Road. The brothers set up Pama in 1967 using the estate agents in Peterborough Road as the offices before relocating to more prestigious premises at 78, Craven Park Road Harlesden. 78 became their retail outlet. Fate conspired to help the brothers cause as several of the companies issuing Jamaican music in the UK were starting to fold or change direction as a subsequence of the ska era being superseded by rocksteady and now the emerging sound of reggae. Harry had already tipped his toe in the water leasing two recordings to Chris Blackwell's Island label one being Joyce Bond's Do The Teasy in 1967, a take on Hopeton Lewis' Take It Easy.

Things were looking promising for the brothers until a set back when little interest was shown towards licensing Clancy Eccles What Will Your Mama Say. Undeterred as they had been about the fire they took the decision to distribute the single independently. Operating from the back room of their estate agents office, the track became the brothers first official release and Pama Records was up and running.

Pama then started issuing soul records from America and home talent with the Mohawks being the most successful - on the blue Pama label - through 'till about the end of '69. One of Pama's first soul releases in 1968 was 'The Champ' by The Mohawks, which has become one of the most sampled tracks in hip hop. Harry had visited Jamaica to establish meaningful relationships with Jamaican producers including Clancy Eccles and paid an advance for records to be produced for Pama. These were sent to England along with some records that had already been hits on the island and then licensed for distribution in the UK on the Pama label. This coincided with the burgeoning skinhead movement who had taken to the sounds of the emerging reggae.

THE LABELS

Pama's inaugural subsidiary label was launched in the spring of '68 with Nu-Beat concentrating on rocksteady from both Jamaica and UK based artists. The name changed to New Beat in 1970 and concentrated on UK artists with Laurel Aitken the main stay of the revamped label. At this time Harry Palmer decided he needed a solid connection to a Jamaican producer and had a chance meting with Bunny Lee on one of his trips to London.

In my 2016 interview with Bunny Lee he talked about the agreement he'd managed to set up with the Palmer brothers when he came to England in '68. *"The three brothers dem come an see me and dem give me bout 700 pound. I go back to Jamaica and start to make some music and the rest is history. They became as big as Trojan, at one point bigger. Wet Dream was a tune I sent to Pama as a B -side."*

The agreement was for Lee to produce tracks that would be issued in both Jamaica and the UK. The name chosen for the joint venture was UNITY with the familiar circular Pama logo sat alongside a similar Lee logo on the JA imprint.

The first release on the Unity label came in the autumn of '68 with Last Flight To Reggae City but it was the second issued from the same batch, Bangarang, that caught the attention with what was described at the time as a jerking organ line and one that everyone wanted including the skinhead. The record is regarded as one of the first true reggae sounds along with Larry And Alvin's Nanny Goat, No More Heartaches from The Beltones and Clancy Eccles Feel The Rhythm. There is no doubt though that UN-503 Wet Dream was the biggest seller for Pama with over 250,000 copies sold despite the radio ban making it to number 10 in the UK chart during August 1969.

Before the end of '68 Pama launched two more subsidiaries namely Crab for Derrick Morgan productions and Gas. The following year saw the launch of Bullet, Camel, Escort, Punch and Success. '69 was also the year of the album with the formula of taking singles that had reached their peak in terms of sales and issuing them as a compilation of a dozen tracks from a subsidiary label on a budget priced L.P. The compilation albums included Bullet, Camel, Crab, Gas, Nu-Beat and Unity. Somewhat at odds to the reggae Pama had also issued an album commemorating the investiture of Price Charles with a Welsh Male Voice Choir and a album featuring the Red Coats at Butlin's holiday camp.

Agitation began to surface when it was apparent that Bunny Lee had licensed Derrick Morgan's Seven Letters to both Pama and Trojan. Another factor was Pama had no licensing arrangements with the legendary Leslie Kong who was producing hit after hit for Trojan and bought in volumes by the skinhead. The Beverley Music on the Pama label had no connection to Beverley's Records. Despite this Pama were still producing good boss sounds as late as 1970 when they set up their final three labels, Ocean, Supreme and Pama Supreme.

The problems with JA producers seemed to escalate in 1971 with much of the labels Jamaican production coming to an end as many producers were now fully committed to supplying Trojan. Several tracks were being sold to both companies at this time with perhaps a slight change of title or artist name and it's estimated that upwards of fifty tracks saw the light of day from both companies.

By the end of 1971 the music that had brought a sense of belonging to the skinhead was changed beyond all recognition, a shift that saw many discerning skinheads lose faith with the music, some who by now were second generation following on from their brothers. Some held on for a resurgence of the boss sound which never came. By the summer of '72 it was all over and the clock was ticking for both Pama and Trojan.

It was announced in 1973 that Pama had gone out of business and Harry Palmer returned to his native Jamaica seemingly disillusioned with a music industry he had so greatly contributed to for over half a decade.

A flurry of singles were released during 1975 with an album ironically titled Reggae Hit The Town issued on PTP 1001 and that was it.

Times winged chariot has moved on but those boss sounds seem as fresh today as they did over fifty years ago.

TELL IT LIKE IT WAS

(The following is an extract from Skinhead Reggae Hit The Town)

The early development of West Indian music in Britain can be traced back to June 1948 with the merchant vessel Empire Windrush arriving at Tilbury carrying 492 passengers from Jamaica, all wishing to start a new life in the United Kingdom. Virgil Jack Williams recalls his arrival in Britain two decades later.

"I arrived in a cold damp London in 1962 having spent my early years growing up bathed by the warmth of the sun blessed West Indies, where blue beat, calypso and mento music always seemed to fill the balmy nights. In London at that time I was not allowed to soak up the night-life in the pubs as all had banned entry with notices stating NO COLOUERED OR IRISH allowed.

Music was an inherent part of the West Indian culture and we would go to big dance hall events in West London, not far from where I was living at the time in Edgware Road. The dance halls were popular venues although no food was served, just drinks and a generous helping of great music, a combination of steel bands, calypso and ska.

I recall with fond memories one evening we had a visit from Cassius Clay, around the time of the great Cooper fight, his appearance caused a real stir and great interest. I was now living with a black family in London and although it was difficult to get hold of we did manage to come by some blue beat and ska records imported from Jamaica. The music was beginning to become more prevalent as the decade went on with ska now being played at the Hammersmith Palais and other clubs such as 'Burtons', a hot spot, and on one occasion Pan's People came to dance.

After the clubs we would go onto 'Blues Parties' often held in someone's house where a large sound system would be pumping out ska and rocksteady into the night, you didn't need to know the address you just had to follow the sound of incessant rhythms booming out. The MC would 'toast' over the music as the drink and food flowed freely including traditional rice peas, jerk chicken and red stripe, with the venues always packed. The opportunity to buy West Indian music was still very limited, and little if any was played on national radio, so the clubs and impromptu parties with their sound systems allowed us to soak up the music with all of our friends.

Towards the end of the decade record shops began to open specialising in the imported hits from Jamaica and would always be crowded on a Saturday, with everyone anxious to hear the latest tunes from back home. The youth both white and black with their cropped hair who rejected the hippie attitude and progressive music took an interest in reggae; much like their elder brothers did with ska earlier in the decade. Add to this mix the birth of record labels in the UK and soon reggae had found its rightful international acclaim. With the sound from the islands available to the mainstream record buying public for the first time, reggae was now charting".

BULLET

BULLET DISCOGRAPHY 1969 - 1973 Prefix BU

BULLET launched in 1969 when Pama was functioning at full capacity with Wet Dream charting. The labels first release for reasons unknown came under prefix BU-399 with Throw Me Corn from Winston Shan.

Bullet was considered by many to be one of Pama's finest, releasing some excellent boss skinhead sounds among its quality output. Dandy Shandy Version 4 on BU-483 is up there with the best, a vibrant offering from Impact All-Stars, as is Motherless Children by Willie Francis on BU-415. The classic Maga Dog delivered with resounding vocals and a pulsating rhythm from Peter Tosh was issued on BU-486 in 1971. Aily And Ailaloo by Niney & Max, Rum Rhythm from Roy Shirley, The Samething For Breakfast by Winston Groovy & Pat Rhoden along with Here Come The Heartaches by Delroy Wilson and Rome by Lloyd Jones are more excellent examples. They were offerings of the purest sound of boss reggae that'd hardened from rocksteady.

An album Bullet - A World Of Reggae was issued on Pama SECO 19 during 1970.

BU-399 Throw Me Corn / Darling Remember - **Winston Shan & The Sheiks** 1969
Produced by: H Robinson / H Robinson
BU-400 (Promo Only)
BU-401 Let Me Tell You Boy - The Ebony Sisters / Mannix - Rythmn Rulers 1969
Produced by: Harry Mudie / Harry Mudie
BU-402 Heart Don't Leap - Dennis Walks / I Am Sorry - The Clarendonians 1969
Produced by: Harry Mudie / Harry Mudie
BU-403 (Promo Only)
BU-404 (Promo Only)
BU-405 No Business Of Yours / Mast It Up - **George Williams** 1969
Produced by: Harry Mudie / Harry Mudie
BU-406 Festival Knocks / Making Love - **The Tennors** 1969
Produced by: G Murphy / G Murphy
BU-407 Tribute To Don Drummond / Japanese Invasion - **Rico** 1969
Produced by: Bunny Lee / Bunny Lee
BU-408 Love Of My Life / Shady Tree - **Dennis Walks** 1969
Produced by: Harry Mudie / Harry Mudie
BU-409 I Am Just A Minstrel / Yesterday - **The Kingstonians** 1969
Produced by: G Murphy / G Murphy
BU-410 V Rocket / Smile - **The Fabions** 1969
Produced by: G Murphy / G Murphy
BU-411 Matilda - Winston Shan / Come To Me - The Harmonians 1969
Produced by: Ranny Williams / Ranny Williams
BU-412 Hog In A Me Minti / Lona Run - **The Hippy Boys** 1969
Produced by: Ranny Williams / Ranny Williams
BU-413 Whats Your Excuse / Tell Me Tell Me - **The Hippy Boys** 1969
Produced by: Ranny Williams / Ranny Williams
BU-414 Cat Woman - Glen Adams / Selassie Seranade - Peter Touch 1969
Produced by: Bunny Lee / Bunny Lee
BU-415 Motherless Children / I Am Not Afraid - **Willie Francis** 1969
Produced by: Willie Francis / Willie Francis
BU-416 Run Nigel Run / Come Home - **The Chuckles** 1969
Produced by: Derrick Harriott / Derrick Harriott
BU-417 Black Soul / Always With Me - **The Imperials** 1969
Produced by: H Robinson / H Robinson
BU-418 (Not Used)
BU-419 Copy Cats - The Clan / Hot Lead - Bunny Lee Allstars 1970
Produced by: Derrick Morgan / Bunny Lee
BU-420 Each Time - The Ebony Sisters / Boss Walk - Bunny Lee Allstars 1970
Produced by: Bunny Lee / Bunny Lee
BU-421 The Feeling Is Fine / Your Killing Me - **Freddie Notes And The Rudies** 1970
Produced by: Derrick Morgan / Derrick Morgan
BU-422 That's My Life / Queen Of My Heart - **Fitz Roy Sterling** 1970
Produced by: F R Sterling / F R Sterling
BU-423 (Promo Only)
BU-424 (Promo Only)
BU-425 Come By Here / Somebody - **Winston and Rupert** 1970
Produced by: Harry Mudie / Harry Mudie
BU-426 Summer Place / Big Boy - **Ranny Williams and The Hippy Boys** 1970
Produced by: Ranny Williams / Ranny Williams
BU-427 Last Date - Hortense Ellis / Cherry Pink - Pat Satchmo 1970
Produced by: Tommy McCook / Tommy McCook
BU-428 Savage Colt / The Clea Hog - **The Eldorados** 1970
Produced by: Ranny Williams / Ranny Williams
BU-429 Rome - Lloyd Jones / Version Of Rome - Rhythm Rulers 1970
Produced by: Harry Mudie / Harry Mudie
BU-430 Na Na Hay Hay Goodbye - The Clan / Musical Bop - King Stitt 1970
Produced by: Derrick Morgan / Ranny Williams
BU-431 Pupa Live On Eye Top / Give Me Faith - **The Reggae Boys** 1970
Produced by: Glen Adams / Glen Adams

BU-432 (Promo Only)

BU-433 (Promo Only)

BU-434 Exposure / Baby Huey - **Lloyd Terrell** 1970
Produced by: Lloyd Charmers / Lloyd Charmers

BU-435 Dollar And Bonds / Sound Familiar - **Lloyd Charmers** 1970
Produced by: Lloyd Charmers / Lloyd Charmers

BU-436 The Return Of Batman / In Action - **Sydney All Stars** 1970
Produced by: Sydney Crooks / Sydney Crooks

BU-437 Outer Space / Full Moon - **Sydney Allstars** 1970
Produced by: Sydney Crooks / Sydney Crooks

BU-438 Freedom Street - Fitzroy Sterling / Version - Fitzroys All Stars 1970
Produced by: Fitzroy Sterling / Fitzroy Sterling

BU-439 Reggae Sounds Are Boss - Fitzroy and Harry / Goodbye My Love -
Fitzroy Sterling 1970
Produced by: Fitzroy Sterling / Fitzroy Sterling

BU-440 Nice Grind - The Rebels / Version Of Grind - Sydney Allstars 1970
Produced by: Sydney Crooks / Sydney Crooks

BU-441 Chariot Coming - The Viceroys / Stackato - Sydney Allstars 1970
Produced by: Sydney Crooks / Sydney Crooks

BU-442 Reggae A Bye Bye / Doctor Jekell - **Lloyd Charmers** 1970
Produced by: Lloyd Terrell / Lloyd Terrell

BU-443 Oh Me Oh My / I Did It - **Lloyd Terrell** 1970
Produced by: Lloyd Terrell / Lloyd Terrell

BU-444 Power Control - The Viceroys / Dip Dip - The Slickers 1970
Produced by: Sydney Crooks / Sydney Crooks

BU-445 Keep Trying - Little Roy / Version II - The Matadors 1970
Produced by: Lloyd Daley / Lloyd Daley

BU-446 I Don't Like To Interfere / Preaching Love - **The Maytones** 1970
Produced by: Alvin Ranglin / Alvin Ranglin

BU-447 Second Pressure / Sammy Dead - **The Rythm Rulers** 1970
Produced by: Harry Mudie / Harry Mudie

BU-448 Set Back - Gregory Isaccs / Version II - Sydney's Allstars 1970
Produced by: Sydney Crooks / Sydney Crooks

BU-449 Coolie Gal - The Slickers / Bawling Baby - Bigie 1970
Produced by: Sydney Crooks / Sydney Crooks

BU-450 Come On Over - The Viceroy / Version II - Sydney's Allstars 1970
Produced by: Lee Perry / Lee Perry

BU-451 (Not Used)

BU-452 Be Strong / Wake Up In The Sunshine - **Solomon Jones** 1970
Produced by: Lee Perry / Derrick Morgan

BU-453 Fancy Cloth - The Viceroys / Jack & Jill - Biggie 1970
Produced by: Sydney Crooks / Sydney Crooks

BU-454 I Wish - Basil Gail / Black Is Black - **Martin Riley** 1970
Produced by: Sydney Crooks / Sydney Crooks

BU-455 Get Out Of This Land - Sammy Morgan / Landmark - Sydney Croods All Stars 1971
Produced by: Sydney Crooks / Sydney Crooks

BU-456 Knock Three Times - Carl / The Whealing Mouse - Sydney Crooks All Stars 1971
Produced by: Sydney Crooks / Sydney Crooks

BU-457 Call Me (PartOne) / Call Me (PartTwo) - **The Cimmerons** 1971
Produced by: The Cimmerons / The Cimmerons

BU-458 Leave A Little Love / My Baby - **The Cimmerons** 1971
Produced by: The Cimmerons / The Cimmerons

BU-459 Just Enough - David Isaacs / Standing - Roy Patin 1971
Produced by: Lee Perry / Lee Perry

BU-460 Can't Reach You - The Untouchables / Natural Woman - Carl Dawkins 1971
Produced by: Lee Perry / Lee Perry

BU-461 All Combine(Part One) / All Combine (Part Two) - **The Upsetters** 1971
Produced by: Harry Palmer / Harry Palmer

BU-462 My Love / Stronger Love - **Rupie Edwards All Stars** 1971
Produced by: Rupie Edwards / Rupie Edwards

BU-463 Shock Attack / Cuban Waltz - **Rad Bryan** 1971
Produced by: Rad Bryan / Rad Bryan

BU-464 Soul Town / Let The Sun Shine On Me - **Bob Marley** 1971
Produced by: Lee Perry / Lee Perry

BU-465 Arawack Version / Guffy Guffy - **The Inner Minds** 1971
Produced by: Ian Smith / Ian Smith

BU-466 Black Man's Pride - Alton Ellis / Grove With It - Leroy Parker 1971
Produced by: Sydney Crooks / A Forgie

BU-467 Nobody Business / Standing By - **Derrick Morgan** 1971
Produced by: Derrick Morgan / Derrick Morgan

BU-468 (Not Used)

BU-469 (Not Used)

BU-470 Rebel Niah / Feel The Spirit - **The Viceroys** 1971
Produced by: Derrick Morgan / Derrick Morgan

BU-471 I Wan'na Be Loved / Get Back Together - **Winston Groovy** 1971
Produced by: Winston Groovy / Winston Groovy

BU-472 Peace Begins Within - Nora Dean / Go Back Home - The Slickers 1971
Produced by: Sid Bucknor / Sid Bucknor

BU-473 Reggae In Wonderland / Wonderland (Version) - **The Charmers** 1971
Produced by: Lloyd Terrell / Lloyd Terrell

BU-474 (Not Used)

BU-475 Something For Breakfast - Winston & Pat / Sweeter Than Honey -
Winston Groovy 1971
Produced by: Winston Groovy - Pat Rhoden / Winston Groovy

BU-476 Never Love Another / Version - **Busty Brown** 1971
Produced by: Sid Bucknor / Sid Bucknor

BU-477 There's A Train / Blue Moon - **Speed** 1971
Produced by: Unknown

BU-478 Mother Oh Mother - Max Romeo / Dreams Of Passion - Morgan All Stars 1971
Produced by: Rupie Edwards / Derrick Morgan

BU-479 Let It Be Me / Dream Dream Dream - **Jamaica Jubilee Stompers** 1971
Produced by: Laurel Aitken / Laurel Aitken

BU-479 (Alternative Issue) **Let It Be Me** / All I Have To Do Is Dream - **Caribos** 1971
Produced by: Laurel Aitken / Laurel Aitken

BU-480 (Not Used)

BU-481 (Not Used)

BU-482 (Not Used)

BU-483 Dandy Shandy Version 4 / Go Back Version 3 - **Impact All Stars** 1971
Produced by: Victor Chinn / Victor Chinn

BU-484 (Not Used)

BU-485 Don't Care / True Born African - **Alton Ellis** 1971
Produced by: Alton Ellis / Sid Bucknor

BU-486 Maga Dog - Peter Tosh / Bull Dog - 3rd And 4th Generation 1971
Produced by: Joe Gibbs / Joe Gibbs

BU-487 (Not Used)

BU-488 Sour Soup / Stranger Cole Medley - **Stranger Cole** 1971
Produced by: Willie Francis / Willie Francis

BU-489 Willie's Rouster / Rouster Version - **Willie Francis** 1971
Produced by: Willie Francis / Stranger Cole

BU-490 Devil Woman / Venn Street Rub - **Ian Smith And The inner Mind** 1971
Produced by: Ian Smith / Ian Smith

BU-491 So Far Away - Bell Techs / So Far Version - Brute Force and Ignorance 1971
Produced by: Unknown

BU-492 One Night Of Sin / Sin (Version) - **The Slickers** 1971
Produced by: Syd Bucknor / Syd Bucknor

BU-493 Lick Samba - Bob Marley And The Wailers / Samba - The Wailers 1971
Produced by: Lee Perry / Lee Perry

BU-494 I'm Gonna Live Some Life - Rupie Edwards / Rock 'In' -
Rupie Edwards All Stars 1971
Produced by: Rupie Edwards / Rupie Edwards

BU-495 (Not Used)

9

BU-496 Tropical Land - Melodians / Love I Bring - Hugh Roy and Slim Smith 1972
Produced by: Tony Brevett / Rupie Edwards
BU-497 So Ashamed - Tony Bravett / My Only Love - Gregory Isaacs 1972
Produced by: Tony Brevett / Gregory Isaacs
BU-498 Three Combine - Syd And Joe / Am I The Nearest One To Your Heart -
Les Foster 1972
Produced by: Ranny Williams / Derrick Morgan
BU-499 Beat Down Babylon - Junior / Ital Version - The Upsetters 1972
Produced by: Lee Perry / Lee Perry
BU-500 Butter And Bread - Lloyd Young / Version Bread And Butter -
Shalimar All Stars 1972
Produced by: M G Mahtani / M G Mahtani
BU-501 High School Serenade - Lennox Brown / On The Track - Winston Scotland 1972
Produced by: Prince Toney / Prince Toney
BU-502 Rum Rhythm - Shirley And Charmers / Rhythm (Version) - Lloyd Charmers 1972
Produced by: Lloyd Charmers / Lloyd Charmers
BU-503 Ally And Ailaloo / Episode 2 - **Niney And Max** 1972
Produced by: Winston Holness / Winston Holness
BU-504 Hard To Believe - Gerry Meggie / Softie - Max Romeo 1972
Produced by: Gerry Meggie / Max Romeo
BU-505 (Not Used)
BU-506 Pure In Heart / Clean Hands - **Bill Gentles** 1972
Produced by: Sir Derrick / Sir Derrick
BU-507 Sad Movies - Barbara Jones / Movies Version - Sir Harry 1972
Produced by: B Brooks / B Brooks
BU-508 Oily Sound / Oily Version - Lloyd Tyrell 1972
Produced by: Lloyd Tyrell / Lloyd Tyrell
BU-509 Dup-Up A Daughter - Dennis Alcapone / Daughter - Tony All Stars 1972
Produced by: Prince Tony / Prince Tony
BU-510 (Not Used)
BU-511 Babylon Falling - Gabby Wilton & Charlie Ace / Make it Love - Charlie Ace 1972
Produced by: Charlie Ace / Charlie Ace
BU-512 Howdy & Tenky - Flowers and Alvin / Sprinkle Some Water - Shorty Perry 1972
Produced by: Alvin Ranglin / Alvin Ranglin
BU-513 The King Is Back - Hofmers Brothers / King Man Version - Shalimar all Stars 1972
Produced by: Glenn Brown / Glenn Brown
BU-514 I Miss My School Days - B.B. Seaton / School Days Version -
The Conscious Minds 1972
Produced by: B Seaton / B Seaton
BU-515 For Once In My Life / Didn't I - **Cornel Campbell** 1972
Produced by: Bunny Lee / Bunny Lee
BU-516 (Not Used)
BU-517 (Not Used)
BU-518 (Not Used)
BU-519 Mr. Parker's Daughter - Sir Harry / On Top Of The Peak - U Roy 1972
Produced by: Rupie Edwards / Alvin Ranglin
BU-520 Here Come The Heartaches / You'll Be Sorry - **Delroy Wilson** 1972
Produced by: Bunny Lee / Bunny Lee

BU-521 Hijack Plane / Shower Of Rain - **Avengers** 1973
Produced by: Kirk Redding / Kirk Redding
BU-522 Ben - Margaret Elaine / Laughing Stock Version -
Ritchie and the Now Generation 1973
Produced by: Pluto Shervington / V Douglas
BU-523 Place In The Sun / Burning Fire - **Slim Smith** 1973
Produced by: Bunny Lee / Bunny Lee
BU-524 The Word Is Black / Town Talk - **King Miguel** 1973
Produced by: Rupie Edwards / Rupie Edwards
BU-525 Go On This Way - Freddie M'Kay / Santic Dub - Santic Allstars 1973
Produced by: C Prehey / C Prehey
BU-526 (Not Used)
BU-527 Take Time Out / Just Like A Log - **Three Tops** 1973
Produced by: Lee Perry / Lee Perry
BU-528 People Get Funny - The Planets / Funny Version - Docbird Allstars 1973
Produced by: Dennis Brown / Dennis Brown
BU-529 Yama Skank - Shorty & The President / Doctor Run Come Quick -
Hugh Roy Junior 1973
Produced by: Rupie Edwards / Rupie Edwards

BULLET SECOND SERIES 1975

BU-550 No Money No Friend - Shelton Walks / Money Dub - Bob Mac All Stars 1975
Produced by: Bob Mac / Bob Mac
BU-551 (Not Used)
BU-552 Step Right Up - I Roy / Banjo Seranade - Andy's Allstars 1975
Produced by: R Anderson / R Anderson
BU-553 (Not Used)
BU-554 Ealing In The Barn Yard / Ealing Dub - **Starlight** 1975
Produced by: Alvin Ranglin / Alvin Ranglin
BU-555 (Not Used)
BU-556 (Not Used)
BU-557 Nyah Chant / Rasta Waltz - **Sons Of Jah** 1975
Produced by: C Davidson / C Davidson

BOSS SOUNDS FROM BULLET

Boss Sounds from BULLET brings some of the highlights from the labels production between 1969 and 1975.

BU-427 Last Date - Hortense Ellis 1970
Produced by: Tommy McCook

A boss tune from a talented lady who toured Jamaica with Byron Lee during the 1960s. The rhythm is taken from Pat Kelly's How Long Will It Take. Hortense released the rousing song I Shall Sing on Gas GAS-166 in 1971.

BU-483 Dandy Shandy Version 4 - Impact All Stars 1971
Produced by: Victor Chinn

The vibrant offering from The Impact All Stars is boss reggae at its best and is a DJ version of Rice And Peas issued on Camel CA-68 credited to Dandy & Shandy.

BU-479(2) Dream Dream Dream - Jamaica Jubilee Stompers 1971
Produced by: Lorenzo (Laurel Aitken)

This one is a mystery as there are two versions of this release both with the same prefix, one credits the Jamaica Jubilee Stompers the other The Cariboes with a change of title to All I Have To Do Is Dream, both are productions from Laurel Aitken. The track is of course a cover of All I Have To Do Is Dream by the Everly Brothers.

BU-462 My Love - Rupie Edwards' All Stars 1971
Produced by: Rupie Edwards

My Love is actually Can't Hide The Feeling, the excellent vocal offering from The Gaylads and produced by B. B. Seaton.

BU-429 Rome - Lloyd Jones 1970
Produced by: Harry Mudie

Rome is better known for the hit instrumental version Leaving Rome by Jo Jo Bennett With Mudies All Stars issued on Moodisc in Jamaica and Trojan but this beautiful vocal rendition is up there with the best boss sounds.

BU-416 Run Nigel Run - The Chuckles 1969
Produced by: Derrick Harriott

Run Nigel Run is actually by Nicky Thomas with his trade-mark vocals and his first UK release. BU-403 and BU-404 featured Cecil Thomas (Nicky Thomas) but both records were only promotional copies. Run Nigel Run with its driving beat is a real boss dance-crasher.

BU-464 Soul Town - Bob Marley 1971
Produced by: Lee Perry

The harmonies are of course provided by Peter Tosh and Bunny Wailer on this DJ cut actually titled Soul Town Reporter with the DJ lyrics courtesy of Johnny Lover.

BU-486 Maga Dog - Peter Tosh 1971
Produced by: Joe Gibbs

Peter Tosh at his best with perhaps the boss version of the song. It doesn't come much better than this. Tosh negotiates the vibrant rhythm with his unmistakable voice, just listen to - Me jus' a do wha' me haffi do -.

BU-502 Rum Rhythm - Shirley And Charmers 1972
Produced by: Lloyd Charmers

Better known as Roy Shirley and Lloyd Charmers. The Jamaican release issued on the Splash label was titled Mucking Fuch and credited to the Muckers.

BU-399 Throw Me Corn - Winston Shan & The Sheiks 1969
Produced by: Ranny Williams

The record that launched the Bullet label by Winston Shan & The Sheiks, a vibrant early reggae beat guaranteed to get you dancing.

BU-475 Samething For Breakfast - Winston & Pat 1971
Produced by: W Groovy - P Rhoden
C/W **Sweeter Than Honey - Winston Groovy**
Produced by: Winston Groovy

A top class Boss sound and definitely not a single with a B side as a filler. Sweeter Than Honey was a change of style for the soulful Winston almost toasting over an infectious beat.

RANNY WILLIAMS

GUITARIST / PRODUCER

Ranford 'Ranny Bop' Williams aka Ranny Williams Jamaican guitarist and producer was born on November 8th 1942. He is believed by many in the know to have created the reggae sound on his guitar. Ranny has played guitar on a plethora of records with a list of artists including but not limited to The Ethiopians, The Versatiles, The Slickers and The Techniques and on the sound track of The Harder They Come. He worked with the great producers including Leslie Kong, Bunny Lee and Duke Reid. His first group in Jamaica were the Jaguars followed by stints with The Pioneers, Tommy McCook And The Supersonics, The Upsetters and of course The Hippy Boys.

During his time at Treasure Isle he worked directly with Duke Reid on arrangements as well as playing guitar. When The Hippy Boys disbanded he moved to the UK to pursue a career as a producer with much of his work released on the Pama label including Bullett.

The linear notes on Bullet - A World Of Reggae refer to Hit Me Back AKA Shocks Of Mighty. Ranny had written and recorded a song I Got A Heart along with Better Must Come and Throw Me Corn. The story goes that Bunny Lee gave a copy of the tape to Lee Perry who changed the title from I Got A Heart to Shocks Of Mighty with Dave Barker on vocals.

Ranny Williams on Bullet.

BU-411 Matilda - Winston Shan / Come To Me - The Harmonians **1969**
Produced by: Ranny Williams / Ranny Williams
BU-412 Hog In A Me Minti / Lona Run - **The Hippy Boys 1969**
Produced by: Ranny Williams / Ranny Williams
BU-413 Whats Your Excuse / Tell Me Tell Me - **The Hippy Boys 1969**
Produced by: Ranny Williams / Ranny Williams
BU-426 Summer Place / Big Boy -
Ranny Williams and The Hippy Boys 1970
Produced by: Ranny Williams / Ranny Williams
BU-428 Savage Colt / The Clea Hog - **The Eldorados 1970**
Produced by: Ranny Williams / Ranny Williams
BU-430(2) Musical Bop - King Stitt 1970
Produced by: Ranny Williams
BU-498 Three Combine - Syd And Joe 1972
Produced by: Ranny Williams

PAMA RECORDS LTD. 16 Peterborough Road, Harrow, Middlesex

PAMA RECORDS LTD. 16 Peterborough Road, Harrow, Middlesex

BULLET- A WORLD OF REGGAE Various Artistes
PAMA SECO 19 1970

Side 1
1. THROW ME CORN - Winston Shand
2. HEART DON'T LEAP - Dennis Walks
3. COPY CATS - The Clan 4. EACH TIME - The Ebony Sisters
5. COME BY HERE - Winston And Rupert 6. WHAT'S YOUR EXCUSE - The Hippy Boys
Side 2
1. SUMMER PLACE - Ranny Williams
2. I AM JUST A MINSTERL - The Kingstonians
3. LOVE OF MY LIFE - Dennis Walks 4. HOG IN A ME MINTI - The Hippy Boys
5. THAT'S MY LIFE (BECAUSE YOU LIED) - Fitzroy Sterling
6. LET ME TELL YOU BOY - Ebony Sisters

The album sleeve notes follow.

ECONOMY   MONO   ECO-19

THE BULLET HITS
VARIOUS ARTISTES

When you are hit with a Bullet you are really hit and when you are hit with the sound of Bullet you are hit harder than ever before by the sheer quality and strength of the records on this most successful Reggae label.

Bullet kicked off with a little thing entitled "Throw Me Corn" which was an instant Hit and is still today after more than a year selling strongly as a single. Good old BU-399. Ranny Williams the principle producer for the Bullet label wasted no time in putting out another similar hit entitled "Hog In A Me Minty", again still selling strongly as a single. Next came a new group, The Clan with "Copy Cats" which stormed the discotheques for many weeks. "Let Me Tell You Boy" and "Each Time" by The Ebony Sisters were also hits and Fitzroy Sterling's "That's My Life" established him among the very hopeful up and coming young stars.

All together "The Bullet Hits" is an album which should not be missed and will find a place among all good record collections. "Hit Me Back" says the man who designed and operates the Bullet label but he is the one who is hitting back with the great sound of "The Bullet Hits".

 PAMA RECORDS LIMITED 78 Craven Park Road London N.W.10 England

Reco moved to the UK in 1961 where he joined live bands including Georgie Fame's Blue Flames and several other reggae bands before recording with his own band, Rico's All Stars, later forming the group Rico and the Rudies who released the 1969 album Blow Your Horn.

RECO IN REGGAE LAND   A TRIBUTE TO DON DRUMMOND   PAMA ECO 14   1969

Side 1
1. TRIBUTE TO DON DRUMMOND 2. ANANCY RUMBA 3. RAINBOW INTO THE RIO MIND
4. SWEET CHAROIT 5. TOM JONES 6. SCAR FACE

Side 2
1. TROMBONE MAN 2. JAPANESE INVASION 3. TOP OF THE CLASS 4. BLACK MILK
5. STRANGER ON THE SHORE 6. PLACE IN THE SUN

ECONOMY   MONO   ECO 14

RECO IN REGGAE LAND

PAYING TRIBUTE TO DON DRUMMOND By: Rodregrez

One name that is very well known in Jazz and Blue Beat Music circles is that of Reco Rodregrez better known to all as Reco.

He is the handsome man on the front cover with his golden trombone and boy can he play that thing. Reco is rated among the best Trombonist in the world and certainly the best from the West Indies. He received his early musical training at Alpha Boys School, the place where all good Jamaican musicians learnt their craft. As a youngster Reco had his choice of instruments and he chose the Trombone. Never has there been a wiser choice as this instrument seems to have been made for him, his lips are formed to suit the mouthpiece and his fingers are shaped to hold the slide in such a way that it is impossible to wrench his instrument away from him without taking his fingers as well. Please do not get the idea however, that Reco is deformed, it's just that he has grown so attached to his Trombone and so all the above peculiarities have developed. This of course helps to make him play all the better as his feel is assured and never a wrong note held. Again you can see from his picture, Reco is only a young man in his late twenties, which at first is a little hard to believe seeing he plays in such an accomplished manner. After saying all that about Reco, it is only fitting that we say a little about the recording and also a few words about the man to whom he is paying tribute Don Drummonds.

Don like Reco attended he Alpha Boys School and he also chose the Trombone as the instrument that he was to gain his livelihood. For many years they jostled between themselves for the number one spot, both seemed equally as good as the other and any year in which Don wasn't chosen number one Trombonist, Reco it was, who would have nipped it and visa versa. For quite a few years this went on between these two young men until five years ago Reco emigrated to England and left Don to reign as King of the Trombone in Jamaica which came to an end with his unfortunate and untimely death earlier this year (1969). Reco was so grieved that he went immediately to his record company PAMA and literally demanded studio time and a good backing band to allow him to pay his respects to his late companion.

When you have listened to this record you will realise the great feeling which Reco put into this session, in memory of his friend and colleague Don Drummonds (departed). The entire recording was done in four hours flat, because of Reco's determination to get his feelings out in the music.

Best of Luck and Happy Listening:- Soul, Soul, Soul and Hail Reco, King of the Trombone.

Satchmo

PAMA RECORDS 78 Craven Park Road London NW10

WINSTON GROOVY   FREE THE PEOPLE   PAMA PMP 2011   1970

Side 1
1. I LIKE THE WAY 2. I GOT TO FIND A WAY TO GET MARIA BACK
3. TO THE OTHER MAN 4. TELL ME WHY 5. NOT NOW 6. I WANNA BE THERE

Side 2
1. DON'T BREAK MY HEART 2. YELLOW BIRD 3. STANDING AT THE CORNER 4. THE FIRST TIME
5. FREE THE PEOPLE 6 . GROOVIN

PAMA / MEDIUM   MONO   PMP 2011

FREE THE PEOPLE
WINSTON GROOVY

Grove me baby, let's go a grooving. My name is Winston Groovy, so nicknamed from school-days because, as they said, I used to sing in a groovy sort of way. There must have been some truth in what they said because now I have grown up and my profession is singing, my name remains Winston Groovy.

Let me first thank you dear fans for your wonderful support, which has given me the chance to prove my worth as a singer and I trust I will never go stale with you.

Living in Birmingham I could not get my desire to sing and make records, until one day that old pro Laurel Aitken (I don't mean old in age, but a long standing name in show business), heard me singing in a Church hall practising for our annual concert. He said "What's your name?" I said "Winston Sir". "Winston what?" said he. "Winston Groovy" I said - Laurel laughed his head off and said "Groovy-Groovy-that's a good one, big headed already eh?"

"No Sir" I said "That's what they call me".

He laughed again and said "never mind I won't call you that but I think you have a good voice and with training you might become something. Would you like me to introduce you to my recording company?" I couldn't believe my ears and jumped at the chance. Well he brought me to his company and here I am one year later making an album.

Laurel I thank you for this introduction, for without you I am sure PAMA wouldn't have given me a chance. Man they are a fussy company.

The first day I met Mr Jeff, he said to Laurel "What sort of country boy is this you asking me to spend money on, he looks so hungry he couldn't even sing for his dinner". I must say he was generous that day because when I finished singing, Mr Jeff himself took me in his car to a restaurant and bought me a wacking great dinner. I am still singing for my dinner although these days I buy my own and thank God I earn very well from my profession.

O.K. I have reminisced enough and I am sure you want to go on and listen to the record. Well it was made for you. I tried my best to please you and I hope you will be. I've got no favourite tracks on it but each one was sung with a special meaning and I just want to go on GROOVIN.

Yours Sincerely
Winston Groovy

PAMA RECORDS 78 Craven Park Road London NW10

SYDNEY CROOKS

ARTIST / PRODUCER

Sydney Crooks et al was born in the Westmoreland area of West Jamaica in 1954 and like so many of his peers have done he moved to Trench Town in his teens and entered the music business in 1962 when ska was taking off. He became a member of The Pioneers along with his brother Derrick and later joined by Winston Hewitt. He began working at Joe Gibbs record shop with the connection allowing the group to gain studio time and with the arrival of a new lead singer Jackie Robinson the group began achieving recognition in Jamaica in 1968.

Their first record Good Nannie featured just Sydney and his brother Derrick. The story goes that while recording another song he needed a backing for the vocals and outside the studio Jackie Robinson just happened to be singing and was invited by Sydney Crooks AKA Norris Cole, Luddy Pioneer to assist with the recording and proved so successful he was invited to join the group. The Pioneers boss reggae years need no preamble as Long Shot Kick De Bucket took the UK by storm with the group performing some of the most endearing songs from the boss reggae period. A move into production for Sydney has elevated the progress and success of many Jamaican artists. He is considered one of the most prolific producers of Jamaican music with a plethora of artists including but not limited to The Viceroys, Gregory Isaacs, The Slickers, Alton Ellis and that's just the productions issued on Pama's Bullet label.

The Sydney Allstars had five tracks released on Bullet, most noticeable were the skinhead boss favourites **Return Of Batman** issued on BU-436 in 1970 and **Outer Space** BU-437 the same year. The flip side of BU-441 released in 1970 featured **Stackato**, an excellent example of Boss Reggae at its best carrying the instrumental version of the A side **Chariot Coming** from The Viceroys, which itself featured on the inaugural Straighten Up in 1971.

THE HIPPY BOYS

LLOYD CHARMERS

Lloyd Charmers was born Lloyd Tyrell one of his aliases whose career bridges the ska and rocksteady years as well as being prolific during the emergence of reggae. He was not only a vocalist but a session musician and producer.

His first introduction to the music business was preforming as a duo with Roy Willis as The Charmers and they were soon taken under the wing of Clement Coxsone Dodd. He eventually formed his own band with an impressive line up of Alva 'Reggie' Lewis, and the brothers Carlton Barrett, the drummer who was the creator of the one drop style and Aston 'Family Man' Barrett and became known as The Hippy Boys. They linked with the up and coming producer Bunny 'Striker' Lee and were used for backing on Bangarang adopting the name Bunny Lee All-Stars. Charmers also had a stint singing with The Uniques. Their reputation for producing driving rhythms for the new reggae beat saw them team up with Lee' Scratch 'Perry who changed their name to the Upsetters for his session work. The group then inadvertently provided Harry Johnson with his massive skinhead hit Liquidator, with the rhythm track laid down for Tony Scott's What Am I To Do. Scott then sold the track to Harry Johnson and Winston Wright. Pama issued work from The Hippy Boys and Charmers on Bullett, Escort, Gas and Supreme with the group credited as The Reggaeites on Harris Wheel issued as the B side to Derrick Morgan's Moon Hop on Crab. Charmers eventually made a move to a solo career releasing several risqué outings.

BU-412 Hog In A Me Minti - The Hippy Boys 1969
Produced by: Ranny Williams
Boss sounds from '69 with a driving rhythm, classic skinhead reggae.

BU-413 What's Your Excuse / Tell Me Tell Me - The Hippy Boys 1969
Produced by: Ranny Williams
More organ led Boss sounds from '69 pulsating reggae at its best, Tell Me Tell Me on the B side takes the nod.

BU-435 Dollars And Bonds - Lloyd Tyrell *(Actually The Hippy Boys)* **1970**
Produced by: Lloyd Charmers
Lloyd Charmers distinctive style with a melodic beat.

BU-473 Reggae In Wonderland / Wonder (Version) -The Charmers 1970
Produced by: Lloyd Tyrell
This melodic tune was issued in Jamaica and credited on the Splash label to the trumpeter Lester Williams from Byron Lee And The Dragonaires. The track is a version of Bert Kaempfert And His Orchestra's Wonderland By Night from 1960.

BU-486 Summer Place - Ranny Williams And The Hippy Boys 1970
Produced by: Ranny Williams
An organ led melody, a cover of the hit Theme From A Summer Place.

WINSTON GROOVY

Winston TUCKER was born in 1946 in Kingston Jamaica, perhaps better known to most as Winston Groovy. His first recording for producer King Edwards titled She's Mine was never released. At the time Edwards ran one of the main three sound systems in Jamaica, the others being Duke Reid and Coxone Dodd.

He moved to England in 1961 to be with his father in Birmingham. While still at school he joined a group called The Ebonites. In 1969 he moved to London and began working with producer Laurel Aitken, a move that resulted in a change of stage name to Winston Groovy and a single Yellow Bird was released on the revamped New Beat label NB-055 in 1970, giving him some recognition. Further singles were issued with I Wanna Be Loved on Bullet BU-471 and Something For Breakfast, a duet with Pat Rhoden on Bullet BU-475, giving him his first real taste of success in 1971.

There were several colour variations on the Bullet label

CAMEL

CA-21 Wonder Of Love / Cinderella - The Inspirations 1969
Produced by: Murphy / Murphy
CA-22 Run For Your Life - Carl Bryan / When We Were Young - The Two Sparks 1969
Produced by: Harry Mudie / Harry Mudie
CA-23 Your Sweet Love / Keep It Moving - **The Soul Cats** 1969
Produced by: Ewan Mc Dermott / Ewan McDermott
CA-24 Midnight Spin - Val Bennett / Money Money - Soul Cats 1969
Produced by: Lee Perry / Lee Perry
CA-25 Girl What You're Doing To Me / Woman A Grumble - **Owen Grey** 1969
Produced by: Derrick Morgan / Derrick Morgan
CA-26 History / Just Be Alone - **Harry and Radcliff** 1969
Produced by: H Robinson / H Robinson
CA-27 Sentimental Reason / Lover Girl - **The Maytones** 1969
Produced by: Alvin Ranglin / Alvin Ranglin
CA-28 No More Tear Drops / Love Me Or Leave Me - **Monty Morris and The Maples** 1969
Produced by: Pama Records Production / Pama Records Production
CA-29 Cat Nip / Cooya - **The Hippie Boys** 1969
Produced by: Pama Records Production / Pama Records Production
CA-30 Confidential - Lloyd Charmers / House In Session - Tommy Cowan 1969
Produced by: Lloyd Charmers / Lloyd Charmers
CA-31 The Warrior - The Sensations / Don Juan - Johny Organ 1969
Produced by: Winston Riley / Winston Riley
CA-32 Power Pack - Winston Wright / Throwing Stones - The Two Sparks 1969
Produced by: Pama Records Production / Pama Records Production
CA-33 Beware Of Bad Dogs / Short Cut - **The Soul Mates** 1969
Produced by: Glen Adams / Glen Adams
CA-34 Dont Take Your Love Away / Two Lovers - **Owen Grey** 1969
Produced by: Derrick Morgan / Derrick Morgan
CA-35 Nobody Knows - Tony Sexton and Junior English / Somewhere - Junior English 1969
Produced by: Harry Palmer / Harry Palmer
CA-36 Bongonyah - The Little Roys / Dad Name - The Creations 1969
Produced by: Lloyd Daley / Lloyd Daley
CA-37 Every Beat Of My Heart / Don't Cry - **Owen Grey** 1969
Produced by: Derrick Morgan / Derrick Morgan
CA-38 Drink And Gamble - Young Freddie / King Of The Road - Lennox Brown and Hue Roy 1969
Produced by: Harry Johnson / Harry Johnson
CA-39 The Three Stooge / The Isle Of Love - **Bunny All Stars** 1970
Produced by: Bunny Lee / Bunny Lee
CA-40 In This World / You Better Call On Me - **The Federals** 1970
Produced by: Derrick / Derrick
CA-41 The Worm - Lloyd Robinson / Afro - Neville Hynes 1970
Produced by: Lloyd Daley / Lloyd Daley
CA-42 Gold Digger - The Little Roys / The Mine - The Matadors 1970
Produced by: Lloyd Daley / Lloyd Daley
CA-43 Scrooge / In The Days Of Old - **Little Roy** 1970
Produced by: Lloyd Daley / Lloyd Daley
CA-44 London Bridge - Neville Hinds / Things And Time - The Scorthers 1970
Produced by: Lloyd Daley / Lloyd Daley
CA-45 Dark Of The Sun / Dreader Than Dread - **The Matadors** 1970
Produced by: Lloyd Daley / Lloyd Daley
CA-46 You Run Come - Little Roy / Skank King - The Little Roys 1970
Produced by: Lloyd Daley / Lloyd Daley
CA-47 Black And White Unite - The Maytones / Jumbo Jet - Glorias Allstars 1970
Produced by: Alvin Ranglin / Alvin Ranglin
CA-48 Jumping Dick / Newsroom - **Glorias Allstars** 1970
Produced by: Alvin Ranglin / Alvin Ranglin
CA-49 Since You Left - The Maytones / Bird Wing - Glorias Allstars 1970
Produced by: Alvin Ranglin / Alvin Ranglin
CA-50 Don't Sign The Paper / Packing Up Lonelyness - **Owen Gray** 1970
Produced by: Derrick Morgan / Derrick Morgan
CA-51 Bring Back Your Love / Got To Come Back - **Owen Gray** 1970
Produced by: Derrick Morgan / Derrick Morgan
CA-52 Fight Them - The Little Roys / Dread Lock - The Matadors 1970
Produced by: Lloyd Daley / Lloyd Daley

CAMEL launched with good quality productions and maintained the classic Pama Boss Reggae sound with offerings from The Techniques with Who You Gonna Run To, the Upsetters A Few Dollars More, The Uniques Watch This Sound and Everybody Bawlin by Dennis Alcapone & Lizzy. Add to those Linger A While from John Holt, Nothing Can Separate Us from Owen Gray, Guilty by Tiger and Strange Whisperings from The West Indians featuring Eric Donaldson' distinctive falsetto voice and you have some of the finest recordings from the era of Boss Reggae.

The label continued production through to 1975 with the yellow artwork introduced towards the end of 1972 on CA-95, making it the second longest running of Pama's subsidiaries.

CAMEL DISCOGRAPHY 1969 - 1975 Prefix CA

CA-10 Who You Gonna Run To / Hi There - **The Techniques** 1969
Produced by: Winston Riley / Winston Riley
CA-11 Down In The Park / Love Oh Love - **The Inspirations** 1969
Produced by: Lee Perry / Lee Perry
CA-12 For A Few Dollars More - The Upsetters / Can't Get No Peace - Monty Morris 1969
Produced by: Lee Perry / Lee Perry
CA-13 "Taste Of Killing" / My Mob - **The Upsetters** 1969
Produced by: Lee Perry / Lee Perry
CA-14 Danny Boy / Reggae Happyness - **Cannon Ball King** 1969
Produced by: Derrick Morgan / Derrick Morgan
CA-15 Sad Mood - Delroy Wilson / Give It To Me - Stranger Cole 1969
Produced by: Bunny Lee / Stranger Cole
CA-16 Strange Whispering - The West Indians / Hard To Handle - Carl Dawkins 1969
Produced by: Lee Perry / Lee Perry
CA-17 Hold On Tight - The Scorchers / 100 Lbs of Clay - The Royals 1969
Produced by: Lloyd Daley / Lloyd Daley
CA-18 Facts Of Life - The Mellotones / I'll Be Waiting - The Termites 1969
Produced by: Lee Perry / Lee Perry
CA-19 Everywhere Everyone / Go Find Yourself A Fool - **The Techniques** 1969
Produced by: Winston Riley / Winston Riley
CA-20 Since You Been Gone - Eric Fatter / Cool Down - Winston Hines 1969
Produced by: Harry Johnson / Harry Johnson

CA-53 Catch This Sound / Suspense - **Martin Riley** 1970
Produced by: Martin Riley / Martin Riley
CA-54 Everyday Tomorrow / Lift Your Head Up High - **Stranger Cole** 1970
Produced by: Stranger Cole / Stranger Cole
CA-55 Feel It - Sisters / Serious - G.G. Allstars 1970
Produced by: Alvin Ranglin / Alvin Ranglin
CA-56 Everbody Bowling / Mr. Brown - **Niney And The Observers** 1970
Produced by: Niney / Niney
CA-57 Selassie Want Us Back -The Little Roys / Make It With You - Roy And Joy 1970
Produced by: Lloyd Daley / Lloyd Daley
CA-58 '1970' / Version Of '70 - **Ron Sig** 1970
Produced by: Ron Sig / Ron Sig
CA-59 You Girl - Roy Edwards / Facts Of Life - Slim Smith & Roy Shirley 1970
Produced by: Ron Sig / Bunny Lee
CA-60 Groove Me / No Other One - **Owen Gray** 1971
Produced by: Sydney Crooks / Sydney Crooks
CA-61 Judas / Mi Nah Tek - **The Maytones** 1971
Produced by: Alvin Ranglin / Alvin Ranglin
CA-62 Donkey Skank - Delroy And The Tennors / Donkey Track - Murphy Allstars 1971
Produced by: G Murphy / G Murphy
CA-63 Hold On - Sisters / Cleanliness - The Maytones
Produced by: Alvin Ranglin / Alvin Ranglin
CA-64 I Will Never Fall In Love Again - Winston Harewood / La-Fud-Dil -
La-Fud-Dil All Stars 1971
Produced by: La-Fud-Dil / La-Fud-Dil
CA-65 Talk About Love - Pat Kelly / Love Music - Phill Pratt All Stars 1971
Produced by: Phill Pratt / Phill Pratt
CA-66 Black Equality / Suffering - **Max Romeo** 1971
Produced by: Unknown
CA-67 Heavy Load / Heavy (Version) - **Pressure Beat** 1971
Produced by: Joe Gibbs / Joe Gibbs
CA-68 Rice And Peas / All The While - **Dandy & Shandy** 1971
Produced by: Keith Chin / Keith Chin
CA-69 Be My Wife - Delroy Wilson / Hit Me Back Baby - Joe Higgs 1971
Produced by: Herman Walters / Herman Walters
CA-70 Guilty / Funny Funny Man - **Tiger** 1971
Produced by: Laurel Aitken / Laurel Aitken
CA-71 Silhouettes / That Did It - **Winston Wright** 1971
Produced by: Lee Perry / Lee perry
CA-72 Crying - Stranger Cole / It Must Come - Delroy & Dennis 1971
Produced by: Byron Smith / Bunny Lee
CA-73 Nothing Can Separate Us / Girl I Want You To Understand - **Owen Gray** 1971
Produced by: Sydney Crooks / Harry Palmer
CA-74 This A Butter - Dennis Alcapone / Butter (Version) - Phil Pratt All Stars 1971
Produced by: Phil Pratt / Phil Pratt
CA-75 Running Back Home -The Rocking Horse / Running Back (Version) -
Soul Syndicate Band 1971
Produced by: H Thomas / H Thomas
CA-76 I Love You The Most / Most (Version) - **Morgan's All Stars** 1971
Produced by: Derrick Morgan / Derrick Morgan
CA-77 When Will We Be Paid - Martin Riley / He's Got The Whole World In His Hands -
Willie Francis 1971
Produced by: Martin Riley / Willie Francis
CA-78 Linger A While - John Holt / Version - Lloyd's All Stars 1971
Produced by: Lloyd Daley / Lloyd Daley
CA-79 Seven In One (Part One) / Seven In One (Part Two) - **The Gaylads** 1971
Produced by: H Chin-Loy & BB Seaton / H Chin-Loy & BB Seaton
CA-80 Freedom Train - The Gladiators / Marcus is Alive - Willie & Lloyd 1971
Produced by: Lloyd Daley / Willie Francis
CA-81 Spanish Harlem / Slipaway - **Slim Smith** 1971
Produced by: Bunny Lee / Bunny Lee
CA-82 The Coming Of Jah / Watch And Pray - **Max Romeo** 1972
Produced by: Winston Holness - Lee Perry /Winston Holness - Lee Perry
CA-83 Put Me Down Easy / I Want To Go Back Home - **The Groovers** 1972
Produced by: F Crossfied / F Crossfield
CA-84 I Am Just A Sufferer / We Want To Know - **Derrick Morgan** 1972
Produced by: Derrick Morgan / Derrick Morgan
CA-85 Rasta Band Wagon / When Jah Speaks - **Max Romeo** 1972
Produced by: Winston Holness / Winston Holness

CA-86 Public Enemy No 1 - Max Romeo / How Long Must We Wait -
Max Romeo & The Prophet 1972
Produced by: Lee Perry / Max Romeo - Glen Lee
CA-87 Black Cinderella - Errol Dunkley / Our Anniversary - Phil Pratt All Stars 1972
Produced by: Jimmy Radway / Phil Pratt
CA-88 Audrey / So Nice - **Winston Shan** 1972
Produced by: Ranny Williams / Ranny Williams
CA-89 Take Me Back / Where Do I Turn - **Slim Smith** 1972
Produced by: Bunny Lee / Bunny Lee
CA-90 Africa Arise - Laurel Aitken / Holy Mount Zion - Gi Ginri 1972
Produced by: Laurel Aitken / G Ginri
CA-91 Ain't No Sunshine - Ken Boothe / You Are Everything - Lloyd & Hortense 1972
Produced by: Lloyd Charmers / Lloyd Charmers
CA-92 The Commandments Of Joshua - Charley Ace / Only Love - Gaby and Wilton 1972
Produced by: Charley Ace / Charley Ace
CA-93 (Not Used)
CA-94 Wonderful World - Alton Ellis / Wonderful Version - Fab Dimension 1972
Produced by: Pete Weston / Pete Weston
CA-95 My Confession - Cornel Campbell / Daddy's Home - Pat Kelly 1972
Produced by: Bunny Lee / Bunny Lee
CA-96 Darling Forever - The Clarendonians / Forever Version - Kenneth Wilson Allstars 1972
Produced by: Peter Austin - Ken Wilson / Peter Austin - Ken Wilson
CA-97 (Not Used)
CA-98 Presenting Cheater - Ansil Collins & Elaine / Official Trombone - Don Wilson 1972
Produced by: Lloyd Parks / Lloyd Parks
CA-99 Ten Times Sweeter Than You / Fat Boy - **Tony Gordon** 1972
Produced by: Rico / Rico
CA-100 Lean On Me - B.B. Seaton / Black Heart - U Roy 1972
Produced by: Lloyd Charmers / Lloyd Charmers
CA-101 Jamaica Song / Out Of Love - **Lloyd Charmers** 1972
Produced by: Lloyd Charmers / Lloyd Charmers
CA-102 The Man In Your Life - Les Foster & Ansil Collins / May Never See My Baby -
Derrick Morgan 1973
Produced by: Derrick Morgan / Derrick Morgan
CA-103 Must I Be Blue / Blue Version - **Owen Thompson** 1973
Produced by: Owen Thompson / Owen Thompson
CA-104 (Not Used)
CA-105 Room Full All Full / Room Version - **Twinkle Brother** 1973
Produced by: Norman Grant / Norman Grant
CA-106 Every Day Is The Same Kind Of Thing - Sister / The Sweat Of Your Brow -
Shortie Perry 1973
Produced by: Alvin Ranglin / Alvin Ranglin
CA-107 Rainy Weather - Roy and Joe / Version - Den Brothers 1973
Produced by: Dennis Brown / Dennis Brown
CA-108 "Baby" Someday I'll Want To Know / Version - **Dennis Brown** 1973
Produced by: Dennis Brown / Dennis Brown

CAMEL SECOND SERIES 1975

CA-2001 Miss Wire Waist - Carl Malcolm / Wire Dub - Justin Hinds 1975
Produced by: Randy Chin / Randy Chin
CA-2002 Wolverton Mountain - Roman Stewart / Version - Carl Pitterson All Stars 1975
Produced by: Carl Pitterson / Carl Pitterson
CA-2003 Knotty Screw Face - Yvonne Harrison / Face Dub - Underground Express 1975
Produced by: Glen Adams / Glen Adams
CA-2004 Lonely Days - Gregory Isaacs / Lonely Dub - G.G. All Stars 1975
Produced by: Hazel Ellis / Hazel Ellis
CA-2005 (Not Used)
CA-2006 Every Night / Ethiopia - **Ruddy & Sketto Ritch** 1975
Produced by: Laurel Aitken / Laurel Aitken
CA-2007 La Vieen Rose / Spanish Eyes - **Laurel Aitken** 1975
Produced by: Laurel Aitken / Laurel Aitken
CA-2008 Dance With Me / Dance Dub - **Gregory Isaacs** 1975
Produced by: Gregory Isaacs / Gregory Isaacs
CA-2009 Everbody's Somebody's Fool - Barbara Jones / Version - The Sunshot Band 1975
Produced by: Phil Pratt / Phil Pratt
CA-70 Guilty / United We Stand - **Tiger** 1975 *
Produced by: Laurel Aitken / Laurel Aitken
* A reissue of the 1971 single using the same prefix but with an alternative B side.

BOSS SOUNDS FROM CAMEL

Boss Sounds from CAMEL brings some of the highlights from the labels production between 1969 and 1975.

CA-47 Black And White Unite - The Maytones 1970
Produced by: (A Gloria Records Production) Alvin Ranglin
Not the Maytones Black And White version of Greyhound's hit but the track used as Straighten Up on Pama's inaugural album in the series. The prominent base-line is accentuated by the concious lyrics to Straighten Up.

CA-55 Feel It - Sisters 1970
Produced by: Alvin Ranglin
Actually by Paulette & Gee and released on Trojan's GG label as Feel It More And More as a B side to Winston Wright's It's Been A Long Time (instrumental version). Organ led introduction and one guaranteed to get you on the dance floor with its wonderful infectious beat.

CA-20 Since You Been Gone - Eric Fatter 1969
Produced by: Pama Camp
A first class single with an excellent beat and outstanding vocals that has appeared on many Boss Reggae albums and featured on The Best of Camel, An Oasis of Sound.

CA-16 Strange Whispering - The West Indians 1969
Produced by: Lee 'Scratch' Perry
Eric Donaldson was the lead singer for the trio and went on to follow a successful solo career. The other members were Hector Brooks and Leslie Burke. A driving beat with Eric's unmistakable falsetto voice dancing around the lyrics.

CA-70 Guilty - Tiger 1971
Produced by: Laurel Aitken
Produced and sung by Laurel as Tiger is in fact Laurel himself. The rhythm track was first used on Nobody But Me, released on the B side of Baby Please Don't Go, both tracks from Laurel were issued on New Beat NB-054 in 1970. Guilty was re issued in 1975 using the same prefix but with an alternate B side.

CA-11 Down In The Park - The Inspirations 1969
Produced by: Lee Perry
The second release on the label was a Lee Perry production from The Inspirations AKA Billy Dyce and Jimmy London. A boss sound from the combination that brought us the classic Tighten Up, although credited to The Untouchables.

CA-25 Girl What You're Doing To Me - Owen Grey 1969
Produced by: A Pama Records Production
Another excellent track from Owen Grey, his trade-mark falsetto vocals ringing out over an hypnotic beat ensured the single sold very well and only just failed to chart.

CA-10 Who You Gonna Run To - The Techniques 1969
Produced by: Winston Riley
The single that launched the label is a pulsating reggae sound but the artists are actually The Shades.

CA-41 The Worm - Lloyd Robinson 1970
Produced by: Lloyd Daley
This is up there with the best, Lloyd Robinson's Jamaican version of Queen Of The World from Lloyd & Claudette issued on Trojan's Big Shot the same year The Jamaican release was issued on Lloyd Daley's Matador Records.

CA-78 Linger A While - John Holt 1971
Produced by: Lloyd Daley
Linger A While needs no introduction from the talented John Holt. The B side has John Holt toasting over an instrumental version although not in the same league as Hugh Roy who he had previously teamed up with on Wear You To The Ball.

CA-85 Rasta Bandwagon - Max Romeo 1972
Produced by: Niney & Lee Perry
A complete change from the boss sounds for Max Romeo with an hypnotic beat and Rastafarian lyrics.

CA-27 Sentimental Reason - The Maytones 1969
Produced by: (A Pama Production) Alvin Ranglin
The duo of Vernon Buckley and Gladstone Grant took their name from their home-town May Pen in Clarendon Jamaica. Sentimental Reason is vibrant early reggae at its very best.

CA-13 "Taste" Of Kiling - The Upsetters 1969
C/W **My Mob - The Upsetters**
Produced by: Scratch
A trade mark Lee Perry production from his studio-band The Upsetters. Both tracks feature on the album Clint Eastwood PSP 1014 released in 1970.

CA-56 Everbody Bowling - Niney And The Observers 1970
Produced by: Winston Holness - Niney
A take on The Melodians and Hugh Roy's Jamaican release of Everybody Bawling from 1969. This time Dennis Alcapone and Lizzy come together to showcase their talents.

THE BEST OF CAMEL Various Artistes   PAMA SECO 18 1970

Side 1
1. STRANGE WHISPERING - The West Indians 2. WHO YOU GONNA RUN TO - The Techniques
3. GIRL WHAT YOU DOING TO ME - Owen Gray 4. THE WARRIOR - The Sensations
5. CONFIDENTIAL - Lloyd Charmers 6. BONGO NYAH - The Little Roys

Side 2
1. EVERY BEAT OF MY HEART - Owen Gray 2. IN THIS WORLD - The Federals
3. GO FIND YOURSELF A FOOL - The Techniques 4. DANNY BOY - Cannon Ball King
5. SINCE YOU'VE BEEN GONE - Eric Fatter 6. YOUR SWEET LOVE - Soul Cats

ECONOMY   MONO   SECO 18

CAMEL AND THE OASIS OF REGGAE

VARIOUS ARTISTES

The Camel is a strong animal and is used as the principle form of transport in the desert lands of the Middle East.

The principle form of Reggae music can be found in one of the strongest labels in the business "Camel" the label that carries a store of strong discotheque material.

We have put together twelve of the strongest numbers released to date on this label and are quite confident that full enjoyment is assured from this album when you listen to hits like "Strange Whispering" from the West Indians, "Who You Gonna Run To" and "Go Find Yourself A Fool" by the fantastic Techniques. The biggest Hits of all on this label to date, Owen Gray's "Girl What You Doing To Me" and Eric Fatter's "Since You've Been Gone". These are just some of the wonderful tracks for your enjoyment on Camels Greatest Hits.

Distributed by: PAMA RECORDS 78 CRAVEN PARK ROAD LONDON NW10 ENGLAND

OWEN GRAY

AKA / OWEN GREY

LLOYD DALEY

PRODUCER

If ever there was list of artists who never received the recognition they deserved then Owen Gray AKA Owen Grey is almost certainly one of them. He released a lot of quality recordings and was among one of the first Jamaican artists Chris Blackwell signed, having the distinction of his recording Patricia being the second record to be released on the Island label back in 1962.

His single Please Let Me Go made it to number one in Jamaica and sold well in the UK which prompted him to relocate to England in 1962. He worked with the top producers including Lesley Kong, Duke Reid, Clancy Eccles and Sydney Crooks. He had another hit with Cupid and a skinhead track Apollo 12. His first release for Pama came with Girl What You're Doing To Me C/W Woman A Grumble on CA-25 in 1969. This was quickly followed up with Don't Take Your Love Away on CA-34. 1970 saw four more singles on Camel with Every Beat Of My Heart, Don't Sign The Paper, Bring Back Your Love and Groove Me. His next release on Camel was Nothing Can Separate Us. Between 69 and 72 he was credited on no less than twenty singles with Pama Records.

The emerging Jamaican ska years had been dominated by a handful of producers including Prince Buster, Clement 'Coxsone' Dodd and Duke Reid and rightly so with their unique contributions. However a new breed of producers were breaking through during the evolving rocksteady reggae scene with Joe Gibbs, Bunny 'Striker' Lee, Leslie Kong and Sonia Pottinger to name but a few. As well as these house-hold names several lesser know but equally important producers were instrumental in the rise of reggae and one was Lloyd 'Matador' Daley. His biggest hit came in 1969 courtesy of his stomping Rasta song Bongo Nyah by The Little Roys released on Lloyd's Jamaican Matador label which remained at the top of the Jamaican charts for some considerable time.

The UK release titled Bongonyah was issued on the Camel label prefix CA-36 the same year. Other Camel highlights include The Worm by Lloyd Robinson issued on CA-41 in 1970 the Jamaican version of Lloyd & Claudette's Queen of The World.

A selection of other productions on Camel.

CA-17 Hold On Tight - The Scorchers 1969
CA-43 Scrooge - Little Roy 1970
CA-44 London Bridge - Neville Hinds 1970
CA-45 Dark Of The Sun - The Matadors 1970
CA-46 You Run Come - Little Roy 1970
CA-52 Fight Them - The Little Roys 1970
CA-57 Sellasie Want Us Back - The Little Roys 1970
CA-80 Freedom Train - The Gladiators 1971

Earl Lowe AKA Little Roy was only sixteen when he had his first hit with Lloyd Daley's produced Bongo Nyah backed by The Hippy Boys in Jamaica.

THE TECHNIQUES

WINSTON RILEY

Winston Delano Riley set out in the music business while he was still at Kingston High School forming The Victors with his friends including one Keith Smith AKA Slim.

The Techniques can be described as a vocal harmony group. Little Did You Know was issued on the Jamaican Treasure Isle label in 1965 and on Island in the UK. Slim Smith left the band in 1966 opting to pursue a solo career and later formed The Uniques initially with Roy Shirley and later Pat Kelly resulting in a plethora of hits during the rocksteady period.

The Techniques line up has transformed over the years with Winston Riley the only constant member. It even including a stint for Dave Barker who went on to achieve a chart topper with Winston Riley's Double Barrel. The group followed Riley who in 1968 had set up his own Techniques label and produced records for many artists. The Techniques had two singles issued on Camel, the labels inaugural release on CA-10 Who You Gonna Run To which was a vibrant early reggae sound and Everywhere Everyone issued on CA-19 in 1969.

PAMA RECORDS LTD. 16 Peterborough Road, Harrow, Middlesex

THE MAYTONES

VERNON BUCKLEY GLADSTONE GRANT

It has long been a Jamaica tradition for a group to form their name reflecting their respective birthplace and The Maytones are no exception. The group were formed in the late 1960s with friends Vernon Buckley, Alvin Ranglin and Gladstone Grant who all grew up in May Pen in the parish of Clarendon, Jamaica. May Pen is an area of Jamaica known for producing several recording artists over the years, perhaps one of its most famous sons was Toots Hibbert who formed the Maytals.

Much of The Maytones early material was produced by Alvin Ranglin who had left the group to become their manager with the Maytones becoming a duo. Their first recording session in 1968 saw the release of Billy Goat a record released in the UK on Trojan's Blue Cat label. It was however the captivating boss reggae track Sentimental Reason issued on the Camel label CA-27 in 1969 that brought their attention to the new found reggae buying public.

The single Black And White Unite with a prominent bass line and conscious lyrics was released in 1970 on Camel CA-47. The track featured on the first volume of Straighten Up with the title changed to Straighten Up for the album.

The follow up single Since You Left was issued on CA-49. The single Serious was issued on Punch PH-35. Two more singles were issued on Camel, Judas CA-61 in 1971 and Cleanliness CA-63 as a B side to Hold On from Sisters.

Two more B sides were issued, one on Escort and one on Punch, before they moved on to release singles on Trojan's GG label. They returned to the fold to release I Am Feeling Lonely on Pama PM-846 in 1972 and their penultimate single As Long As You Love Me on Pama Supreme PS-353. In 1973 Pama released the impressively vibrant Rasta chanting All Over The World People Are Changing on PM-781.

CRAB DISCOGRAPHY 1968 - 1971 Prefix CRAB

CRAB-1 Children Get Ready / Someone To Love - **The Versatiles** 1968
Poduced by: Lee Perry / Eric Barrett

CRAB-2 Fire A Mus Mus Tail / Blacker Black - The Eathopians 1968
Produced by: H Robinson / Bobby Kalphat

CRAB-3 River To The Bank - Derrick Morgan / Reggie Limbo - Peter King 1968
Produced by: Derrick Morgan / Derrick Morgan

CRAB-4 Reggie Hit The Town / Ding Dong Bell - The Eathopians 1968
Produced by: H Robinson / H Robinson

CRAB-5 Spread Your Bed / Worries A Yard - **The Versatiles** 1968
Produced by: Lee Perry / Lee Perry

CRAB-6 Reggae City - Val Bennett / Mellow Trumpet - Cannon King 1969
Produced by: Bunny Lee / Derrick Morgan

CRAB-7 I'm A King / What A Big Surprise - **The Eathopians** 1969
Produced by: H Robinson / H Robinson

CRAB-8 Seven Letters - Derrick Morgan / Lonely Heartaches - The Tartons 1969
Produced by: Derrick Morgan / Ken Lack

CRAB- 9 Private Number / Another Chance - **Ernest Wilson** 1969
Produced by: Derrick Morgan / Derrick Morgan

CRAB-10 Run Girl Run - G.G. Grossett / The Drifter - Dennis Walks 1969
Produced by: Harry Mudie / Harry Mudie

CRAB-11 The First Taste Of Love - Derrick Morgan / Dance All Night - The Tartans 1969
Produced by: Derrick Morgan / Ken Lack

CRAB-12 Work It / You Mean So Much To Me - **The Viceroys** 1969
Produced by: Lloyd Daley / Lloyd Daley

CRAB-13 Take Your Hand From My Neck / Equality And Justice - **The Paragans** 1969
Produced by: Lloyd Daley / Lloyd Daley

CRAB-14 Please Please - The Caribbeans / The Destroyer - The Matadors 1969
Produced by: Lloyd Daley / Lloyd Daley

CRAB-15 When There Is You - The Melodians / My Woman's Love - The Uniques 1969
Produced by: Winston Lowe / Winston Lowe

CRAB-16 Walking By - Vincent Gordon / Promises Promises - The Viceroys 1969
Produced by: Lloyd Daley / Lloyd Daley

CRAB-17 Freedom Train - Ernest Wilson / You Should Never Have To Come -
Stranger Cole 1969
Produced by: Lee Perry / Duke Reid

CRAB-18 Don't Play That Song / How Can I Forget - **Derrick Morgan** 1969
Produced by: Derrick Morgan / Derrick Morgan

CRAB-19 Hold Down - The Kingstonians / Who Will She Be - Barry York 1969
Produced by: Derrick Harriott / Derrick Harriott

CRAB-20 Tears On My Pillow / I Am Trapped - **Rudy Mills** 1969
Produced by: Derrick Harriott / Derrick Harriott

CRAB-21 Just Once In My Life - Ernest Wilson & Freddie / Mighty Organ - Glen Adams 1969
Produced by: Bunny Lee / Bunny Lee

CRAB-22 Mek It Tand Deay / Come What May - **Derrick Morgan** 1969
Produced by: Derrick Morgan / Derrick Morgan

CRAB-23 Send Me Some Loving / Give Me Back - **Derrick Morgan** 1969
Produced by: Derrick Morgan / Derrick Morgan

CRAB-24 A Heavy Load / Wholesale Love - **Rudy Mills** 1969
Produced by: Derrick Harriott / Derrick Harriott

CRAB-25 Brother Ram Goat - T. Beckford / What A Condition - The Starlighters 1969
Produced by: T Beckford / T Beckford

CRAB-26 Baff Boom / Feel Bad - **The Tennors** 1969
Produced by: G Murphy / G Murphy

CRAB-27 (Promo Only)

CRAB-28 Hard Time - Derrick Morgan / Death Rides A Horse - Roy Richards 1969
Produced by: Derrick Morgan / Stranger Cole

CRAB-29 True Brothers / Sign Of The Times - **The Tennors** 1969
Produced by: G Murphy / G Murphy

CRAB-30 Man Pon Moon - Derrick Morgan / What A Thing - **Derrick Morgan** 1969
Produced by: Derrick Morgan / Pama Records Production

CRAB-31 (Promo Only)

CRAB. The latter part of 1968 saw Pama full of activity with the Crab label brought into the fold and continuing production through to 1971. Crab was launched to cater for productions from Derrick Harriott, Lee Perry, Rupie Edwards, Lloyd Daley and Harry Mudie. It was however Derrick Morgan who became the conquering ruler of the label in terms of performance and productions with almost a third of the output credited to Derrick. Crab was seen by many as being Pama's most prolific with the skinhead in mind, releasing Boss sounds that appealed to the youth of the day.

The pinnacle of the labels success has to be Moon Hop from Derrick Morgan issued on CRAB-32 with music backing from The Rudies. The Jamaican release on Unity of Man Pon Moon featured Moon Hop on the B side but there remains doubt as it may well have featured What A Thing, replicating the B side of Man Pon Moon from Derrick issued on CRAB-30. Moon Hop was selling well on the back of the Apollo 11 moon landing and had reached 49 in the UK chart on 17 January 1970. The progress was however hampered with the release of Skinhead Moonstomp by Symarip from the Trojan stable. Alongside the original Moon Hop Crab issued many classic tracks such as River To The Bank, Hard Time, and Make It Tand Deay from Derrick Morgan. The Ethiopians spelt Eathopians on the label came in with their Reggae Hit The Town and I'm A King along with The Kingstonians Hold Down, The Versatiles Children Get Ready and Spread Your Bed contributing greatly to the labels success.

The album Crab's Biggest Hits was issued on ECO 2 in 1969.

CRAB-32 Moon Hop - Derrick Morgan / Harris Wheel - Reggaeites 1969
Produced by: Derrick Morgan / G Murphy

CRAB-33 Greater Sounds / Live The Life I Love - **G.G. Grossett** 1969
Produced by: Harry Mudie / Harry Mudie

CRAB-34 (Promo Only)

CRAB-35 Long Lost Love / Uncertain Love - **Rupie Edwards** 1969
Produced by: Rupie Edwards / Rupie Edwards

CRAB-36 I Want Everything / Cherry - **The Tennors** 1969
Produced by: G Murphy / G Murphy

CRAB-37 Quaker City / Double Up - **Eric Barnett** 1969
Produced by: Eric Barnett / Eric Barnett

CRAB-38 Devil Woman / Nobody Cares - **The Tender Tones** 1969
Produced by: - Unknown

CRAB-39 Without My Love - Little Roy / Here I Come Again - Winston Samuels 1969
Produced by: Lloyd Daley / Lloyd Daley

CRAB-40 Big Thing - Winston Blake / Exclusively Yours - Rupie Edwards 1969
Produced by: Rupie Edwards / Rupie Edwards

CRAB-41 Never Miss / Redemption - **Rupie Edwards Allstars** 1969
Produced by: Rupie Edwards / Rupie Edwards

CRAB-42 My Elusive Dreams - Ernest Wilson / Hee Cup - Sir Harry 1970
Produced by: Lee Perry / Lee Perry

CRAB-43 (Promo Only)

CRAB-44 A Night At The Hop / Telephone - **Derrick Morgan** 1970
Produced by: Derrick Morgan / Derrick Morgan

CRAB-45 Sentimental Man / Its A Lie - **Ernest Wilson** 1970
Produced by: Bunny Lee / Bunny Lee

CRAB-46 Oh Babe - Derrick Morgan / The Rat - The Thunderbirds 1970
Produced by: Derrick Morgan / Derrick Morgan

CRAB-47 Need To Belong / Let's Have Some Fun - **Derrick & Jennifer** 1970
Produced by: Derrick Morgan / Derrick Morgan

CRAB-48 The Pill - Bim-Bam & Clover / Spring Fever - Tommy McCook 1970
Produced by: Derrick Morgan / Bunny Lee

CRAB-49 (Promo Only)

CRAB-50 Thinking About My Baby / I Wonder - **U.B. Barrett** 1970
Produced by: Derrick Morgan / Derrick Morgan

CRAB-51 I Wish I Was An Apple / The Story - **Derrick Morgan** 1970
Produced by: Derrick Morgan / Derrick Morgan

CRAB-52 Take A Letter Maria - Derrick Morgan & Owen Grey / Just A Little Loving - Derrick Morgan 1970
Produced by: Derrick Morgan / Derrick Morgan

CRAB-53 Rain Is Going To Fall / This Game Ain't Fair - **Denzil Dennis** 1970
Produced by: Derrick Morgan / Derrick Morgan

CRAB-54 Rocking Good Way / Wipe These Tears - **Derrick & Jennifer** 1970
Produced by: Derrick Morgan / Derrick Morgan

CRAB-55 Tennants - Jennifer Jones / Western Standard Time - Reco Rodriguez 1970
Produced by: Derrick Morgan / Derrick Morgan

CRAB-56 I Am Disgusted / Fire In Me Wire - **Bim and Clover** 1970
Produced by: Derrick Morgan / Derrick Morgan

CRAB-57 My Dickie -The Commentator / Brixton Hop - The Kuraas 1970
Produced by: Derrick Morgan / Pama Records Production

CRAB-58 I Can't Stand It No Longer / Beyond The Hill - **Derrick Morgan** 1970
Produced by: Derrick Morgan / Derrick Morgan

CRAB-59 Endlessly / Who's Making Love - **Derrick Morgan** 1970
Produced by: Derrick Morgan / Derrick Morgan

CRAB-60 Having A Party / Man With Ambition - **D.D. Dennis** 1971
Produced by: Derrick Morgan / Derrick Morgan

CRAB-61 Band Of Gold - Joan Ross / Midnight Sunshine - The Hammers 1971
Produced by: Derrick Morgan / Derrick Morgan

CRAB-62 Hurt Me / Julia - **Derrick Morgan** 1970
Produced by: Derrick Morgan / Derrick Morgan

CRAB-63 I Like The Way (You Hug And Kiss Me) / Tell Me Why - **Winston Groovy** 1971
Produced by: Winston Groovy / Winston Groovy

CRAB-64 I've Got To Find A Way To Win Mary Back / Wanna Be There - **Winston Groovy** 1971
Produced by: Winston Groovy / Winston Groovy

CRAB-65 In The Ghetto / Something Sweet - **Rip 'N' Lan** 1971
Produced by: Lorenzo (Laurel Aitken) / Lorenzo (Laurel Aitken)

CRAB-66 Birmingham Cat / Now You Are On Your Own - **The Invitations** 1971
Produced by: Lorenzo (Laurel Aitken) / Lorenzo (Laurel Aitken)

CRAB-67 Searching So Long - Derrick Morgan / Drums Of Passion - Morgan All-Stars 1971
Produced by: Derrick Morgan / Morgan

BOSS SOUNDS FROM
CRAB

Boss Sounds from CRAB brings some of the highlights from the labels perhaps lesser well known productions from over sixty singles issued between 1968 and 1971.

CRAB-15 When Ever There Is You - The Melodians 1969

Produced by: Winston Lowe

The track from The Melodians carried their trade-mark vocals over a strong reggae beat. The group recorded a handful of singles for Pama issued on various labels, namely Punch, Bullet and Gas.

CRAB-32(2) Harris Wheel - The Reggaites 1969

Produced by: Pama Records Production

Harris Wheel is a vibrant organ led track from The Reggaeites *(actually The Hippy Boys)* backed by The Rudies and was issued as the B side to Derrick Morgan's Moon Hop. The track is an instrumental version of Uncle Joe by Austin Faithful.

CRAB-6 Reggae City - Val Bennett 1969

Produced by: Harry Robinson

The boss reggae sound features a strong melodic organ rhythm accompanied by Val Bennett's trade-mark saxophone. The tenor saxophonist had previously performed with Prince Buster's band before joining Bunny Lee's All Stars.

CRAB-19 Hold Down - The Kingstonians 1969

Produced by: Derrick Harriott

Hold Down is very much in the same rhythm as Sufferer which was a huge hit in Jamaica and another skinhead favourite. The Kingstonians also released I am Just A Minstrel on Bullet BU-409.

CRAB-54 Rocking Good Way - Derrick & Jennifer 1970

Produced by: Derrick Morgan

Derrick and Jennifer Jones with a reggae version of the song recorded in 1960 as a pop and R&B duet by Dinah Washington and Brook Benton.

CRAB-45 Sentimental Man - Ernest Wilson 1970

Produced by: Pama Records

Ernest Wilson was originally a member of the vocal group The Clarendonians. In 1969 he teamed up with Freddie McGregor. Sentimental Man was his fifth release on the Crab label.

CRAB-5(2) Worries A Yard - The Versatiles 1969

Produced by: Lee Perry

A good blast of skinhead reggae from The Versatiles issued as a B side to Spread Your Bed. Strong vocals over an hypnotic driving beat.

CRAB-37 Quaker City - Eric Barnett 1969

Produced by: Eric Barnett

An infectious rhythm from Eric with Winston Wright on organ on this instrumental version of The Kingstonians You Don't Remember, a true boss reggae sound.

CRAB-9 Private Number - Ernest Wilson 1969

Produced by: Derrick Morgan

An early release on Crab from Ernest Wilson. A good infectious danceable early reggae beat and a cover of a song first recorded by American soul singers Judy Clay and William Bell in 1968.

CRAB-7 I'm A King - The Eathopians 1969

Produced by: H. Robinson

The Ethiopians follow up to Reggie Hit The Town continuing with their tenor vocals over an early up-tempo reggae beat.

CRAB-8(2) Lonely Heartaches - The Tartons 1969

Produced by: H. Robinson

The rocksteady-reggae tune Lonely Heartaches featured as the B side to Derrick Morgan's legendary Seven Letters. The label credits the recording to The Tartons however the artists were in fact The Clarendonians.

CRAB'S BIGGEST HITS Various Artistes PAMA ECO 2 1969

Side 1
1. PRIVATE NUMBER - Ernest Wilson 2. RUN GIRL RUN - G.G. Grossett
3. FIRE A MUSS MUSS TAIL - The Eathopians 4. CHILDREN GET READY - The Versatiles
5. SEVEN LETTERS - Derrick Morgan 6. REGGAE HIT THE TOWN - The Eathopians

Side 2
1. WORK IT - The Viceroys 2. RIVER TO THE BANK - Derrick Morgan
3. SPREAD YOUR BED - The Versatiles 4. WHAT A BIG SURPRISE - The Eathopians
5. REGGAE CITY - Val Bennett 6. LONELY HEARTACHES - The Tartons

The album carried comprehensive sleeve notes as was the case on many of the early Pama albums.

ECONOMY   MONO   ECO 2

CRAB'S BIGGEST HITS
VARIOUS ARTISTES   VOLUME ONE

Reggae music was first introduced into great Britain on the CRAB label and with its very first release too: - "CHILDREN GET READY" by the fabulous group "The Versatiles". This number was an instant hit because of the difference it introduced to the Blue Beat field.

Crab has since then gone on from strength to strength and can be one of the few labels to boast that it has never had a miss yet - and the way things are going it doesn't seem likely to have one ever.

The album contains all hit tunes ranging from the reggae version of "Private number" by Ernest Wilson a promising young Jamaican singer, through to numbers like "Run Girl Run" by the music maestro himself Mr. G. G. Grosett, "Fire a Muss Muss Tail" "Reggae Hit The Town" "Big Surprise" - by The Eathopians a group of talented singers known to all and has frequently toured the world giving concerts with their unique brand of music. From there we move on to Derrick Morgan with his biggest ever hit tune - "SEVEN LETTERS" and another of his great ones entitled "RIVER TO THE BANK". "Work It" is dished up by the Viceroys - a group of boys who sure know how to do their thing. Then we move on to "Reggae City" by an old campaigner "Val Bennett" and "Lonely Heartaches" by The Tartons coming back finally to "Spread Your Bed" by the instigators of the label "The Versatiles".

Yes Sir/Madam Crab is offering all this to you on this budget line "Economy LP. entitled "CRAB'S BIGGSET HITS" and for about one pound sterling - you couldn't do better could you?

Just remember however, that this gesture is made to enable you to have a proper introduction to "CRAB" - so get and buy some of the others on this label with the great line of hit tunes.

Come on then, Hip-Hip-Hurrah three million cheers for the fantastic CRAB Record label and for Volume One of its greatest Hits. Have Fun.

DONALD LEE

A Pama / Crab Records Production - London England and Kingston Jamaica

 Distributed by:- PAMA RECORDS 78 CRAVEN PARK ROAD LONDON NW10 ENGLAND

DERRICK MORGAN IN LONDON   PAMA ECO 10 1969

Side 1
1. SEVEN LETTERS 2. FIRST TASTE OF LOVE 3. HOW CAN I FORGET 4. STAND BY ME
5. DON'T PLAY THAT SONG 6. TOO BAD

Side 2
1. ONE MORNING IN MAY 2. COME WHAT MAY 3. SEND ME SOME LOVING
4. MAKE IT TAN DEAY 5. GIVE ME BACK 6. RIVER TO THE BANK

All tracks were produced in Jamaica contrary to the title however the album sleeve notes are comprehensive from George Cordale.

ECONOMY   MONO   ECO 10

DERRICK MORGAN in LONDON

As soon as a singer makes a hit he gets the inevitable invitation to tour and Derrick's case is no exception. Derrick Morgan a twenty-six year old singer from Jamaica first toured the U.K. in 1963 when he had a hit entitled "She's Gone". Now five years later in 1969 he is once again on tour promoting his recent hit "Seven Letters" but luckily for him another of his records has also just hit, this one is called "Make It Tan Deay" on CRAB-22. So Derrick is busy promoting not one but two hits at the same time. Maybe like me you don't envy him and his work but I do envy him for the loot he is sure to collect from royalty.

Now back to this album. Some very clever people have got together and done a very clever thing, they have produced Derrick in two faces. (1) He is on the great Ben E. King lines doing tunes like of course "Seven Letters" - "First Taste Of Love" - "How Can I Forget" - "Stand By Me" - "Don't Play That Song" and "Too Bad", all are on one side. (2) The other side contains songs more in his usual reggae style - "One Morning In May" - "Come What May" - "Send Me Some Loving" - "Make It Tan Deay" - "Give Me Back" and "River To The Bank".

All these fabulous songs have been picked from Derrick's repertoire which he uses for his stage performances during his present tour of the U.K. and Europe.

The tour has been a tremendous success (to the time of going to press with these notes) and he has played in most of the major Ballrooms in the major cities of the United Kingdom to packed houses of screaming fans shouting frantically for more, more, more of your great numbers with the reggae treatment.

Fans are continuously being turned away from most of the venues at which he appears because of overcrowding and the promoters are laughing all the way to their Banks.

I am sure that before this tour ends Derrick will be re-invited to make another tour of Great Britain. This gentleman is a fantastic singer and a great performer and although he is literally blind his communication with his audience is very strong indeed.

One thing you can be sure of and that is full enjoyment from the contents of this album, twelve great songs well performed to very excellent backing provided by his own touring Band, the complete recording being done at the famous "Club West Indies" here in Harlesden N.W.10. Great Sound - Great Recording. O.K. Derrick - We are listening.

GEORGE CORDALE

Distributed by:- PAMA RECORDS, 78, CRAVEN PARK ROAD, LONDON, N.W.10. ENGLAND

MOON HOP   DERRICK MORGAN   PAMA PSP 1006   1970

Side 1
1. NIGHT AT THE HOP 2. OH BABE 3. LET'S HAE SOME FUN 4. MAN PON MOON
5. JUST A LITTLE LOVIN 6. MOON HOP

Side 2
1. DERRICK TOP THE POP 2. GIVE ME LOVIN' 3. THE STORY 4. THIS AIN'T MY LIFE
5. WIPE THESE TEARS 6. TELEPHONE

CRAB-30 Man Pon Moon 1969
Produced by: Derrick Morgan

CRAB-32 Moon Hop 1969
Produced by: Derrick Morgan

CRAB-44 A Night At The Hop 1970
Produced by: Derrick Morgan

RUDY MILLS REGGAE HITS   PAMA SECO 12 1969

Side 1
1. A HEAVY LOAD 2. WITH EVERY BEAT OF MY HEART 3. JOHN JONES
4. I'M TRAPPED 5. WHOLE-SALE LOVE

Side 2
1. TEARS ON MY PILLOW 2. HANG YOUR HEART TO DRY
3. PLACE CALLED HAPPINESS 4. TIME ON MY SIDE 5. A LONG STORY

The original "John Jones" (You Son Of A Gun) was issued on the Jamaican Move & Grove label in 1968. Described at the time as having an unstoppable rhythm with aggressive lyrics the track soon became a major hit with the skinheads.

"JOHN JONES"
(YOU SON OF A GUN)
-D. HARRIOTT - R. MILLS-
RUDY MILLS

ECONOMY   STEREO   SECO 12

RUDY MILLS REGGAE HITS

The shape of things to come for singing star Rudy Mills is-hit, after hit, after hit. The singer who records for Crystal Records but whose records now appear on the PAMA label, is highly enthused about his career as a singer and often dreams of the day when he will be recognised as Rudy Mills of Rock Steady and Reggae fame and also as an international singing star, sought after by millions. The story of Rudy's emergence into show and record business does not go very far back, one thing is quite sure - he has completely broken through on the record scene as a soloist. Prior to this, he had sung with several vocal groups throughout the country, and by so doing, has amassed an abundance of show-business techniques.

On this LP Rudy has dual-tracked an extremely attractive Reggae effort - "John Jones" (You Son Of A Gun) - the feature tune - and this tune has simply won its appeal to a big, big market - locally and abroad.

Rudy Mills the person - is a descent clean cut "Kat", who has already taken the necessary steps in life to gain an asset, that today - is of vital importance as eating and drinking. The asset? Education - for he has gone through school and college and has made good grades while doing so.

Another thing about this singer - is that he still has his right religious up-bringing in mind. He embraces religion and is an ardent church-goer.

"RUDY MILLS REGGAE HITS" is Rudy's first LP and it offers everything for an evening of real life fun.

JACKIE ESTICK

RECORDED AT: FEDERAL RECORDING STUDIO. SUPERVISION & PRODUCTION: DERRICK HARRIOTT. RECORDING ENGINEER: BUDDY DAVIDSON. VOCAL ACCOMPANIMENT: KEITH & TEX, DERRICK HARRIOTT. BRASS ARRANGEMNTS: BOBBY ELLIS. MUSICAL ACCOMPANIMENT: THE CRYSTALITES. PHOTO-GRAPH & ART DESIGNS: JACKIE ESTICK. ART IMPRESSIONS: GUY COOMBES

Distributed by:- PAMA RECORDS 78 CRAVEN PARK ROAD LONDON NW10 ENGLAND

DERRICK MORGAN

ARTIST / PRODUCER

Derrick Seymour Morgan was born on the 27th March 1940 in the parish of Clarendon, Jamaica. At the age of just seventeen he entered a talent show which he won, receiving a rousing reception. Two years later he began recording for Duke Reid who at the time was resourcing new talent for his Treasure Isle label. One of Morgan's early records, Fat Man, gave him a popular hit in Jamaica. The record was released on the Blue Beat label, then later re worked in 1970 and issued as the flip side of Return Of Jack Slade on Pama's Unity label, UN-546. During the early years of ska Derrick worked alongside Desmond Dekker, Bob Marley and Jimmy Cliff and it was a meeting with Jimmy Cliff that led to a fruitful relationship with producer Leslie Kong.

Derrick created a different record in 1960 being the only artist to hold the top seven positions in the Jamaican chart simultaneously. The following year brought another massive hit for him in his homeland with the release of You Don't Know, a Leslie Kong production later re titled Housewife's Choice, a track now synonymous with the name Derrick Morgan. The record launched a rivalry between him and Prince Buster who accused Derrick of stealing his ideas. Buster released Blackhead Chiney Man taking a swipe at Kong. A counter release was quick to come from Derrick Morgan titled Blazing Fire. Listen to the tracks and you will see how intense the rivalry was. Further releases and counter releases followed including Thirty Pieces Of Silver from Buster with Morgan responding with No Raise No Praise. Clashes often erupted amongst the respective followers to such an extent the government of the day had to step in. A photo shoot was arranged appearing in the Jamaican Daily Gleaner portraying the rivals as friends.

He continued to release first class quality material including Tougher Than Tough, The Conqueror and Seven Letters cited by some as the first true reggae record, although a fact disputed by others. By this time Island in the UK had picked up on Derrick's records releasing tracks like Gimme Back.

Bunny 'Striker' Lee, Derrick's brother in law, who Derrick helped to set up in the music business in 1968 released Hold You Jack in the UK on Island The same year. The record became a huge hit for Derrick in Jamaica and with an up-tempo melodic rhythm track it was utilised for Wet Dream.

A track produced by Bunny Lee that exasperated the great rivalry already existing between Pama and Trojan was Derrick's Seven Letters, released during 1969 in the UK on CRAB-8, as Lee had licensed the track to both companies.

MAN ON THE MOON was the headline from 21st July 1969 and launched a succession of reggae hits. One being Derrick Morgan's Man Pon Moon on Pama's CRAB-30. Moon Hop came next issued on CRAB-32 and with the popularity of reggae in the UK taking off due to the skinheads indulgence Derrick moved to England with Bunny Lee in 1969 to work with Harry, Jeff and Carl at Pama, who were now giving Trojan some serious competition and finally achieving recognition in the UK with the release of the skinhead anthem. Moon Hop with backing provided by London based musicians The Rudies entered the UK chart at number 49 but remained for only one week, no doubt hampered by lack of airplay amongst other things.

CRAB SINGLES DISCOGRAPHY 68-72

CRAB-3 River To The Bank 1968
CRAB-8 Seven Letters 1969
CRAB-11 The First Taste Of Love 1969
CRAB-18 Don't Play That Song 1969
CRAB-22 Make It Tand Deay 1969
CRAB-23 Send Me Some Loving / Give Me Back 1969
CRAB-28 Hard Time 1969
CRAB-30 Man Pon Moon 1969
CRAB-32 Moon Hop 1969
CRAB-44 Night At The Hop 1970
CRAB-46 Oh Babe 1970
CRAB-47 Need To Belong - *Derrick & Jennifer* 1970
CRAB-51 I wish I Was An Apple 1970
CRAB-52 Take A Letter Marie - *Derrick & Owen Grey* 1970
CRAB-54 Rocking Good Way - *Derrick & Jennifer* 1970
CRAB-57 My Dickie (*Label credits The Commentator*) 1970
CRAB-58 I Can't Stand It No Longer 1970
CRAB-59 Endlessly 1970
CRAB-62 Hurt Me 1970
CRAB-67 Searching So Long 1971

PAMA ALBUM DISCOGRAPHY 68-72

ECO 10 Derrick Morgan In London 1969
PSP 1006 Moon Hop 1970

THE ETHIOPIANS

REGGAE HIT THE TOWN

THE VERSATILES

The Ethiopians spelt Eathopians on early Crab labels had an influence on Jamaican music dating back to the days of ska. The famous trio consisted of Leonard Dillon, Stephen Taylor and Aston Morris. With a succession of hits during the ska and rocksteady period they were among one of the first Jamaican acts to tour the U.K. The group perhaps best known for their harmonies emerged toward the end of the ska period. Dillon moved to Kingston having written a number of songs in search of work as a teenager. Living at the time in Trench Town he met up with Peter Tosh who eventually introduced him to Studio One where the Wailers were recording as Peter was impressed with Dillon's original material. Eventually the trio took shape and it was Clement 'Coxsone' Dodd who suggested the that the name Ethiopians would be appropriate. In 1966 they released the classic early rocksteady track Owe Me No Pay Me produced by Lloyd Daley.

The trio became a duo for a short time with Albert Griffiths eventually replacing songwriter Aston Morris.

The group were certainly on the right track in 1967 when they recorded and self produced their chart hit Train To Skaville. Despite no airplay the single reached the top 50 in the UK chart where it stayed for six weeks, peaking at a respectable number 40 on 26th September. Further stand out tracks followed including Engine 54 and The Whip. The success of Train To Skaville brought them to the UK for a short tour in 1968 with a re-run in 1969. Fire A Mus Mus Tail was the groups first release with Pama on CRAB-2 in 1968. With the transition from rocksteady to reggae the group had another single produced by Harry Robinson in Jamaica that was picked up by Pama and issued on CRAB-4 titled Reggae Hit The Town although the label reads Reggie Hit The Town - The Eathopians. A further release followed with I'm A King on CRAB-7 in 1969.

Reggae Hit The Town and Fire A Mus Mus Tail featured on Crab's Biggest Hits ECO 2 in 1969. Satan Girl produced by Lloyd Daley issued on GAS-142 featured on Pama's Birth Control album issued on SECO 32 in 1970. Reggae Hit The Town had an outing on the album Reggae Hits 69 Volume 1 ECO 3 and The Lovely Dozen PSP 1001 both released in 1969.

The vocal trio was formed in 1967 by Keith Byles, Earl Dudley and Louis Davies. Their debut single, Just Can't Win, was recorded at Joe Gibbs Amalgamated Studio. In 1968 the group entered the famous Jamaican Song Festival set up in 1966 with The Time Has Come, which earned them runners-up to Desmond Dekker And The Aces Music Like Dirt (Intensified 68). The trio initially recorded under the name Byles after the lead vocalist who left to pursue a solo career recording under the name Junior Byles. The Crab label was launched with their Children Get Ready and soon followed up with Spread Your Bed, both tracks appearing on Crab's Biggest Hits album and Reggae hits 69 Volume One and Two respectively. The Versatiles disbanded during the mid seventies but remain perhaps one of the most underrated bands of the boss reggae era.

Pama singles:

CRAB-1 Children Get Ready 1968
Produced by: Lee Perry
Good backing and fine lyrics on this early reggae beat from a group that has been together since school days.

CRAB-5 Spread Your Bed 196
C/W **Worries A Yard**
Produced by: Mrs Barnett
Their first was a hit but this is even better, what a follow up, a stomping boss sound, skinhead reggae at its best. The B side is also a sensation and found its way onto Trojans Big Shot label as Worries.

NB-060 Pick My Pocket 1970
Produced by: Laurel Aitken
A different label and producer but still good enough for an outing on Straighten Up Volume 1.

NB-076 Give It To Me 1971
Produced by: Laurel Aitken
Reminiscent of good early reggae.

"JOHN JONES"
(YOU SON OF A GUN)
-D. HARRIOTT - R. MILLS-
RUDY MILLS

RUDY MILLS

ARTIST / AKA JOHN JONES

Discovered by Derrick Harriott Rudolph 'Rudy' Mills was a talented musician but some-what of a late-comer compared to most of his peers, performing with The Progressions and releasing a handful of singles during the rocksteady era with two singles released on Crab in 1969, Tears On My Pillow CRAB-20 and A Heavy Load CRAB-24. Fair Deal from The Progressions featured on the album Reggae To The UK With Love PSP 1004. However Ruddy is probably best known for his massive skinhead hit John Jones. The original Jamaican release in 1968 produced by Derrick Harriott issued on the Move And Groove label prefix-2017 carries the full title as John Jones (You Son Of A Gun). It was issued in the UK on Trojan's Big Shot label finding its way onto the iconic Tighten Up Volume 2 and features on his Pama album Rudy Mills Reggae Hits, along with both Crab singles.

ESCORT

ESCORT is perhaps one of Pama's lesser know labels to the uninitiated albeit with a handful of gems and one oddity which was of course ES-824 an initial release of the original Jamaican cut of Bob And Marcia's Young Gifted And Black, minus the strings of Trojans sweetened version. The vivacious strings added track became a massive hit for Trojan, a formula that worked for Nicky Thomas' Love Of The Common People. The oddity was Pama removed Bob And Marcia's JA cut and replaced it with the same title from Denzil And Jennifer still using the same prefix ES-824 but with a different B side. Some of the Escort gems were Man From Carolina from G.G. Allstars issued as a B side on ES-835, Elisabeth Serenade from Sweet Confusion and What Am I To Do from Tony Scott.

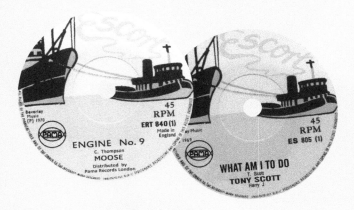

ESCORT DISCOGRAPHY 1969 - 1971 Prefix ES / ERT

ES-801 Hold The Pussy - Kid Gungo / Wha Pen - King Connon 1969
Produced by: Harry Johnson / Harry Johnson
ES-802 Adults Only / Calalue - **Calypso Joe** 1969
Produced by: Harry Johnson / Harry Johnson
ES-803 Shine Eye Gal / Who Nest - **Vincent Foster** 1969
Produced by: Harry Johnson / Harry Johnson
ES-804 Rich In Love - Glen Amams / Zumbelly - The Woodpeckers 1969
Produced by: Harry Johnson / Harry Johnson
ES-805 What Am I To Do / Bring Back That Smile - **Tony Scott** 1969
Produced by: Harry Johnson / Harry Johnson
ES-806 Early In The Morning / Mr Lonely - **The Jamaicans** 1969
Produced by: Harry Johnson / Harry Johnson
ES-807 My Love - Stranger & Patsy / Windsor Castle - Sweet Confusion 1969
Produced by: Stranger Cole / Stranger Cole

ES-808 Don't Let Me Down - Marcia Griffiths / Romper Room - The Reggaeites 1969
Produced by: Harry Johnson / Harry Johnson
ES-809 Elisabeth Serenade / Don At Rest - **Sweet Confusion** 1969
Produced by: Stranger Cole / Stranger Cole
ES-810 Pretty Cottage / To Me - **Stranger "Soul" Cole** 1969
Produced by: Stranger Cole / Stranger Cole
ES-811 Why Did You / Do You Remember - **Stranger Cole and Patsy** 1969
Produced by: Stranger Cole / Stranger Cole
ES-812 Hotter Scorcher / Conquer Lion - **Sweet Confusion** 1969
Produced by: Stranger Cole / Stranger Cole
ES- 813 (Promo Only)
ES-814 Please Stay - Lascelles Perkins / Voyage From Moon - The Matadors 1969
Produced by: Lloyd Daley / Lloyd Daley
ES-815 (Not Used)
ES-816 Darling If You Love Me / Saturday Night - **Tony Scott** 1969
Produced by: Tony Scott / Tony Scott
ES-817 Bandit - Errol Wallace / Family Man Mood - Aston Borrot 1970
Produced by: Aston Barratt / Aston Barratt
ES-818 Boss A Moon - S.S. Binns / Brotherly Love - Bunny Lee Allstars 1970
Produced by: Derrick Morgan / Bunny Lee
ES-819 Leana Leana - Stranger Cole / Nana Na Na Nana - Stranger "Soul" Cole 1970
Produced by: Stranger Cole / Stranger Cole
ES-820 Soul of England / Shang I - **Lloyd Charmers** 1970
Produced by: Lloyd Charmers / Lloyd Charmers
ES-821 Mango Tree / The Removers - **J.J. All Stars** 1970
Produced by: JJ Johnson / JJ Johnson
ES-822 Fight For Your Right - Busty Brown / Soul Fight - Medetators 1970
Produced by: Martin Riley / Martin Riley
ES-823 It Grows / We Had A Good Thing Going - **Martin Riley** 1970
Produced by: Martin Riley / Martin Riley
ES-824 Young Gifted And Black - Bob and Marcia / My Cheri Amour - Barrington Biggs 1970
Produced by: Harry Johnson / Harry Johnson
ES-824 Young Gifted And Black - Denzil and Jennifer / I Am Satisfied - Owen Grey 1970
Produced by: Derrick Morgan / Derrick Morgan
ES-825 Stampeed - The Kuraas / You Were Meant For Me - King Stitt 1970
Produced by: Graham Hawk / Clancy Eccles
ES-826 Remember / Loneliness - **Stranger Cole** 1970
Produced by: Stranger Cole / Stranger Cole
ERT-827 Pop A Top Train / Doing The Moon Walk - **Fitzroy and Harry** 1970
Produced by: Fitzroy Sterling / Fitzroy Sterling
ERT-828 (Promo Only)
ERT-829 Bits And Pieces / Nimrod Leap - **The Pacesetters** 1970
Produced by: G Murphy / G Murphy
ERT-830 Little Things / Till The Well Runs Dry - **Stranger Cole** 1970
Produced by: Stranger Cole / Stranger Cole
ERT-831 Everything With You / Picture On The Wall - Stranger Cole 1970
Produced by: Stranger Cole / Stranger Cole
ERT-832 Pussy / Let Me In - **Stranger Cole** 1970
Produced by: Stranger Cole / Stranger Cole
ERT-833 While There Is Life - Gregory Isaac / Come On Over - Harry Young 1970
Produced by: Gregory Isaacs / Gregory Isaacs
ERT-834 Midnight Sunshine - Family Man / You Are My Sunshine - Gregory and Sticky 1970
Produced by: Roy Smith / Gregory Isaacs
ERT-835 African Melody / Man From Carolina - **G.G. Allstars** 1970
Produced by: Alvin Ranglin / Alvin Ranglin
ERT-836 Hi Shan / Soul At Large - **Lloyd Charmers** 1970
Produced by: Lloyd Terrell / Lloyd Terrell
ERT-837 Crock Iron / Memphis Bop - **Ranny Bop** 1970
Produced by: Ranny Williams / Ranny Williams
ERT-838 Lonesome Feeling - Barbara Andrews / Hop Scotch - Ranny Bop 1970
Produced by: Ranny Williams / Ranny Williams

ERT-839 **Women A Love In The Night Time** / The World On A Wheel - **Lord Spoon and David** 1970
Produced by: Alvin Ranglin / Alvin Ranglin
ERT-840 **Engine No. 9 - Moose** / Do It - The Kukaas 1970
Produced by: Unknown / Derrick Morgan
ERT-841 (Not Used)
ERT-842 **To The Rescue** / Run For Cover - **The Wailers** 1970
Produced by: Bob Morley/ Bob Morley
ERT-843 **A Day Will Come -The Tartans** / Version II - Robi's Allstars 1970
Produced by: Bunny Lee / Bunny Lee
ERT-844 **Work It - The Mellotones** / Good Lover - Soul Man 1970
Produced by: Lee Perry / Lee Perry
ERT-845 **Man Short - Busty Brown** / She Want It - Dave Barker 1970
Produced by: Sonia Pottinger / Sonia Pottinger
ERT-846 **Me A Tell Yuh - The Victors** / More Echo - Lloyd's All Stars 1971
Produced by: Lloyd Daley / Lloyd Daley
ERT-847 **Knock On Your Door - John Holt** / Set Me Free - Uriel Aldridge 1971
Produced by: Bunny Lee / Harry Johnson
ERT-848 **Burn Them** / Poor Boy - **Willie Francis** 1971
Produced by: Willie Francis / Willie Francis
ERT-849 **Chicken Thief - Lloyd Clarke** / Tomorrow - Stranger Cole 1971
Produced by: Bunny Lee - Pat Kelly / Clancy Eccles
ERT-850 **Yester-Me Yester-You Yesterday - Little Roy** / Yes Sir - Matador All Stars 1971
Produced by: Lloyd Daley / Lloyd Daley
ERT-851 (Not Used)
ERT-852 **Life Keeps Turning** / My Conversation - **Slim Smith** 1971
Produced by: Slim Smith / Bunny Lee
ERT-853 **Bachelor Boy - Bill Gentles** / Colour Rites - The Scorpions 1971
Produced by: Derrick Morgan / Derrick Morgan
ERT-854 **Love Brother (Vocal) - Herman** / Love Brother (Inst) - Aquarius 1971
Produced by: Aquarius Productions / Aquarius Productions
ERT-855 **One Woman - Lloyd Terrell** / What Should I Do - **The Charmers** 1971
Produced by: Lloyd Terrell / Lloyd Terrell
ERT-856 (Not Used)
ERT-857 **Peace Treaty** / Brain Wash - **The Conscious Minds** 1971
Produced by: H Seaton / H Seaton
ERT-858 **Girl Tell Me What To Do** / Be Careful - **Fitzroy Sterling** 1971
Produced by: Sydney Crooks / Sydney Crooks
ERT-859 **My Girl - Slim Smith** / Plus One - Reco 1971
Produced by: Sid Bucknor / Sid Bucknor
ERT-860 **Rasta Never Fails -The Charmers** / Rasta (Version) - Charmers All Stars 1971
Produced by: Lloyd Terrell / Lloyd Terrell
ERT-861 **Love & Unity - Cynthia Richards** / Wah Noh Dead - The Maytones 1971
Produced by: Lloyd Daley / Alvin Ranglin
ERT-862 **African Museum** / African Version - **Sounds Combine** 1971
Produced by: Errol Dunkley / Errol Dunkley
ERT-863 **Bend Down Low** / The Burning Feeling - **Groovers** 1971
Produced by: Derrick Morgan / Derrick Morgan

BOSS SOUNDS FROM ESCORT

Boss Sounds from ESCORT brings some of the highlights from the labels production between 1969 and 1971.

ES-809 Elisabeth Serenade - Sweet Confusion 1969
Produced by: Unknown
Elisabeth Serenade (Elizabethan Serenade) is a cover of a composition by Ronald Binge originally titled Andante Cantabile but was altered by the composer to reflect the New Elizabethan Age. Byron Lee released an early version with and update to Elizabethan Reggae on Duke in 1969 eventually credited to Boris Gardiner and seen by many as one of the best reggae instrumentals of all time, Elisabeth Serenade is also up there with them.

ES-824 Young Gifted And Black - Bob And Marcia 1970
Produced by: Harry Johnson
Another of those tracks almost certainly promised to both companies although Pama released the original JA Mix which is far removed from the string laden Trojan version.

ES-824 Young Gifted And Black - Denzil And Jennifer 1970
Produced by: Pama Records Production
The hastily recorded version from Pama by Denzil & Jennifer, better known as Denzil Dennis and Jennifer Jones, still with the same prefix.

ES-805 What Am I To Do - Tony Scott 1969
Produced by: Harry J
Actually produced by Tony Scott this is the vocal version of the revered Liquidator issued before the celebrated instrumental cut from Winston Wright that reached number 9 in November the same year and became a firm favourite on the football terraces as well as at a stomp.

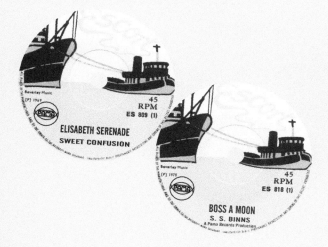

HARRY JOHNSON
PRODUCER / AKA HARRY J

ES-818 Boss A Moon - SS Binns 1970

Produced by: A Pama Records production / Derrick Morgan

Boss A Moon is an organ cut of Derrick Morgan's Moon Hop laid down by Freddie Notes & The Rudies with Sony Binns on organ.

ES-810 Pretty Cottage- Stranger "Soul" Cole 1969

Produced by: Stranger Cole

A vocal led single with a catchy rhythm. Stranger on this occasion was accompanied by Gladdy Anderson. The single featured on the album This Is Reggae PSP 1003.

ERT-849 Chicken Thief - Lloyd Clarke 1971

Produced by: Bunny Lee

The track appears on Max Romeo's Let The Power Fall so is it Max? The lyrics are up-to date as he mentions an electric car. On The Trojan album release of Let The Power Fall it's titled Fowl Thief.

ERT-853 Bachelor Boy - Bill Gentles 1971

Produced by: Derrick Morgan

Bill Gentles was a talented singer and impersonator and could double as Desmond Dekker, Max Romeo and Derrick Morgan to name a few and probably did. This time he comes up with his own catchy version of a Cliff Richard hit.

ERT-860 Rasta Never Fails - The Charmers 1971

Produced by: Lloyd Charmers

The Boss sounds have moved on with this vocal rendition from Ken Boothe and Lloyd Charmers over an hypnotic rhythm.

ERT-844 Work It - The Mellotones 1970

Produced by: Lee Perry

A good Boss reggae tune from The Mellotones.

ERT-835 African Melody - GG Allstars 1970

Produced by: Alvin Ranglin

B side features Man From Carolina from GG Allstars.

Harry Zephaniah Johnson better known as Harry J was born on July 6th 1945 in Westmoreland, Jamaica. He found success as a producer during the reggae era.

His first introduction to the music business was playing the bass with a group called The Virtues but he soon moved on taking a stint as an insurance salesman. A return to the music industry in 1968 saw his first appearance as a record producer setting up his own record label Harry J and releasing No More Heartaches by The Beltones, one of the first reggae songs ever recorded at the same time as Studio One produced Nanny Goat by Larry & Alvin. He had an agreement with Coxsone Dodd allowing him to use the facilities at Studio One where he also produced Cuss Cuss by Lloyd Robinson, a track that has been sampled many times.

It was Lloyd Charmers Hippy Boys who inadvertently provided Harry Johnson with his massive skinhead hit Liquidator. The big international hit starts out with Tony Scott's What Am I To Do released on the Escort label ES-805 in 1969. Scott then sold the track to Harry Johnson. With the help of Winston Wright Harry Johnson created the legendary piece of music with its distinctive organ melody reaching number 9 in the UK chart in November 1969, a boss tune and a record that became an anthem with the emerging skinhead. The song soon became a favourite anthem on the football terraces and remains so over half a century later. The opening bars were used as the introduction on a hit for the Staple Singers, I'll Take You There.

By far the lion's share of early singles released on Escort were Harry J productions. The inaugural ES-801 was Pussy from King Cannon who was actually Sir Lord Comic. This was followed up by Adults Only from Calypso Joe. ES-804 carried Rich In Love credited to Glen Amams but is actually Glen Adams. His Young Gifted And Black first Escort pressing needs no further introduction aside from to say it was the original Jamaican cut. In 1972 he sold his record shop to set up his own studio on Roosevelt Avenue in Kingston, Jamaica. The Harry J Studio became a recording Mecca for many artists including Bob Marley And The Wailers and The Rolling Stones. Chris Blackwell, founder of Island spent a great deal of time at Harry J's before moving to England and Blackwell sent Bob Marley back to Roosevelt Avenue to record the classic album Catch A Fire. The studio also featured in the reggae movie Rockers.

YOUNG GIFTED AND BLACK Various Artistes   PAMA ECO 35 1970

Side 1

1. YOUNG GIFTED AND BLACK - Denzil and Jennifer 2. TAKE ME BACK - Laurel Aitken
3. IN THIS WORLD - The Federals 4. STANDING AT THE CORNER - Winston Groovy
5. RETURN OF JACK SLADE - Derrick Morgan 6. GOLD DIGGER - Little Roys

Side 2

1. ARTIBELLA - Ken Boothe 2. DOLLARS AND BONDS - Lloyd Charmers
3. DOGGY IN THE WINDOW - Doreen Shaffer 4. SCROOGE - Little Roy
5. THE CENSUS TAKER - Rupie Edwards 6. NEED TO BELONG - Derrick And Jennifer

HOUSE IN SESSION LLOYD CHARMERS AND THE HIPPY BOYS PAMA SECO 25 1970

Side 1
1. SOUL AT LARGE 2. SOUL OF ENGLAND 3. AFRICAN ZULU
4. CONFIDENTIAL 5. HOUSE IN SESSION *(Tommy Cowan And The Hippy Boys)* 6. COOYAH

Side 2
1. SHANG I 2. EVERYBODY NEEDS LOVE 3. STRONGER
4. SWEET SWEET 5. LING TONG TING 6. YES SA

ECONOMY   STEREO   SECO 25
ELECTRONICALLY REBALANCED
(PLAYABLE ON MONO)

HOUSE IN SESSION
By Lloyd Charmers

Lloyd Charmers the boss man who has been responsible for quite some time for both the arrangements and Organ playing on the majority of records from the Reggae-land of Jamaica has at last found time to be selfish enough to feature himself fully on an entire album for the pleasure of you and I. Skinheads number 1,2,3 to 15,000. The name Charmers was adopted by this man whose real name, believe it or not, is The Right Honourable Lloyd Tyrell - Mr Bang Bang Lulu himself.

To the majority of his British fans it must be hard to believe that a man who writes and sings such songs as "Bang Bang Lulu", "Lulu Returns", "Birth Control" etc. could be the same person who writes and plays such fantastic melodies as are found on this album in titles such as:- "Soul At Large", "African Zulu", "Soul Of England", " Confidential", "Cooyah", "Shang I", "Everybody Needs Love", "Stronger", "Sweet Sweet", "Ling Tong Ting" etc.

Charmers is no new-comer to the scene because many years back he began his recording career in a group called The Uniques which featured himself, Slim Smith and Martin Riley. May hit tunes have come from that group and even in those by-gone days, Charmers was the sole arranger and instigator of the tunes which "The Uniques" made popular. In session after session, for whatever producer they may be, he is continually and fully employed to play both the piano and the organ in the recordings made in Jamaica. His talents therefore are unlimited as you will certainly discover when you have listened to Charmers At Large - on this album "House In Session". He is of course the Boss.

We know you may want to know something about Charmers, so we tell you. His charming personality first of all won him the name of Charmers, as divorced from Tyrell. He is no mean cat with the girls and like most Jamaicans likes driving fast cars and does in fact own a racing Lotus Cortina, in which I had the privilege and delight of being driven by Mr. Charmers when I was last in Jamaica. He is now twenty-three years of age, unmarried to date and as it would now look has a great musical future in front of him.

Surely I have sung his praises in no mean way but be warned, you will too when you have discovered the great talents of this man. Believe me Reggae Brothers this is possible once you have set your pick-up on the first track of this album and which I am sure you will not take off until you have listened to the entire twelve tracks.

Get going then, what are you waiting for? The House is in Session.

Harry Dee

Distributed by:- PAMA RECORDS 78 CRAVEN PARK ROAD LONDON NW10 ENGLAND

STRANGER COLE

Wilburn Theodore Cole AKA Stranger Cole was born in Kingston in 1945 with his family heartlessly giving him the nickname Stranger as he didn't resemble any family member. He found some early success writing songs and It was Duke Reid who gave him his first break in the music industry during the heyday of ska, giving him a hit with Rough And Tough and When You Call My Name, a duet with Patsy Todd. He performed several duets with his soulful voice as a result of his shyness to perform alone.

Stranger had released a vast amount of material during the ska and rocksteady period with his first two recordings for Pama issued on Unity UN-501 Last Flight To Reggie City with Tommy McCook, using a re-working of a rhythm used on Just Like A River (Stranger Cole And Gladdy) from 1968, and UN-502 Bangarang with Lester Sterling. The Escort connection begins with Pretty Cottage issued on ES-810, a vocal led offering with a catchy rhythm accompanied by Gladdy Anderson.

Other Stranger Cole singles issued on Escort.

ES-807 My Love - Stranger & Patsy 1969
Produced by: Stranger Cole
**ES-819 Leana Leana - Stranger Cole / Nana Na Na Nana -
Stranger "Soul" Cole** 1970
Produced by: Stranger Cole / Stranger Cole
ES-826 Remember / Loneliness - Stranger Cole 1970
Produced by: Stranger Cole / Stranger Cole
ERT-830 Little Things / Till The Well Runs Dry - Stranger Cole 1970
Produced by: Stranger Cole / Stranger Cole
ERT-831 Everything With You / Picture On The Wall - Stranger Cole 1970
Produced by: Stranger Cole / Stranger Cole
ERT- 832 Pussy / Let Me In - Stranger Cole 1970
Produced by: Stranger Cole / Stranger Cole
ERT-849(2) Tomorrow - Stranger Cole 1971
Produced by: Clancy Eccles

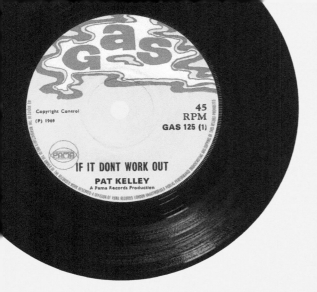

GAS

GAS-107 Pictures Of You / Searching For My Baby - **Nola Campbell** 1969
Produced by: Harry Palmer / Harry Palmer
GAS-108 Ring Of Gold / You've Got It - **The Melodians** 1969
Produced by: Winston Lowe / Winston Lowe
GAS-109 Choo Choo Train / The Load - **Soul Cats** 1969
Produced by: Harry Mudie / Harry Mudie
GAS-110 Workman Song / Never Give Up - **Pat Kelly** 1969
Produced by: H Robinson / H Robinson
GAS-111 The Weight - Stan Hope / Tell Me Now - **Marcia Griffiths** 1969
Produced by: Coxson Dodd / Coxson Dodd
GAS-112 1,000 Tons Of Megaton / Musical Resurrection - **Roland Alphonso** 1969
Produced by: Bunny Lee / Bunny Lee
GAS-113 Soul Call / Musical Gate - **Soul Rhythms** 1969
Produced by: Joe Sinclair / Joe Sinclair
GAS-114 Walking Proud - Martin Riley / Why Baby - Lloyd Charmers 1969
Produced by: Winston Lowe / Winston Lowe
GAS-115 How Long Will It Take / Try To Remember - **Pat Kelley** 1969
Produced by: Bunny Lee / Bunny Lee
GAS-116 Personally Speaking / Trouble Trouble - **The Melodians** 1969
Produced by: Winston Lowe / Winston Lowe
GAS-117 Too Proud To Beg / Love And Devotion - **The Uniques** 1969
Produced by: Bunny Lee / Bunny Lee
GAS-118 Wanted - Baba Dise / I'll Always Love You - **The Sensations** 1969
Produced by: Winston Riley / Winston Riley
GAS-119 Never Gonna Give You Up / Let Me Remind You - **The Shades** 1969
Produced by: Winston Riley / Winston Riley
GAS-120 Throw Me Corn (Instrumental) - Ronny Williams / Temptation - The Hippy Boys 1969
Produced by: Ranny Williams / Hippy Boys
GAS-121 Janet - Tony and The Hippy Boys / Beleive Me - **The Harmonians** 1969
Produced by: Ranny Williams / Ranny Williams
GAS-122 (Promo Only)
GAS-123 (Promo Only)
GAS-124 Festival Time (Part 1) / Festival Time (Part 11) - **Pat Kelley** 1969
Produced by: Bunny Lee / Bunny Lee
GAS-125 If It Dont Work Out / I Am Coming Home - **Pat Kelley** 1969
Produced by: Bunny Lee / Bunny Lee
GAS-126 I Who Have Nothing / You Send Me - **Nellie** 1969
Produced by: Derrick Morgan / Derrick Morgan
GAS-127 (Promo Only)
GAS-128 (Promo Only)
GAS-129 People Are Wondering / Long Time - **The Show Boys** 1969
Produced by: Rupie Edwards / Rupie Edwards
GAS-130 (Not Used)
GAS-131 When I Am Gone / She Bring Me Joy - **The Clarindonians** 1969
Produced by: Unknown / Unknown
GAS-132 The Vow - Slim Smith and Doreen / Why Didn't You Say - James Nephew 1969
Produced by: Bunny Lee / Bunny Lee
GAS-133 Stagger Back / The Creeper - **Cannon Ball King** 1969
Produced by: A.G. Murphy / A. G. Murphy
GAS-134 Waking The Dead - Carl Bryan / Got What You Want - Trevor and Keith 1969
Produced by: Harry Mudie / Harry Mudie
GAS-135 Ba Ba - Reggae Boys / Power Cut - Glen Adams 1969
Produced by: Lee Perry / Lee Perry
GAS-136 Too Much Loving / Roaring Twenties - **Mood Reaction** 1969
Produced by: Unknown / Unknown
GAS-137 (Not Used)
GAS-138 Sail Away / Fight A Broke - **The Marvells** 1970
Produced by: Derrick Morgan / Derrick Morgan
GAS-139 Someday We'll Be Together - The Marvels / The Rhythm - The Mohawks 1970
Produced by: Derrick Morgan / Derrick Morgan
GAS-140 (Promo Only)
GAS-141 Leaving On A Jet Plane - Glen Adams & The Reggae Boys / Phrases - The Reggae Boys 1970
Produced by: Glen Adams / Glen Adams

GAS was launched in 1968 following in the footsteps of Unity, Nu-Beat and Crab. although the label appeared to lack the purposeful direction of its forerunners it did turn out several first-rate Bunny Lee productions, curious as Lee already had his Unity label in full swing. The label released upward of seventy singles between 1968 and 1971 with the inaugural release on GAS-100 of the excellent instrumental The Horse by Eric Barnet. The record was a hit in the clubs but just failed to make an impact in the conventional charts. The label was an outlet for Pat Kelly with his stand-out How Long Will It Take released on GAS-115, another single that sold well but never charted as the sales were predominantly from non chart return shops, a destiny that held back many excellent Pama singles. Other stand-out singles included 1,000 Tons Of Megaton from Roland Alphonso and The Melodians evocative Ring Of Gold.

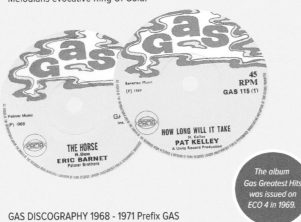

The album *Gas Greatest Hits* was issued on ECO 4 in 1969.

GAS DISCOGRAPHY 1968 - 1971 Prefix GAS

GAS-100 The Horse / Action Line - **Eric Barnet** 1968
Produced by: E Barnet / Lee Perry
GAS-101 Gimme Little / Trip To Warland - **Junior Smith** 1968
Produced by: J Smith / J Smith
GAS-102 Got To Play It Cool / Jezabel - **Fitzroy Sterling** 1968
Produced by: R Docker / R Docker
GAS-103 Reggie In The Wind - Lester Sterling / Try Me One More Time - The Soul Set 1968
Produced by: Bunny Lee / Palmer Brothers Production
GAS-104 Long Life - Billy Gentle / O Tell Me - The Schoolboys 1969
Produced by: H Robinson / H Robinson
GAS-105 Diana / English Talk - **Alton Ellis** 1969
Produced by: Jeff - Alton / Alton - Johnny
GAS-106 Te Ta Toe - Eric Barnet / Lonely And Blue - Milton Boothe 1969
Produced by: Eric Barnet / Eric Barnet

GAS-142 Satan Girl - The Eathopians / The Pum - The Matadors 1970
Produced by: Lloyd Daley / Lloyd Daley
GAS-143 Change Of Heart / Run Away Man - **Mood Reaction** 1970
Produced by: Loyla / Loyla
GAS-144 Tammy / I Am Not Your Guy - **Pat Kelly** 1970
Produced by: Pat Kelly / Pat Kelly
GAS-145 Striving For The Right / When A Boy Falls In Love - **Pat Kelly** 1970
Produced by: Pat Kelly / Pat Kelly
GAS-146 Something Sweet The Lady - Pete Western & His Orchestra / Love Letters - Bim and Clover 1970
Produced by: Pete Weston / Derrick Morgan
GAS-147 Bumper To Bumper / Fat Turkey - **Eric Barnet** 1970
Produced by: Alvin Ranglin / Alvin Ranglin
GAS-148 Something On Your Mind / I Need Love - **Errol Dixon** 1970
Produced by: Errol Dixon / Errol Dixon
GAS-149 (promo Only)
GAS-150 What Kind Of Life - Slim Smith / It's All In The Game - Martin Riley 1970
Produced by: Slim Smith / Sydney Crooks
GAS-151 Suzie / Denver - **Alton Ellis and The Flames** 1970
Produced by: Alton Ellis / Alton Ellis
GAS-152 Lift Your Head Up High (Original) / Everyday Tomorrow (Version) - **Stranger Cole** 1970
Produced by: Stranger Cole / Stranger Cole
GAS-153 So Alive / Mercy Mr. D.J. - **G.G. Allstars** 1970
Produced by: Alvin Ranglin / Alvin Ranglin
GAS-154 I Love You Madly - Busty Brown / A Blue Summer - Lloyd Charmers 1970
Produced by: Lloyd Terrell / Lloyd Terrell
GAS-155 Pipe Dream / Suck Suck - **Ranny Bop** 1970
Produced by: Ranny Williams / Ranny Williams
GAS-156 Daddy Daddy Don't Cry / I Like It - **Tony King** 1970
Produced by: Ranny Williams / Ranny Williams
GAS-157 I Just Don't Know What To Do With Myself / What's He Got That I Ain't Got - **Pat Kelly** 1970
Produced by: Bunny Lee / Bunny Lee
GAS-158 Teach Me - Pat / Sea Breeze - Rythm Rulers 1970
Produced by: Earl George / Earl George
GAS-159 It's Christmas Time Again / If I Could See You - **Norman T. Washington** 1970
Produced by: Derrick Morgan / Harry Palmer
GAS-160 To The Other Woman - Hortense Ellis / Rain Drops - Music Blenders 1970
Produced by: Winston Riley / Harry Palmer
GAS-161 Deliver Us - Alton Ellis / Originator - Neville Hinds 1970
Produced by: Lloyd Daley / Lloyd Daley
GAS-162 Hotter Than Scorcher / Someday - **The Hammers** 1970
Produced by: Tom of Brixton / Tom of Brixton

GAS-163 Work Out / Too Long - **Donald Lee** 1970
Produced by: Bunny Lee / Bunny Lee
GAS-164 Back To Africa - Alton Ellis / Delivered - Neville Hinds 1971
Produced by: Lloyd Daley /Lloyd Daley
GAS-165 Greedy Boy - Nora Dean / Please Stay - Keith 1971
Produced by: Bunny Lee / Bunny Lee
GAS-166 I Shall Sing / Stand By Your Man - **Hortense Ellis** 1971
Produced by: Winston Riley / Winston Riley
GAS-167 Blood And Fire - Niney / 33-66 - Roland Alpfanso 1971
Produced by: Winston Holness / Bunny Lee
GAS-168 What You Gonna Do About It - Ernest Wilson / Halfway To Paradise - Dobby Dobson 1971
Produced by: Rupie Edwards / Rupie Edwards
GAS-169 Give It To Me - Ken Boothe / Why 1971
Produced by: Phil Prat / Phil Prat
GAS-170 (Not Used)
GAS-171 Love / With All Your Heart - **Pat Kelly** 1971
Produced by: Pat Kelly / Pat Kelly

BOSS SOUNDS FROM GAS

Boss Sounds from GAS brings some of the highlights from the labels production between 1968 and 1971. Often referred as the label without direction it nevertheless produced several gems.

GAS-100 The Horse - Eric Barnet 1968
Produced by: E Barnet

What a statement to launch a label with a Boss driving sound, the instrumental a take on Ronald Russell's Rhythm Hips.

GAS-115 How Long Will It Take - Pat Kelley 1969
Produced by: Bunny Lee

Pat Kelley (Kelly) left The Techniques to pursue a solo career in late '68. Working with Bunny Lee How Long Will It Take was released in 1969 and became a strong seller for Pama. In Jamaica - How Long - made the top spot issued on the Jamaican Pama imprint. As has been stated it would have been a UK chart hit for Pama had it not sold in predominantly non chart return outlets

GAS-145 Striving For The Right - Pat Kelly 1970
Produced by: Pat Kelly

This one is self produced by Pat Kelly whose falsetto voice finds its way around an infectious melodic reggae beat, one guaranteed to get the dance-floor stomping. This one is up there with his best.

GAS-112 1,000 Tons Of Megaton - Roland Alphonso 1969

Produced by: Bunny Lee

Roland Alphonso comes up with a boss saxophone performance on a another take of Slim Smith's Everybody Needs Love rhythm.

GAS-142 Satan Girl - The Eathopians 1970

Produced by: Lloyd Daley

The Ethiopians still being spelt Eathopians Satan Girl found its way onto the album Birth Control released on SECO 32 in 1970.

GAS-151 Suzie - Alton Ellis and The Flames 1970

Produced by: Alton Ellis

A fabulous reggae beat and vocals from Alton Ellis backed by The Flames whose former members including Winston Jarrett reformed as The Righteous Flames.

GAS-116 Ring Of Gold - The Melodians 1969

Produced by: Winston Lowe

A trade mark vocal rendition from Brent Dowe, Trevor McNaughton and Tony Brevett AKA The Melodians.

GAS-144 Tammy - Pat Kelly 1970

Produced by: Pat Kelly

A fast paced rhythm is enhanced with the soulful falsetto voice of Pat Kelly one of twelve tracks featured on his Pama album Pat Kelly Sings PMLP 12.

GAS-109 Cho Cho Train - Soul Cats 1969

Produced by: M Mudie

A driving rhythm and intermittent vocals makes for a stand out boss sound continuing on from the the successful ska theme of trains. Features on Gas Greatest Hits ECO 4.

GAS-106 Te Ta Toe - Eric Barnet 1969

Produced by: Eric Barnet

A pulsating instrumental rhythm. The provenance has been questioned as the Jamaican release credits Theo Beckford, but whoever the track is still a boss sound.

GAS-120 Throw Me Corn (Instrumental) - Ronny Williams 1969

Produced by: Ranny Williams

The instrumental version of the record that launched the Bullet label, a vibrant early reggae beat guaranteed to get you dancing. Credited to Ronny Williams the producer the track is actually Cannon Ball Special by Cannon Ball King.

PAT KELLY
SINGER / PRODUCER

Born in 1949 Horatious Adolphus AKA Pat Kelly (Kelley) the soulful man of reggae was heavily influential during the rocksteady years. After a brief spell as a soloist he found himself replacing Slim Smith, who'd left The Techniques, teaming up with Bruce Ruffin and Winston Riley at a time when the ska beat was shifting to rocksteady. Kelly's falsetto voice influenced by Sam Cooke ensured The Techniques maintained the success the group had enjoyed with Slim Smith with classics such as My Girl and Love Is Not A Gamble. He decide to pursue a solo career in 1968 at a time when the beat was shifting into reggae.

In 1969 he cut some tracks for Lee 'Scratch' Perry and Bunny Lee and it was the Lee production How Long Will It Take that really launched his career. The record was the biggest selling Jamaican single of 1969 and believed to be the first reggae song to be overdubbed with strings when it was released in UK on Pama's Gas label. A deal was signed with Pama and the album Pat Kelly Sings PMLP 12 engineered by Lee Perry was released in 1969. It is well documented Kelly was offered a contract with Apple Records. The deal was said to be worth £25,000 but Slim was unable to accept due his contractual arrangements with Pama

As well as a talented singer Pat Kelly also had a hand in production. He was responsible for several singles issued on Pama.

Pat Kelly singles issued on Gas.

GAS-110 Workman Song / Never Give Up **1969**
Produced by: H Robinson / H Robinson
GAS-115 How Long Will It Take / Try To Remember **1969**
Produced by: Bunny Lee / Bunny Lee
GAS-124 Festival Time (Part 1) / Festival Time (Part 11) **1969**
Produced by: Bunny Lee / Bunny Lee
GAS-125 If It Don't Work Out / I Am Coming Home **1969**
Produced by: Bunny Lee / Bunny Lee
GAS-144 Tammy / I Am Not Your Guy **1970**
Produced by: Pat Kelly / Pat Kelly
GAS-145 Striving For The Right / When A Boy Falls In Love **1970**
Produced by: Pat Kelly / Pat Kelly
GAS-157 I Just Don't Know What To Do With Myself /
What's He Got That I Ain't Got **1970**
Produced by: Bunny Lee / Bunny Lee
GAS-171 Love / With All Your Heart **1971**
Produced by: Pat Kelly / Pat Kelly

How Long Will It Take released in 1969 became a strong seller for Pama. In Jamaica - How Long - made the top spot issued on the Jamaican Pama imprint.

GAS GREATEST HITS Various Artistes   PAMA ECO 4 1969

Side1
1. 1,000 TONS OF MEGATON - Roland Alphonso
2. HOW LONG WILL IT TAKE - Pat Kelley 3. REGGAE IN THE WIND - Lester Sterlin
4. WALKING PROUD - Martin Riley 5. TOO PROUD TO BEG - The Uniques 6. THE HORSE - Eric Barnett

Side 2
1. SOUL CALL - Soul Rhythms 2. WANTED - The Scorchers 3. NEVER GIVE UP - Pat Kelley
4. TE TA TOE - Eric Barnett 5. RING OF GOLD - The Melodians 6. CHOO CHOO TRAIN - The Soul Cats

Comprehensive sleeve notes from Lord Reggae follow the Pama format.

ECONOMY   MONO   ECO 4

GAS GREATEST HITS

VARIOUS ARTISTES

GAS - is a Gas and with the Greatest Hits on the Gas label being pooled together on one album nothing could be gassier.

This album contains twelve of the best reggae numbers ever to be released in the U.K. and if you want to learn how to do this new dance, investing in this record is a sure way to success.

If you speak to people who know, Sound System Operators, Disc Jockeys and Discotheque owners, they will give you full assurance regarding the high standard of the recordings on this album, both from the Artistes and material angles.

On this record you have Artistes like - Roland Alphonso doing a powerful knock-out tune entitled - "1,000 TONS OF MEGATON", what tremendous blowing, exciting phrasing and ingenious backing. Fabulous. Then we move to tracks like "REGGAE IN THE WIND" from Mr. Versatile himself - Lester Sterlin followed by "WALKING PROUD" by Martin Riley and "THE HORSE" by Eric Barnett, the number that broke open the R&B Charts for Reggae, plus a gift or two from Jamaica's greatest singer - Pat Kelly, offering such things like "NEVER GIVE UP" and would you belive it ? "HOW LONG WILL IT TAKE".

Yes, Sir, this album is too much, far too much so do your part Reggae Brothers and spread the tidings. After all, you do owe it to your fellow men to give them the full story of the greatest Reggae ever played.

LORD REGGAE

 PAMA RECORDS LTD 78, CRAVEN PARK ROAD, LONDON, N.W.10 ENGLAND

PAT KELLEY SINGS   PAMA PMLP 12 1969

Side 1
1. SINCE YOU ARE GONE 2. TROUBLING MIND 3. TRACKS OF MY YEARS
4. HOW LONG WILL IT TAKE 5. A THOUSAND YEARS
6. TRY TO REMEMBER

Side 2
1. DARK END OF THE STREET 2. FESTIVAL TIME
3. WORKMAN SONG 4. IF IT DON'T WORK OUT
5. THE GREAT PRETENDER 6. NEVER GIVE UP

PAMA   MONO   PMLP -12
(This Record is playable on both Mono and Stereo)

PAT KELLEY SINGS

Mr. PAT KELLEY

"HOW LONG WILL IT TAKE" and other great hits for Pat are included on this album, his very first and we do hope you will enjoy the great singing and talent of this very fine Artiste.

This album is an introduction to the finest quality reggae recordings available to date and offers value for money in any language you wish to interpret it.

Kelley is Jamaican, twenty-six years of age and is a Radio Engineer as well as a Singer Entertainer. His voice has been compared quite favourably to that of the late Sam Cooke.

Peter Peters

Distributed by:- PAMA RECORDS 78 CRAVEN PARK ROAD LONDON NW10 ENGLAND

ROCKSTEADY
ALTON ELLIS
THE GODFATHER OF ROCK STEADY

Known as the GODFATHER OF ROCK STEADY Alton Nehemiah Ellis was born in 1938 in Kingston Jamaica into a musical family in down town Trench Town with his sister Hortense Ellis. He was destined to become one of Jamaica's finest vocalists. His first recording was as early as 1959 for Blue Beat. He worked with John Holt before Holt joined The Paragons. Alton then formed The Flames with Winston Jarrett, David Gordon and his brother Leslie. The initial plan was for the trio to back Alton but they released singles as Alton & The Flames. A man of many talents he had a stint as a studio musician with his voice used numerous times as backing vocals. In 1967 he toured the UK with Soul Vendors.

It was the rock steady era that saw Alton shine with vocal harmonies now more suited to the slowed down tempo and is credited with the first song to use the term rock steady with Rock Steady - *get ready come do rock steady* - issued on the Jamaican Trojan / Treasure Isle label in 1966 and in the UK on Treasure Isle the following year.

Signing for Duke Reid provided Alton Ellis & The Flames an outlet in the UK on Trojan and Gas. He recorded many classic tracks between 1966 and 1968 including his signature song Girl I Have Got A Date issued in Jamaica on Treasure Isle in 1967 and on Doctor Bird in the UK as I've Got A Date. He then released several singles, some were cover version of romantic hits including Bye Bye Love and La La Means I Love You on Nu Beat in 1968. The first single released on Gas was Diana issued on GAS-105 in 1969. Other classics followed on Pama including Moon River on Pama Supreme PS-347 in 1972. Pama issued seventeen singles spread over seven labels including the main Pama imprint between 1968 and 1972.

The original film credits confirm that Alton featured in the 1972 film The Harder They Come playing the stunt double for Jimmy Cliff.

Alton Ellis singles issued on Gas.

GAS-105 Diana / English Talk - Alton Ellis 1969
Produced by: Jeff - Alton / Alton - Johnny
Alton delivers his version on a song written and first performed by Paul Anka in 1957 over a driving reggae beat accompanied by Tommy McCook & The Supersonics.

GAS-151 Suzie / Denver - Alton Ellis and The Flames 1970
Produced by: Alton Ellis / Alton Ellis
Suzie is classic boss reggae from Alton and The Flames.

GAS-161 Deliver Us - Alton Ellis 1970
Produced by: Lloyd Daley
Alton's vocals compliment the hypnotic beat.

GAS-164 Back To Africa - Alton Ellis 1971
Produced by: Lloyd Daley
A Catchy delivery of the classic tune in Alton's inimitable vocal style.

NU-BEAT

NU-BEAT was the first subsidiary label launched in the spring of 1968 specifically to release Jamaican and UK produced rocksteady. The recently formed London Based band The Rudies set the label in motion with Train To Vietnam issued on NB-001 C/W Skaville To Rainbow City with production credited to Palmer Brothers.

Dandy approached Pama with an album worth of material with a view to issuing his work on Nu-Beat but the burgeoning Trojan offered Dandy his own Downtown label. One of Dandy's singles did feature, Engine 59 released on NB-005 and credited to The Rudies with R Thomson as the composer and clearly performed by Dandy. By 1969 Nu-Beat had become an outlet for Laurel Aitken reflecting a change of policy to focus on UK productions and a change of name to New Beat. An album Nu-Beat's Greatest Hits was issued on ECO 6 in 1969 with all tracks issued under the original moniker.

NU-BEAT DISCOGRAPHY 1968 - 1970 Prefix NB (FIRST LABEL)

NB-001 Train To Vietnam / Skaville To Rainbow City - **The Rudies** 1968
Produced by: Palmer Brothers / Palmer Brothers
NB-002 Rain And Thunder / Swing Baby Swing - **Soul Tops** 1968
Produced by: Dickie Wong / Dickie Wong
NB-003 Cover Me / Darling - **Fitz & The Coozers** 1968
Produced by: Jeff Palmer / Jeff Palmer
NB-004 Rocksteady Cool - Fredrick Bell / I Have Changed - Carlton Alphonso 1968
Produced by: Carl Bradford / Carl Bradford
NB-005 Engine 59 / My Girl - **The Rudies** 1968
Produced by: Jeff Palmer / Jeff Palmer
NB-006 This Festival ' 68 / I Really Love You - **Clancy Eccles** 1968
Produced by: Clancy Eccles / Clancy Eccles
NB-007 Rhythm & Soul - Bobby Kalphat / True Romance - Bunny & Ruddy 1968
Produced by: Ken Lack / Ken Lack
NB-008 Hey Boy, Hey Girl - Derrick & Patsy / Music Is The Food Of Love - Derrick Morgan 1968
Produced by: Derrick Morgan / Derrick Morgan
NB-009 (Promo Only)
NB-010 I Can't Stand It / Tonight - **Alton Ellis** 1968
Produced by: C Bough / C Bough
NB-011 On The Town - Bunny & Ruddy / Simple Simon - Monty Morris 1968
Produced by: Ken Lack / Clancy Eccles
NB-012 Young Love / Days Like These - **The Imperials** 1968
Produced by: H Robinson / H Robinson
NB-013 Bye Bye Love - Alton Ellis / My Lonely Days - Monty Morris 1968
Produced by: Clancy Eccles / Clancy Eccles
NB-014 La La Means I Love You / Give Me Your Love - **Alton Ellis** 1968
Produced by: Alton Ellis / C Bough
NB-015 (Promo Only)
NB-016 I Love You - Derrick Morgan / Searching - Junior Smith 1968
Produced by: Derrick Morgan / Roy Smith

NB-017 Push Push / Girls - **The Termites** 1968
Produced by: Eric Barnett / Eric Barnett
NB-018 (Promo Only)
NB-019 Rhythm Hips - Ronald Russell / Deltone Special - Soul Rhythms 1968
Produced by: E Barnett / E Barnett
NB-020 Mini Really Fit Them / Soul Train - **The Soul Flames** 1968
Produced by: Alton Ellis / Alton Ellis
NB-021 Let's Have Some Fun / Making Love - **Devon And The Tartons** 1969
Produced by: H Robinson / H Robinson
NB-022 Blowing In The Wind - Max Romeo / Money Girl - Larry Marshall 1969
Produced by: H Robinson / H Robinson
NB-023 Mr Ryha / After Dark - **Lloyd Tyrell** 1969
Produced by: Winston Lowe / Winston Lowe
NB-024 Woppi King / Mr Soul - **Laurel Aitken** 1969
Produced by: Laurel Aitken / Laurel Aitken
NB-025 Suffering Still / Reggae 69 - **Laurel Aitken** 1969
Produced by: Laurel Aitken / Laurel Aitken
NB-026 Another Heartache / Come On Little Girl - **Winston Sinclair** 1969
Produced by: Winston Sinclair / Winston Sinclair
NB-027 I'll Do It / Give You My Heart - **Derrick & Paulett** 1969
Produced by: Derrick Morgan / Derrick Morgan
NB-028 You've Lost Your Date / Little Girl - **The Flames** 1969
Produced by: E Barnett / E Barnett
NB-029 Rescue Me - The Reggae Girls / Unity Is Strength - The Soul Mates 1969
Produced by: H Mudie / Bunny Lee
NB-030 Rodney's History - Carl Dawkins / Drumbago - The Dynomites 1969
Produced by: Clancy Eccles / Clancy Eccles
NB-031 My Testamony - The Maytals / One Dollar Of Soul - The Johnson Boys 1969
Produced by: A Johnson / A Johnson
NB-032 Hailes Selaise - Laurel Aitken / Blues Dance - Girlie & Laurel Aitken 1969
Produced by: Laurel Aitken / Laurel Aitken
Laurel Aitken 1969
Produced by: Laurel Aitken / Laurel Aitken
NB-034 Crimson And Clover / What A Situation - **The Uniques** 1969
Produced by: Winston Lowe / Winston Lowe
NB-035 Run Powell Run - Laurel Aitken / A Message To You - Reco 1969
Produced by: Laurel Aitken / Laurel Aitken
NB-036 Splash Down / Finders Keepers - **The Crystalites** 1969
Produced by: Derrick Harriott / Derrick Harriott
NB-037 I'll Make You Love Me / Lovers Prayer - **The Uniques** 1969
Produced by: Winston Lowe / Winston Lowe
NB-038 Buss You Mouth - The Eathopians / Rough Rough Way Ahead - Reggae Boys 1969
Produced by: JJ Johnson / Glen Adams
NB-039 Save The Last Dance / Walk Right Back - **Laurel Aitken** 1969
Produced by: Laurel Aitken / Laurel Aitken
NB-040 Don't Be Cruel / John B - **Laurel Aitken** 1969
Produced by: Laurel Aitken / Laurel Aitken
NB-041 Island In The Sun / Work It Up - **Winston Gruvy** 1969
Produced by: Laurel Aitken / Laurel Aitken
NB-042 Josephine / Champagne & Wine - **Winston Gruvy** 1969
Produced by: Laurel Aitken / Laurel Aitken
NB-043 Shoo Bee Boo Bee / Baby Lon Gone - **Laurel Aitken** 1969
Produced by: Laurel Aitken / Laurel Aitken
NB-044 Landlords & Tenants / Everybody Suffering - **Laurel Aitken** 1969
Produced by: Laurel Aitken / Laurel Aitken
NB-045 Jesse James / Freedom - **Laurel Aitken** 1969
Produced by: Laurel Aitken / Laurel Aitken
NB-046 Pussy Price / Give Me Back Me Dallar - **Laurel Aitken** 1969
Produced by: Laurel Aitken / Laurel Aitken
NB-047 Skinhead Train - Laurel Aitken / Kent People - The Gruvy Beats 1969
Produced by: Laurel Aitken / Laurel Aitken
NB-048 Mr Popcorn / Share Your Popcorn - **Laurel Aitken** 1970
(Issued on Nu-Beat and New Beat)
Produced by: Laurel Aitken / Laurel Aitken
NB-049 (Issued on New Beat) 1970
NB-050 Scandal In Brixton Market - Laurel and Girlie / Soul Jerker - Girlie 1969
Produced by: Laurel Aitken / Laurel Aitken

NB-051 Frankenstein - King Horror / I Can't Stand It - Winston Grievy 1969
Produced by: Laurel Aitken / Laurel Aitken
NB-052 - NB-058 (Issued on New Beat)
NB-059 Election - The Freedom Singers / Tomorrow's World -
Fleece And The Live Shocks 1970
Produced by: Laurel Aitken / Laurel Aitken
NB-060 Pick My Pocket - The Versatiles / Freedom - The Freedom Singers 1970
Produced by: Laurel Aitken / Laurel Aitken
NB-061 Same Old Feeling / So Much Love - **The Classics** 1970
(Issued on Nu-Beat and New Beat)
Produced by: Laurel Aitken / Laurel Aitken
NB-062 Nobody Else But You - Joel Lace / Version Of Nobody - The Live Shocks 1970
Produced by: Laurel Aitken / Laurel Aitken

BOSS SOUNDS FROM
NU-BEAT

Boss Sounds from NU-BEAT brings some of the highlights from production between 1968 and 1970.

NB-019 Rhythm Hips - Ronald Russell 1968
Produced by: E Barnett
The vocal version of Eric Barnett's The Horse, both celebrated tracks produced by Eric Barnett himself. This is one that has to be checked out with its fast paced beat and vocals telling a story of mini skirted girls.

NB-005 Engine 59 - The Rudies 1968
Produced by: Jeff Palmer
Dandy et al with a rare outing on Pama.

NB-011 On The Town - Bunny & Ruddy 1968
Produced by: Ken Lack
A vocal rendition with a good hypnotic beat and another well worth checking out.

NB-007 Rhythm & Soul - Bobby Kalphat 1968
C/W **True Romance - Bunny & Ruddy**
Produced by: Ken Lack
The instrumental maintains a good pace with a melodic rhythm from Bobby Kalphat. He started out singing pre ska years with a stint on keyboard before moving into production in the late 60s. Oddly the B side features a vocal rendition from Bunny & Ruddy with True Romance.

NB-047 Skinhead Train - Laurel Aitken 1969
Produced by: Laurel Aitken
This would have to be a Boss tune with that title. A riveting number from Laurel Aitken. Laurel who must be Mr Nu-Beat sings a few nursery rhymes but unlike Judge Dread he keeps it clean. Skinhead reggae at its best.

NB-046 Pussy Price - Laurel Aitken 1969
Produced by: Laurel Aitken
A risqué outing from Laurel singing about inflation. The track had an outing on Birth Control SECO 32. Laurel's Benwood Dick also featured on the album but was only issued as a promo copy on Nu-Beat.

NB-041 Island In The Sun - Winston Gruvy 1969
Produced by: Laurel Aitken
This traditional Jamaican song gets the reggae treatment from Winston Groovy credited on his early releases on Pama as Gruvy. The song was originally written for and performed by Harry Belafonte in the 1957 film of the same name.
Chris Blackwell's Island record label was named after the song in 1959.

NB-036 Splash Down - The Crystalites 1969
Produced by: Derrick Harriott
Splash Down is an instrumental take on Sufferer from The Kingstonians.

NB-040 Don't Be Cruel - Laurel Aitken 1969
C/W **John B - Laurel Aitken**
Produced by: Laurel Aitken
Both sides are excellent covers with the trade-mark Laurel vocals and a Boss beat. Both tracks feature on the excellent album The High Priest Of Reggae issued on PSP 1012 in 1970.

NB-008 Hey Boy, Hey Girl - Derrick & Patsy 1968
Produced by: Derrick Morgan
Hey Boy, Hey Girl carries an infectious beat with impressive vocals from Derrick Morgan and Patsy Todd and featured on Nu-Beats Greatest Hits and Reggae Hits 69 Volume One. It was also used as the title track for the album issued on PSP 1002 in 1969 - Hey Boy, Hey Girl.

NB-025 Suffering Still - Laurel Aitken 1969
Produced by: Laurel Aitken
Another from Laurel this time a prominent organ riff with an incessant beat and delightful patois chatter accompanied by Girlie.

NU-BEAT GREATEST HITS Various Artistes   PAMA ECO 6   1969

Side 1
1. LA LA MEANS I LOVE YOU - Alton Ellis   2. RESCUE ME - The Reggae Girls
3. ANOTHER HEARTACHE - Winston Sinclair   4. RHYTHM HIPS- Ronald Russel
5. HAILES SELAISE - Laurel Aitken   6. MY TESTIMONY - The Eathopians

Side 2
1. TRAIN TO VIETNAM - The Rudies   2. HEY BOY, HEY GIRL - Derrick & Patsy
3. BLOWING IN THE WIND - Max Romeo   4. RHYTHM AND SOUL - Bobby Kalphat
5. SUFFERING STILL - Laurel Aitken   6. GIVE YOU MY HEART - Derrick & Paulette

ECONOMY   MONO   ECO 6

NU-BEAT'S GREATEST HITS

VARIOUS ARTISTES

NU-BEAT is by far one of the most progressive labels in the Blue Beat - Reggae field. This label was launched by Pama Records nearly two years ago and was surely a welcome change for the shop-keepers who were used to seeing only one colour label on records, especially those issued by Blue Beat companies. The sound too was different, because it carried with it something of interest and progressiveness and the record buyers and music lovers showed their appreciation by buying great quantities of each record issued on this new label.

Too very often has NU-BEAT gone close to breaking through on the National Charts but regretfully missed narrowly with numbers like "RHYTHM & SOUL", "HEY BOY-HEY GIRL", "LA LA MEANS I LOVE YOU", "RHYTHM HIPS", "BLOWING IN THE WIND", "WHOPPIE KING", "SUFFERING STILL" and many other such great numbers. Nevertheless they always scored high on the Blue Beat and R&B charts, thanks to the great public who always support the good sounds of NU-BEAT and its Reggae Hits.

NU-BEAT has far to go and with the line-up on this present album with Artistes like Alton Ellis, The Reggae Girls, Winston Sinclair, Ronald Russel, Laurel Aitken, The Ethiopians, The Rudies, Derrick & Patsy, Max Romeo and Bobby Kalphat, it's clear to see that as always NU-BEAT has continued to give value for money and a little more.   Two years of releases have been searched through and nothing but the best of NU-BEAT Hits are included hereon. So do enjoy yourself and look out for the other great records on this very exciting label.

THE REGGAE AND NU-BEAT ARE HERE TO STAY.

William Harrison

Distributed by:- PAMA RECORDS 78 CRAVEN PARK ROAD LONDON NW10 ENGLAND

PAMA SPECIAL   MONO   PSP 1012

THE HIGH PRIEST OF REGGAE

LAUREL AITKEN

THE HIGH PRIEST OF REGGAE   LAUREL AITKEN   PAMA PSP 1012 1970

Side 1
1. JESSE JAMES 2. Mr. POPCORN 3. I GOT TO HAVE YOUR LOVE
4. JOHN B. 5. SHOO BEE SHOO BEE 6. HAILES SELAISE

Side 2
1. LANDLORDS AND TENANTS 2. SAVE THE LAST DANCE 3. WALK RIGHT BACK 4. DON'T BE
CRUEL 5. WOPPI KING 6. SUFFERING STILL

PAMA SPECIAL   MONO   PSP 1012

THE HIGH PRIEST OF REGGAE
LAUREL AITKEN

There are many different religious sects and creeds covering every corner of the world. in every Land the people have their own beliefs and serve their own gods, some serve Allah, some serve Mohammed, some serve Buddha, some serve idols, and the majority of us serve the one true God, The almighty Father the Creator of the Universe, the giver of life and all true blessings which surround us.

Reggae is not a religion, it is music, a beat music with a calypso type of rhythm and it originated in Jamaica the sunny isle of the Caribbean. Many many years ago this music was created, then it was called Blue Beat. The founder of the new sound, who rightly claims to be its High Priest, is a little Cuban emigrant to Jamaica, name of Laurel Aitken.

Way back in the fifties, the emigrants from the West Indies living in England, got a taste of their "back home" music in a number entitled "Little Shelia". Yes this was the first Blue Beat, or Reggae as it is now called, and was written and sung by no other than the founder himself, Maestro Laurel Aitken. His worship, as he is better known, has the best of two worlds in the reggae business. He does his recording in the Reggae workshop of Pama Records which is based in Harlesden, London, Reggae City No. 1, and (believe it or not, with all his fame and money, he has not deserted his- original fans and supporters). He lives in Reggae City No. 2, Brixton. Some people may argue that Brixton is the No.1 Reggae City, but last Reggae polling day, when Laurel was returned to High Priest of Reggae his greatest support came from Harlesden, beating Brixton by two votes, 1,234,567 (One Million Two-hundred and Thirty-four Thousand, Five-hundred and Sixty-seven) Brixton, 1,234,569 (One Million Two-hundred and Thirty-four Thousand, Five-hundred and Sixty-nine) Harlesden. Some people say that Laurel and his wife voted twice, once on the Brixton side and then on the Harlesden side, causing it to be a tie. others say it was actually Mr. Palmer who got the doorman of his club, the new "London Apollo", to vote three times giving Harlesden the lead. But whatever it was Harlesden won the title from Brixton, and His Worship was once again re-elected "High Priest of Reggae". As the Pope is true to his religion, so is Laurel to Reggae and from the authenticity to the sound of this record, rightfully entitled "High Priest of Reggae". You will understand why it is true that Mr. Aitken must have been the founder of this music and why for so many years, despite stiff competition from some very good newcomers like Derrick Morgan, Owen Gray, Stranger Cole, Rico Rodrequez, Max Romeo, Pat Kelly, Slim Smith, The Mohawks, The Marvells, Lloyd Tyrell, Busty Brown, Ernest Wilson, David Isaacs, Winston Grovy, Pat Rhoden, Denzil Dennis, Sketto Rich and al the many many Artistes, Laurel has remained and will forever be "THE HIGH PRIEST OF REGGAE".

PAMA RECORDS LIMITED, 78, Craven Park Road, London, N.W.10, England

Signed **DERRICK MORGAN**

SCANDAL IN A BRIXTON MARKET GIRLIE AND LAUREL AITKEN   PAMA ECO 8 1969

Side1

1.SCANDAL IN A BRIXTON MARKET - Girlie & Laurel Aitken 2. MADAME STREGGAE - Girlie & Laurel Aitken
3. STUPID MARRIED MAN - Laurel Aitken 4. TAMMERING - Girlie & Laurel Aitken
5. HAVE MERCY - Girlie & Laurel Aitken 6. NIGHT CRICKET - Laurel Aitken

Side 2

1. RUN POWELL RUN - Laurel Aitken 2. TEDDY BEAR - Laurel Aitken 3.MR .SOUL - Laurel Aitken
4. WOKE UP THIS MORNING - Laurel Aitken 5. BABELON - Girlie & Laurel Aitken
6. STOP THE WAR IN VIETNAM - Girlie & Laurel Aitken

ECONOMY   MONO   ECO 8

At a time when artist albums were still considered a rarity in 1969 Pama issued Scandal In A Brixton Market from London based Laurel Aitken. The album included five previously released singles and presented seven new recordings.
Guest appearances on the album were from artists Girlie and Rico Rodriguez. The sleeve notes - Fictional Story - was a unique breath of fresh air when released, following on the tradition of Pama's seemingly unique trait.

SCANDAL IN A BRIXTON MARKET
SHORT STORY BOUT BRIXTON *By Raglan Gungo Peas*

One day in de col col month of January about half pass four in de evening a big fight bruck out in-a Brixton Market between de man Larel Akin and is wife Girly - Well she not im wife really but dem bin living together no far bout eight years and so we acep dem as being marid. He still keep shen altho she have other man wid im but im really don't care cause im have another sweet gal imself.

So this day Mass Larel go into de market fe but de week's provision when to im great suprise, a who you tink im see in de? no Girly sah an wid har man to a ug up an a chat sweet chat. Altho im is a quiet man most a de time dis time im couldn't take no more cause all im fren dem bin a tell im bout she an dis man Paddy.

All this time de Paddy im go on like im have nothing fe do wid it and if you look pan de front cover you can see im looking quite unconcerned in a im glasses wid im two han dem in a im packet. Me also hear seh a fe im de last pikiny dat Girly have and weh she and Larel a quarrel bout on de record "Scandal in-a Brixton Market". To me im really look gilty, a wah you tink?

Anyhow Nat Cole im no like de fus in front a im place so in de confusion om call de law. You can see im (de cappa) a lik down all de Black people dem wid im big stick and believe me sah, im lik hard fe true cause one catch me. At the same time pan de font you can see Girly a hole Larel in a im wase like a teef an she even bruck a backle over im head just because im talk bout she nasty teet man. She even treaten to hand im over to de police because im did tek weh all de money fram de dance and she no get notin out of it, even a curry goat weh she boil wid har own two han dem and dem sell it aff at de dance. He did also get some money from Pama fe rayalty af de record "Whoppi King" weh im sing fe dem and by de way, de boy is a good singer to you know! A all hit dem im a mek like "Suffering" "Blues Dance" "Powel" "Lawd Doctor" and im and Girly sing "Scandal In-a Brixton Market".

A weh me was wid de story again - Oh yes she was going to squeel pon im to de cappa but after all she well love im, so she didn't bother altho de two a dem gat lak up and Nat imself had fe go down and bail dem out of de Nick, seeing im is a upstanding and well liked man especially in de Brixton area. So wen dem get out dem go ome and lived appily ever after quite up until de nex day when in come fram work early and cetch Girly and de same man a lie down pon fe im own bed, once again a ug up and a......., so im lef dem de and go round to Paddy yard and start telling im wife bout de afare and convincing har to start on wid im to fe mek every ting fair and square between de two families and de two races. It worked and so dem swap omes now-but believe it or nat dem still a cheat one another wid de other one woman or dem own as de case may be - you sort it out fe your self - after you listen dis very good recard wid de crazy Reggae Beat of Girlie and Laurel Aitken.

Yes sah - look out me a come back again - Yours sweet as ever. Gungo Peas

(FICTION)

A Pama Records Production, London.

LAUREL AITKEN

THE GODFATHER OF SKA ARTIST / PRODUCER

About the same time as man landed on the moon Laurel Aitken had established himself by far as Britain's favourite Jamaican performer with both the West Indian community and the burgeoning reggae loving skinhead subculture. He was highly sought after by several record companies who had enjoyed a fierce and bitter rivalry so it was a coup when he signed for Pama. Unlike many of his reggae peers Laurel was born on the island of Cuba in April 1927.

He moved across the water with his family to Kingston when he was eleven years old and soon influenced by the islands clubs and sound systems. He'd released several records before the sixties dawned including Little Shelia for Chris Blackwell's emerging Jamaican based Island records. Little Shelia became the first Jamaican popular music single to be issued in the UK on the Starlite label. Laurel moved to London where he worked with various record companies. Ska had slowed to rock steady in '66 but as the decade was drawing to a close the music was evolving into reggae, and as fate conspired the new growing skinhead movement would take reggae to its heart. Laurel being based in London found his services were in great demand, initially releasing singles on Dotor Bird before his accomplished journey with Pama Records, along the way releasing some of the very best all time boss skinhead sounds. His success gained him the title The Godfather of Ska and for some Boss Skinhead.

It was Laurel who introduced Winston Groovy to Pama but also Ian Smith's The Inner Mind, described as the Greatest White Reggae Band on Earth. As the twilight of the skinhead era faded away Laurel adapted with live performances and as the decade came to an end he found favour once more with a new wave of ska and reggae fans.

Several of Laurel's singles have been covered in Boss Sounds from Nu-Beat but that's only part of the story as he produced many classic singles amongst almost fifty released on the Nu-Beat and New Beat imprint between '69 and '71.

NB-045 Jesse James - Laurel Aitken 1969
Produced by: Laurel Aitken
Shades of Alcapone on this chugging infectious beat with intermittent gun fire and Laurel declaring Jesse James rides again. The single made it onto the renowned album This Is Reggae issued on PSP 1003 in 1970.

NB-024 Woppi King - Laurel Aitken 1969
Produced by: Laurel Aitken
The incessant beat is talked over by Laurel the philosopher.

NB-050 Scandal In Brixton Market - Laurel & Girlie 1969
Produced by: Laurel Aitken
The title track for Laurel's 1969 album
Scandal In A Brixton Market issued on ECO 8.

NB-060 Pick My Pocket - The Versatiles 1970
Produced by: Laurel Aitken
One of the last to appear on the original moniker and good enough for an outing on Straighten Up Volume One.

NB-062 Nobody Else But You - Joel Lace 1970
Produced by: Laurel Aitken
The incessant melodic rhythm and the laid back lyrics made for a good underrated song.

NB-061 Same Old Feeling - The Classics 1970
Produced by: Laurel Aitken
The London based Classics included Denzil Dennis and Eugene Paul. This track was one of just a few issued on Nu-Beat and New Beat and a complete change of pace and vocals from the early trade-mark boss sounds on Nu-Beat.

NB-059 Election - The Freedom Singers 1970
Produced by: Laurel Aitken
A story about the pressure of an election with an good beat.

NEW BEAT

NB-048 Mr Popcorn / Share Your Popcorn - **Laurel Aitken** 1970
Produced by: Laurel Aitken / Laurel Aitken
NB-049 I Got To Have Your Loving - Laurel Aitken / Blue Mink - Aitken Gruvy Beats 1970
Produced by: Laurel Aitken / Laurel Aitken
NB-052 Souls Of Africa / Dallas Texas - **Tiger** 1970
Produced by: Laurel Aitken / Laurel Aitken
NB-053 Standing At The Corner / You Send Me - **Winston Gruvy** 1970
Produced by: Laurel Aitken / Laurel Aitken
NB-054 Baby Please Don't Go / Nobody But Me - **Laurel Aitken** 1970
Produced by: Laurel Aitken / Laurel Aitken
NB-055 Yellow Bird / For Your Love - **Winston Groovy** 1970
Produced by: Laurel Aitken / Laurel Aitken
NB-056 I'll never Love Any Girl (The Way I Love You) / The Best I Can - **Laurel Aitken** 1970
Produced by: Laurel Aitken / Laurel Aitken
NB-057 Reggae Popcorn / Take Me Back - **Laurel Aitken** 1970
Produced by: Laurel Aitken / Laurel Aitken
NB-058 Here Is My Heart - Winston Groovy / Birds And Flowers - Groovy Beats 1970
Produced by: Laurel Aitken / Laurel Aitken
NB-061 Same Old Feeling / So Much Love - **The Classics** 1970
(Issued on New Beat and Nu-Beat)
Produced by: Laurel Aitken / Laurel Aitken
NB-063 Baby I Need Your Loving / Think It Over - **Laurel Aitken** 1970
Produced by: Laurel Aitken / Laurel Aitken
NB-064 Musical Scorther / Three Dogs Night - **Tiger** 1970
Produced by: Laurel Aitken / Laurel Aitken
NB-065 Sex Machine / Since You Left - **Laurel Aitken** 1970
Produced by: Laurel Aitken / Laurel Aitken
NB-066 Groovin / Sugar Mama - **Winston Groovy** 1970
Produced by: Laurel Aitken / Laurel Aitken
NB-067 Witchcraft Man / Night In Cairo - **The Inner Mind** 1970
Produced by: Ian Smith / Ian Smith
NB-068 (Not Used)
NB-069 Pum Pum Girl / Freedom - **The Inner Mind** 1970
Produced by: Ian Smith / Ian Smith
NB-070 (Not Used)
NB-071 History Of Africa / Honey Bee - **The Classics** 1970
Produced by: Laurel Aitken / Laurel Aitken
NB-072 Pachanga (Part1) / Pachanga (Part 2) - **Laurel Aitken** 1970
Produced by: Laurel Aitken / Laurel Aitken
NB-073 Tennessee Waltz / Oldman Trouble - **Winston Groovy** 1970
Produced by: Laurel Aitken / Laurel Aitken
NB-074 Your Testamony / Train Coming - **Freedom Singers** 1971
Produced by: Laurel Aitken / Laurel Aitken
NB-075 African Beat / Black Man Land - **Tiger** 1971
Produced by: Laurel Aitken / Laurel Aitken
NB-076 Give It To Me - The Versatiles / Hot - Tiger And The Versatiles 1971
Produced by: Laurel Aitken / Laurel Aitken
NB-077 (Promo Only)

NB-078 True Love / The Best I Can - **Laurel Aitken** 1971
Produced by: Laurel Aitken / Laurel Aitken
NB-079 Only Heaven Knows - Shiela / Freedom Psalm - Grant & Richards 1971
Produced by: Laurel Aitken / Laurel Aitken
NB-080 Monkey Spanner - Larry & Lloyd / Monkey Spanner (Version) 2 - Larry & Lloyd All Stars 1971
Produced by: Laurel Aitken / Laurel Aitken
NB-081 Co Co / Hey Girl Don't Bother Me - **The Marvels** 1971
Produced by: Sydney Crooks / Sydney Crooks
NB-082 Black Man / Tell The People - **Rupie Edwards All Stars** 1971
Produced by: Rupie Edwards / Rupie Edwards
NB-083 Love & Emotions / Love (Version) Two - **The Rightious Flames** 1971
Produced by: Derrick Morgn / Derrick Morgan
NB-084 Mary - The Jamaicans / Soldier Boy - The Conscious Minds 1971
Produced by: Tom Cowan / Tom Cowan
NB-085 (Not Used)
NB-086 Walk A Little Prouder - Carl Dawkins / Walk (Version) - Youth Professionals 1971
Produced by: Unknown / Unknown
NB-087 Mother Radio - Joe Higgs / Little Deeds - Dawn Sharon 1971
Produced by: Rupie Edwards / Rupie Edwards
NB-088 Have You Ever Been Hurt / Our Day Will Come - **Tiger** 1971
Produced by: Laurel Aitken / Laurel Aitken
NB-089 Can't Stop Loving You / El-Passo - **Laurel Aitken** 1971
Produced by: Laurel Aitken / Laurel Aitken
NB-090 Hold Them One / Two Three Four - **Roy Shirley** 1971
Produced by: Lloyd Tyrell / Lloyd Tyrell
NB-091 Three In One - Errol Dunkley / One In Three - Rupie Edward's All Stars 1971
Produced by: Rupie Edwards/ Rupie Edwards
NB-092 Valley Of Tears / Because I Love - **Cock and The Woodpeckers** 1971
Produced by: Laurel Aitken / Laurel Aitken
NB-093 Every Day & Every Night / I Fall In Love Everyday - **Cock and The Woodpeckers** 1971
Produced by: Laurel Aitken / Laurel Aitken
NB-094 I Will Never Let You Down / This Majic Moment - **Lorenzo** 1971
Produced by: Lorenzo/ Lorenzo
NB-095 (Promo Only)

BOSS SOUNDS FROM
NEW BEAT

Boss Sounds from NEW BEAT brings you some of the highlights from the labels production between 1970 and 1971. Although Nu-Beat issued the lions share of the true boss reggae sound there were still some gems to come from the relaunched label now issuing only UK productions.

NB-080 Monkey Spanner - Larry & Lloyd 1971
Produced by: Laurel Aitken

The Laurel Aiken produced version of the famous hit Monkey Spanner isn't a straight cover, the tempo is upped and includes Monkey Spanner in the lyrics. The original was always going to be a hard act to follow so the shift in vocals and tempo was a good call from Lorenzo.

NB-055 Yellow Bird - Winston Groovy 1970
Produced by: Laurel Aitken

The original Haitian song first appeared on a calypso album in 1957 and is now given an excellent reggae treatment from Winston Groovy.

NB-069 Pum Pum Girl - The Inner Mind 1970
Produced by: Ian Smith

"Pum Pum Girl was the Dreams Of Yesterday backing track with suggestive words added. I lived in Thornhill Lees Dewsbury at the time. I caught the bus to Huddersfield one night to get to Mat's two track recording studio, nothing posh, just primitive, simple and great. I wrote the lyrics on the bus on the way there! So, had the mood taken me, it could've ended up a sentimental love song!"

(Ian 'Smithy' Smith - extract from Skinhead Reggae Hit The Town)

NB-075 African Beat - Tiger 1971
Produced by: Laurel Aitken

The rhythm is reminiscent of The Pioneers Catch The Beat issued on Amalgamated in 1968. Tiger doesn't sound much like Laurel this time out with falsetto style vocals negotiating the way around nursery rhymes.

NB-081 Co Co - The Marvels 1971
C/W **Hey Girl Don't Bother Me - The Marvels**
Produced by: Sydney Crooks

A rare production for Sydney Crooks on New Beat with British based band The Marvels. Performing since 1962 the band consisted of Alex 'Dimple' Hinds, Cornell 'Ornell' Hinds and Eddie Smith and specialised in Doo-wop harmonies. Co Co is a cover of the 1971 hit from Sweet and the B side a cover of The Tams original 1966 release that finally gave a chart hit for The Tams in 1971. The Marvels feature on the cover of This Is Reggae Volume 3 PMP 2008 released in 1971.

NB-090 Hold Them One - Roy Shirley 1971
Produced by: Lloyd Tyrell

Hold Them One is a medley of Roys Shirley's earlier releases with side one using the rhythm lifted from his hit A Sugar. Hold Them was said to be the first record to slow down the infectious ska beat, thus creating rocksteady in 1966.

NB-078 True Love - Laurel Aitken 1971
Produced by: Laurel Aitken

AKA Let True Love Begin is performed admirably by Laurel undertaking a cover version of Nat King Cole's 1961 hit.

THE INNER MIND

THE GREATEST WHITE REGGAE BAND

During the late 60s there were just a handful of Jamaican musicians living in London who would support stop-over recording stars from Jamaica on tour, including the likes of Prince Buster. By 1969 with reggae now charting other artists arrived in Britain with Desmond Dekker leading the way, although The Aces refused to travel with him. Within a few months the bustling capital became home to Derrick Morgan, Jimmy Cliff, Owen Gray, sometimes known as Grey, and of course Laurel Aitken.

Most of the artists were unknown in Britain, apart that was from their recording talents and many a promoters tale has been told of the same artist topping the bill at different far apart venues on the same night.

The backing for many of the artists new UK releases were from British based musicians and one group from Yorkshire, The Inner Mind, were destined to become one of Pama's backing bands, earning the title as The Greatest White Reggae Band on Earth. The group had formed in '69 and comprised Ian R Smith, Organ and Piano, Jimmy Walsh on drums, Dave Tattersall on bass and Finley Topham guitar. The Inner Mind backed many of Pama's established reggae acts such as Laurel Aitken, Owen Gray, Winston Groovy and Alton Ellis.

The Inner Mind had releases on Pama's New Beat label with one of their biggest coming in 1970 Pum Pum Girl NB-069, although erroneously credited as a Laurel Aitken production on the label. Singles on Bullet BU-465 Arawack Version, and Devil Woman BU-490 were released in 1971. Without doubt Ian's biggest success came in 1973 after the skinhead era had run its course with the release on his Hot Lead label of Doggie Bite Postman, under the guise of Smithy, a record it was said to have sold faster than it could be pressed.

Ian recalled his memories from the skinhead reggae years in the book Skinhead Reggae Hit The Town and the following is an extract.

"It was somewhat of a strange coincidence that we ended up recording for Pama Records. Basically, besides our own show, over the months we'd backed Laurel Aitken (a lot), Owen Gray (several times), Winston Groovy (twice) & Alton Ellis, so Pama had heard of us and our reputation. We'd done a gig in High Wycombe with Owen and on the following night, we'd taken a gig at Pama's Apollo Club in Harlesden - just The Inner Mind. When we got there, there seemed to be a sort of strange atmosphere and the boss (Jeff Palmer) started getting awkward with me. We set up our gear and then he said he wasn't going to pay us our full fee, no reason given. It was obvious he was just 'trying it on'; as we were down there from Yorkshire, reluctantly I said OK, we'll take the reduction; ten minutes later, he tried it on again saying he would pay us less. At that, the Yorkshire white reggae band said 'Stuff you', packed up and went north!

Don Auty persuaded us to give it one more try and we became a regular at the Apollo, on an agreed fee and billed as 'The Greatest White Reggae Band on Earth', somewhat of a change of heart on Jeff Palmer's part"!

OCEAN

BOSS SOUNDS FROM
OCEAN

OCEAN was one of the last to be set up by Pama in 1970. The label issued only three singles by the end of the year. The first one came from Sol Ray who appeared in the sitcom Desmond's - *Norman Beaton played a character called Desmond Ambrose who's barber shop set in Peckham was a meeting place for a variety of local characters* - The second single came from Danny Williams with the third coming from Pat Kelly with Martin Luther And John on OC-1003. The original colourful label stood out but even that was replaced.

A low-key revival came in 1975 in the form of the re-issue of Max Romeo's Wet Dream on OC-003 followed by just five more singles including Can't You Understand from Larry Marshall - and that was it.

OCEAN DISCOGRAPHY FIRST SERIES 1970 - SECOND SERIES 1975 Prefix OC

OC-1001 Welcome Stranger / Until Then - Sol Raye 1970
Produced by: Danny Williams / Danny Williams
OC-1002 Fare Ye Well - Separate Ways / A Girl Like You - **Danny Williams** 1970
Produced by: Danny Williams / Danny Williams
OC-1003 Martin Luther And John / Never Could It Be - **Pat Kelly** 1970
Produced by: Unknown / Unknown
OC-003 Wet Dream / She's But A Little Girl - **Max Romeo** 1975
Produced by: H Robinson / J Smith
OC-004 Can't You Understand - Larry Marshall / Locks Of Dub - King Tubby 1975
Produced by: C Patterson / C Patterson
OC-005 Tonight Is The Night - Claudette Miller / Tonight Dub - Contrust Mind 1975
Produced by: Duke Reid / Duke Reid
OC-006 Dreadlocks Power / Black Lash - **Carlton Patterson** 1975
Produced by: C Patterson / C Patterson
OC-007 Never Found A Girl - Denzil Dennis / Version - The Inmates 1975
Produced by: Denzil Dennis / Denzil Dennis
OC-008 (Not Used)
OC-009 It De Hay - Freddie McKay / Bub De Hay - Phil Pratt Allstars 1975
Produced by: Phil Pratt / Phil Pratt

Still room for some good boss tunes among the labels minimal output.

OC-004 Can't You Understand - Larry Marshall 1975
Produced by: C Patterson

Back in 1968 Larry teamed up with Alvin Lewis and recorded as Larry & Alvin. They scored a massive hit in Jamaica with Dodd's production of Nanny Goat which began the shift from rocksteady to early reggae and regarded by many as the first real reggae record. Can't You Understand had an outing on the album Reggae Hit The Town issued on PTP 1001 in 1975.

OC-006 Dreadlocks Power - Carlton Patterson 1975
Produced by: C Patterson

Dreadlock vocals over on an hypnotic beat sampling Train To Skaville from The Ethiopians. The infectious harmonic rock steady tune was a boss sound and the rhythm works well on this record from producer an artist Carlton Patterson.

OC-003 Wet Dream - Max Romeo 1975
Produced by: H Robinson

Max claimed that the 1968 song was telling the story of his leaking roof, he was asking for his girlfriend to get out of the way as he tried to push a broom up in the hole to stop the leak.

The label released over fifty soul records on the PM prefix issued on a blue label. The most relevant by far was The Champ from Alan Hawkshaw's The Mohawks on PM-719 in 1968. A record that has been sampled over 700 times.

The comprehensive discography from the Pama imprint highlights SOUL releases appropriately in blue.

PAMA DISCOGRAPHY
First Series 1967 - 1973 Prefix PM Second Series 1975 Prefix PM

PM-700 Where In This World / Peace Makers - **Carlton Alphonso** 1967
Produced by: Roy Bennett / Roy Bennett
PM-701 What Will Your Mama Say / Darling Don't Do That - **Clancy Eccles** 1967
Produced by: Clancy Eccles / Clancy Eccles
PM-702 Let's Get Married / Around The World - **Little John and the Shadrocks** 1967
Produced by: Palmer Brothers / Palmer Brothers
PM-703 Western Organ / Mothers Advice - **The Clancy Set** 1967
Produced by: Clancy Eccles / Clancy Eccles
PM-704 Bad Mind People - Miss Jane / My Heart Is Aching - Trails 1968
Produced by: Clancy Eccles / Clancy Eccles
PM-705 (Not Used)
PM-706 It's Not Unusual / Soul Man - **Rico Rodrecez** 1968
Produced by: Palmer Brothers / Palmer Brothers
PM-707 The Message / Some Talk - **Alton Ellis** 1968
Produced by: Alton Ellis / Alton Ellis
PM-708 (Not Used)
PM-709 (Not Used)
PM-710 Bang Bang Lulu - Lloyd Terrel / I Never Knew - Mrs. Miller 1968
Produced by: Lynford Anderson / Lynford Anderson
PM-711 Heart Beat - Ernest Ranglin / Birds Of The Air - The Coolers 1968
Produced by: Clancy Eccles / Clancy Eccles
PM-712 The Fight / Great - **Clancy Eccles** 1968
Produced by: Ernest Ranglin / Ernest Ranglin
PM-713 (Not Used)
PM-714 (Not Used)
PM-715 Tenderfoot Ska / Memories - **Rico Radregez** 1968
Produced by: Jeff Palmer / Jeff Palmer
PM-716 Mr. Pitiful / That's How Strong My Love Is - **Beverley Simmons** 1968
Produced by: Harry Palmer / Harry Palmer
PM-717 My Time Is The Right Time - Alton Ellis / Tribute To Sir Alex - Johnny Moore 1968
Produced by: Ellis - Moore / Ellis - Moore
PM-718 Back To School - Joyce Bond / They Wash - The Joyce Bond Show 1968
Produced by: Carl Palmer / Carl Palmer
PM-719 The Champ / Sound Of The Witchdoctors - **The Mohawks** 1968
Produced by: J Palmer / J Palmer
PM-720 Fiddle Sticks / Please Stay - **Tommy McKenzie & His Orchestra** 1968
Produced by: Harry Palmer / Clancy Eccles
PM-721 Say What You Say / Tears In Your Eyes - **Monty Morris** 1968
Produced by: Clancy Eccles / Clancy Eccles
PM-722 C.N. Express (Part One) / C.N. Express (Part 2) - **Clancy's All Stars** 1968
Produced by: Clancy Eccles / Clancy Eccles
PM-723 Soul Food / Music Flames - **Lynn Tait And The Jets** 1968
Produced by: Lynford Anderson / Lynford Anderson
PM-724 (Not Used)
PM-725 I Know It's Alright / Surrender - **The Crowns** 1968
Produced by: Harry Palmer / Harry Palmer
PM-726 Afro Blue / Empty Little Shadow - **Diana Landor** 1968
Produced by: Unknown / Unknown
PM-727 (Not Used)
PM-728 Don't Change Your Mind (About Me) / Anytime Man - **Anthony Deeley** 1968
Produced by: David Osborn / David Osborn
PM-729 Push It Up / Two Of A Kind - The Termites 1968
Produced by: H Robinson / Clancy Eccles
PM-730 Same Thing All Over / You've Been Cheating - **Norman T. Washington** 1968
Produced by: Carl Palmer / Carl Palmer

PAMA. Harry Palmer visited Jamaica to establish links with producers before setting up the label, one being Clancy Eccles. What Will Your Mama Say by Clancy was the second record issued on the label just a month behind a relatively fruitless first release of Where In This World from Carlton Alphonso. Clancy's What Will Your Mama Say PM-701 enjoyed healthy sales and a few airings on Radio One. The recordings then came thick and fast including Lloyd Tyrell's AKA Lloyd Chalmers, Lloyd Terell or Lloyd Terrell's suggestive Bang Bang Lulu on PM-710. Over one hundred and fifty singles were released on the Pama label up to the end of 1973. Gems included PM-835 Way Down South from U. Roy and PM-856 Good Hearted Woman from The Clarendonians.

Birth Control from Lloyd Terrell was issued on PM-792 in 1970, the precursor for the album of the same title issued on SECO 32. Continuing the risqué theme another single that was never going to receive airplay was Sex Education by The Classics released on PM-830, although the record produced by Harry Palmer in 1971 was always a firm favourite at the school disco.

PM-731 You're Mine / What A Guy - **Little Beverley** 1968
Produced by: Harry Palmer / Harry Palmer
PM-732 (Not Used)
PM-733 "Sick & Tired" (Oh Babe) / "Treat Me Nice" - **The Milwaukee Coasters** 1968
Produced by: Harry Palmer / Harry Palmer
PM-734 Lament To Bobby Kennedy / If You Were My Girl -
Knights Of The Round Table 1968
Produced by: Unknown / Unknown
PM-735 Broadway Ain't Funky No More / I Met My Match -
Bobby Patterson & The Mustangs 1968
Produced by: Unknown / Unknown
PM-736 Jerking The Dog / Keep Me Going - **The Crowns** 1968
Produced by: Harry Palmer / Harry Palmer
PM-737 (Not Used)
PM-738 Show Me The Way / What Can I Do - **The Termites** 1968
Produced by: R Bennett / Roy Bennett
PM-739 "Baby Hold On" (Part 1) / "Baby Hold On" (Part 2) - **The Mohawkes** 1968
Produced by: A Hawkshaw / A Hawkshaw
PM-740 How Come - Lloyd Terrel / Oh My Lover - **Mrs. Miller** 1968
Produced by: F. Lindo / F. Lindo
PM-741 Tip Toe / Don't Hang Around - **Norman T. Washington** 1968
Produced by: Palmer Brothers / Palmer Brothers
PM-742 "If I Love You" / Loving You - **The Butter Cups** 1968
Produced by: Harry Palmer / Harry Palmer
PM-743 The Good Ol Days / Don't Be So Mean - **Bobby Patterson & The Mustangs** 1968
Produced by: Jet Star / Jet Star
PM-744 "Dr. Goldfoot And His Bikini Machine" / "Where Do I Go From You" -
he Beas 1968
Produced by: Al Simms / Al Simms
PM-745 "She Ain't Gonna Do Right" / I Need Your Lovin - **The Crowns** 1968
Produced by: Harry Palmer / Harry Palmer
PM-746 Beverley / Wait For Me Baby - **Eldridge Holmes** 1968
Produced by: Allen Toussaint / Allen Toussaint
PM-747 (Not Used)
PM-748 "Only Your Love Can Save Me" / I Feel Good (All Over) - **Betty Lavette** 1968
Produced by: Don Gardner / Don Gardner
PM-749 Jumping Jack Flash / Spinning - **Norman T. Washington** 1968
Produced by: Palmer Brothers / Palmer Brothers
PM-750 When / Go - Roy Docker 1968
Produced by: Roy Smith / Roy Smith
PM-751 Sweet Soul Music / Hip jigger - **The Mohawks** 1968
Produced by: Palmer Brothers / Palmer Brothers
PM-752 Lulu Returns - Lloyd Terrell / I Feel The Music - **Mrs. Miller** 1968
Produced by: Lynford Anderson / Roy Smith
PM-753 Peace On Earth - Premo & Joseph / Guilty Of Love - The School Boys 1968
Produced by: H Robinson / Bunny Barrett
PM-754 Busy Busy Bee / Sweet Taste Of Love - **Bobby Patterson & The Mustangs** 1968
Produced by: Jet Star / Jet Star
PM-755 (Not Used)
PM-756 Everyday Will Be Like A Holiday / I'm An Outcast - **Roy Docker** 1969
Produced by: Harry Dee / Harry Dee
PM-757 Mony Mony / Pepsi - **The Mohawks** 1969
Produced by: Palmer Brothers / Palmer Brothers
PM-758 Ride Your Pony / Western Promise - **The Mohawks** 1969
Produced by: Palmer Brothers / Palmer Brothers
PM-759 Call Me / Since You Been Gone - **The Crowns** 1969
Produced by: Harry Palmer / Harry Palmer
PM-760 "Come Put My Life In Order" / If I Love You - **The Buttercups** 1969
Produced by: Harry Palmer / Harry Palmer
PM-761 I Need Your Love So Bad / I'm Coming Too - **Billy Bass** 1969
Produced by: Stan Watson / Stan Watson
PM-762 Under Dog Back Street / Just Like A Woman - **Warren Lee** 1969
Produced by: Big Q / Big Q
PM-763 T.C.B Or T.Y.A. / What A Wonderful Night For Love - **Bobby Patterson** 1969
Produced by: Abnak Music / Abnak Music

PM-764 (Not Used)
PM-765 Sock It To 'Em Soul Brother / Sock It To 'Em Soul Brother (Instr) - **Bill Moss** 1969
Produced by: Bill Moss / Bill Moss
PM-766 Walk On Judge / Lose The One You Love - **Soul Partners** 1969
Produced by: Bill Moss / Bill Moss
PM-767 Action / What Would It Take - **The Showmen** 1969
Produced by: Moses Dillard / Moses Dillard
PM-768 You Don't Know / Ode To Billy Joe - **Anna Walker and The Crownettes** 1969
Produced by: Randy Irwin / Randy Irwin
PM-769 Oh Happy Day / Can't Get Along Without You - **Conroy Cannon Mission** 1969
Produced by: Unknown / Unknown
PM-770 (Not Used)
PM-771 Mr. Pitiful / Let's Get Married - **Joyce Bond & Little John** 1969
Produced by: Harry Palmer / Harry Palmer
PM-772 The Sun Gotta Shine In Your Heart (If You Want Happiness) /
I Only Have Eyes For You - **The Persians** 1969
Produced by: Beywes Production / Beywes Production
PM-773 My Thing Is Your Thing (Come Get It) / Keep It In The Family -
Bobby Patterson 1969
Produced by: Abnak Music / Abnak Music
PM-774 Who's Got The Ball (Y'all) / Half Time -
Roosevelt Grier and The Fearsome Foursome 1969
Produced by: Chips Moman / Chips Moman
PM-775 I Am Not Going To Work Today / A Shot of Rhythm And Blues -
Clyde McPhater 1969 *Produced by: Rick Hall / Rick Hall*
PM-776 - PM-783 (Not Used)
PM-784 C'mon Cupid / High Society Woman - **Roosevelt Grier** 1969
Produced by: Chips Moman / Chips Moman
PM-785 Let's Get Together / Little Girl - **The Other Brothers** 1969
Produced by: Dale Hawkins / Dale Hawkins
PM-786 Karate / I've Got To Have Her - **The Emperor's** 1969
Produced by: George Brown - Phil Gaber / George Brown - Phil Gaber
PM-787 (Not Used)
PN-788 (Not Used)
PM-789 Give Peace A Chance / She - **The Rudees** 1969
Produced by: Derrick Morgan / Derrick Morgan
PM-790 (Not Used)
PM-791 (Not Used)
PM-792 Birth Control - Lloyd Terrell / Return To Peace - Val Bennett 1970
Produced by: Lloyd Terrell / Lynford Anderson
PM-793 You Turn Out The Light / Good Humour Man - **Clifford Curry** 1970
Produced by: Buzz Cason / Buzz Cason
PM-794 I'm A Poor Man's Son / That's How Much I Love You - **Spencer Wiggins** 1970
Produced by: Q Claunch - R Russell / Q Claunch - R Russell
PM-795 Say You Need Me / Unlovable - **Barbara Perry** 1970
Produced by: Q Claunch - R Russell / Q Claunch - R Russell
PM-796 Number One - Bill Moss / Landscape - **The Mohawks** 1970
Produced by: Bill Moss / Alan Hawkshaw
PM-797 I Can't Get Hold Of Myself / Ain't No Danger - **Clifford Curry** 1970
Produced by: Buzz Cason / Buzz Cason
PM-798 Skin Head Shuffle - The Mohawks / Red Cow - Reco Rodregez 1970
Produced by: Graham Hawk / Coxsone Dodd

PM-799 Close Shave - Kirk Redding / Prisoner Of Love - The Untouchables 1970
Produced by: Kirk Redding / E McLeod
PM-800 Down On The Corner / Who Is That Stranger - **Sid & Joe with The Moharks** 1970
Produced by: Graham Hawk / Graham Hawk
PM-801 What A Woman / Sleepy Cat - **Bill Jentles** 1970
Produced by: Bunny Lee / Bunny Lee
PM-802 Jeff Barns Thing - Jeff Barns / Lover's Mood - Lennox Brown 1970
Produced by: Bunny Lee / Bunny Lee
PM-803 Annie Pama / Mr Mago - **Lee's Allstars** 1970
Produced by: Bunny Lee / Bunny Lee
PM-804 Reggae And Shout - The Black Beatles / The Green Hornett - Lennox Brown 1970
Produced by: Derrick Morgan / Bunny Lee
PM-805 Take Back Your Nicket - Ferdinand and Dill / Blue Berry Hill - Ferdinand 1970
Produced by: Derrick Morgan / Derrick Morgan
PM-806 Hound Dog / Black Girl - **Sketto Rich** 1970
Produced by: Derrick Morgan / Derrick Morgan
PM-807 Confussion / We Got To Have Loving - **Noel And The Fireballs** 1970
Produced by: Derrick Morgan / Derrick Morgan
PM-808 Can't Turn You Loose / Skinny Legs - **Noel And The Fireballs** 1970
Produced by: Derrick Morgan / Derrick Morgan
PM-809 True True Train - Bill Jentles / Give And Take - Jeff Barns 1970
Produced by: Bunny Lee / Bunny Lee
PM-810 Sugar Dumpling / I Don't Know Why - **Owen Gray** 1970
Produced by: Sydney Crooks / Sydney Crooks
PM-811 Maybe The Next Time / Got To See You - **Pat Rhoden** 1970
Produced by: Derrick Morgan / Derrick Morgan
PM-812 Here Comes The Night - Solomon Jones / Jaded Ramble - Rico Rodriques 1970
Produced by: Derrick Morgan / Derrick Morgan
PM-813 Love One Another / Falling Rain - **The Marvels** 1970
Produced by: Derrick Morgan / Derrick Morgan
PM-814 Soul And Inspiration / Stand By - **The Blossoms** 1970
Produced by: Bill Medley / Bill Medley
PM-815 The Choking Kind / Chocolate Candy - **Sonny Cox** 1970
Produced by: Richard Evans / Richard Evans
PM-816 Got To Get You Off My Mind / So High So Wide So Low - **Shell Altermann** 1970
Produced by: Harry Palmer / Harry Palmer
PM-817 Don't Let Her Take Your Love From Me / La La La - The Marvels 1970
Produced by: Derrick Morgan / Derrick Morgan
PM-818 Mary's Boy Child - Laurel Aitken / Mary's Boy Child - Rupie Edwards Allstars 1970
Produced by: Laurel Aitken / Laurel Aitken
PM-819 Oh Lord, Why Lord - The Marvels / Love Letters - Nellie 1970
Produced by: Derrick Morgan / Dimple Hinds
PM-820 My Sweet Lord / Darling That's Right - **Fitzroy Sterling** 1971
Produced by: Sydney Crooks / Sydney Crooks
PM-821 (Promo Only)
PM-822 Love Bug / My Dickie - **Derrick Morgan** 1971
Produced by: Derrick Morgan / Derrick Morgan
PM-823 Heaven Help Us / Can't Do Without Your love - **Winston Groovy** 1971
Produced by: Sydney Crooks / Sydney Crooks
PM-824 Jesus Keepeth My Soul / Fire Fire - **The Youth** 1971
Produced by: Harry Palmer / Harry Palmer
PM-825 No More Lonely Teardrops / My Mama Told Me - **Joan Ross** 1971
Produced by: Harry Palmer / Harry Palmer
PM-826 Grooving Out Of Life - Hopeton Lewis / Grooving Out Of Life (Part 2) - M Squad 1971
Produced by: Winston Blake / Winston Blake
PM-827 Don't Break My Heart / How Long Will This Go On - **Winston Groovy** 1971
Produced by: Sydney Crooks / Sydney Crooks
PM-828 Jesamine - Junior English / The Flash - Sydney Crooks All Stars 1971
Produced by: Sydney Crooks / Sydney Crooks
PM-829 Oh What A Mini / Mini (Version) 2 - **Willie Francis** 1971
Produced by: Willie Francis / Willie Francis

PM-830 Sex Education - The Classics / Soul Flash - The Power 1971
Produced by: Harry Palmer / Harry Palmer
PM-831 (Not Used)
PM-832 Do You Know You Have To Cry / Love Power - **The Marvels** 1971
Produced by: Harry Palmer / A Hinds
PM-833 You Don't Care - Lloyd Sparks / Must Care - Tony All Stars 1972
Produced by: Tony Robinson / Tony Robinson
PM-834 Living In Sweet Jamaica - Jackie Brown / Sweet Jamaica (Version) - Tony All Stars 1972
Produced by: Tony Robinson / Tony Robinson
PM-835 Way Down South - Hugh Roy / Be My Guest - Billy Dyce 1972
Produced by: Alvin Ranglin / Alvin Ranglin
PM-836 Night Angel (Wet Dream - Max Romeo Bang Bang Lulu - Lloyd Tyrell / Birth Control - Llloyd Tyrell Sex Education - The Classics) 1972 *(E.P.)*
Produced by: Bunny Lee / Lloyd Tyrell / Lloyd Tyrell / Harry Palmer
PM-837 (not Used)
PM-838 Beautiful Sunday / Take Care Son - **Eugene Paul** 1972
Produced by: Ranny Williams / Ranny Williams
PM-839 Come What May - Fermena / Come What May (Version) - Fermena And Ranny 1972
Produced by: Ranny Williams / Ranny Williams
PM-840 Girl Have Got A Date / Eat Bread - **Alton Ellis** 1972
Produced by: Alton Ellis / Alton Ellis
PM-841 Miss Playgirl / Once In My Life - **Junior English** 1972
Produced by: Ellis Breary /Ellis Breary
PM-842 Rocket Man / I'm All Broke Up - **In Flames** 1972
Produced by: Ranny Williams / Ranny Williams
PM-843 You've Lost That Loving Feeling - The Heptones / Feeling Version - The Underground People 1972
Produced by: Rupie Edwards / Rupie Edwards
PM-844 Shake It Loose - Ken Parker / Shaking Version - Timmy McCook & Ken Parker 1972
Produced by: Duke Reid / Duke Reid
PM-845 3 x 7 Rock & Roll - Slim Smith / I'll Always Love You - John Holt 1972
Produced by: Bunny Lee / Stranger Cole
PM-846 I Am Feeling Lonely / Lonely Version - **The Maytones** 1972
Produced by: Alvin Ranglin / Alvin Ranglin
PM-847 This Is My Story - Clarendonians / Caledonia - Val Bennett 1972
Produced by: Bunny Lee / Bunny Lee
PM-848 The House Where Bombo Lives / Our High School Dance - **Stranger Cole** 1972
Produced by: Bunny Lee / Bunny Lee
PM-849 (Not Used)
PM-850 The Time Has Come - Slim Smith / Version - The Aggrevators 1972
Produced by: Bunny Lee / Bunny Lee
PM-851 Feel Good All Over - Phill Pratt Allstars / Dangerous - Keble Drummond 1972
Produced by: Phill Pratt / Phill Pratt
PM-852 Pledging My Love - John Holt / I Will Know What To Do - James Brown 1972
Produced by: Bunny Lee / Bunny Lee
PM-853 Big Seven - Charlie & Fay / Ace & The Professionals Version - Youth Professional Band 1972
Produced by: Charlie Ace / Charlie Ace
PM-854 Cow Town Skank - I Roy / Version - Augustos Pablo 1972
Produced by: Bunny Lee / Bunny Lee
PM-855 (Not Used)
PM-856 Good Hearted Woman - Clarendonians / What Happens - Cornell Campbell 1972
Produced by: Bunny Lee / Bunny Lee
PM-857 Fever - Junior Byles / Soul Sister - The Groovers 1972
Produced by: Lee Perry / Lee Perry
PM-858 (Not Used)

REGGAE TOP 50
REGGAE TOP 50
PAMA RECORDS
BOSS SOUNDS ON PAMA
REGGAE TOP 50

PM-859 **At The End** / Good Night My Love - **Chenley Duffas** 1972
Produced by: Lee Perry / Lee Perry
PM-860 **Sound Doctor - Bobby Floyd** / Doctor Skank - Young Dellinger 1972
Produced by: Lee Perry / Lee Perry
PM-861 (Not Used)
PM-862 **The Godfather - Jerry Lewis** / Some Day - Alton Ellis 1972
Produced by: Bunny Lee / Bunny Lee
PM-863 **Big Eight - Lloyd Terrell** / Auntie Lu Lu - Junior Byles 1973
Produced by: Lloyd Charmers / Lee Perry
PM-864 **I Want Justice - B.B. Seaton** / Version Of Justice - Rupie Edwards Allstars 1973
Produced by: Rupie Edwards / Rupie Edwards
PM-865 (Not Used)
PM-866 **I Don't Want To Die** / Land Of Sea And Sun - **Junior English** 1973
Produced by: Ellis Breary / Ellis Breary
PM-867 (not used)
PM-868 (Not Used)
PM-869 **Daniel** / Perfidia - **Junior English** 1973
Produced by: Ellis Breary / Ellis Breary
PM-870 (Not Used)
PM-871 **All Over The World People Are Changing - The Maytones** / Dubwise - Volcano 1973
Produced by: Alvin Ranglin / Alvin Ranglin
PM-872 **Dedicated To Illiteracy - Glady & Stranger** / Dub - G.G. Allstars 1973
Produced by: Alvin Ranglin / Alvin Ranglin
PM-873 **True Believer - Larry Marshall** / Water Your Garden - The Flames 1973
Produced by: Lee Perry / Lee Perry
PM-874 **Woman Smarter - Billy Dice** / Standing On The Hill - Chenley Duffas 1973
Produced by: Lee Perry / Lee Perry
PM-875 **Pussy Watchman - Max Romeo** / You Are My Sunshine - Cornell Campbell 1973
Produced by: Bunny Lee / Bunny Lee
PM-876 **Village Ram** / Push It Inna - The Twinkle Brothers 1973
Produced by: Norman Grant / Norman Grant
PM-877 **Big Nine - Father Sketto** / Old Lady - The Untouchables 1973
Produced by: Ranny Williams / Ranny Willians
PM-878 **Education Rock - Junior Byles** / Nobody Knows - Ken McKay 1973
Produced by: P Morrison / P Morrison
PM-879 **Wonderful Dreams (Erestu)** / Version (Wonderful Dreams) - **Fermena** 1973
Produced by: Palmer Brothers / Palmer Brothers
PM-4000 **Sing About Love** / Love Version - Pat Kelly 1975
Produced by: Phil Pratt / Phil Pratt
PM-4001 **Sinners Where Are You Going To Hide** / If It's Love You Need - **Justin Hinds** 1975
Produced by: Duke Reid / Duke Reid
PM-4002 **Darling Is You** / Car Pound - **Bill Gentles** 1975
Produced by: Bill Gentles / Bill Gentles

BOSS SOUNDS FROM
PAMA

Boss Sounds from PAMA brings some of the highlights from the labels production between 1967 and 1973.

PM-834 Living In Sweet Jamaica - Jackie Brown 1972
Produced by: Tony Robinson
Jackie Brown moved to Kingston when he was fifteen to pursue a singing career and gained success as a balladeer in the 70s. The rhythm track for Living In Sweet Jamaica is sampled from Love Of The Common People.

PM-835 Way Down South - Hugh Roy 1972
Produced by: Alvin Ranglin
Hugh Roy or U Roy was known for his unique melodic style of toasting and comes up trumps with a resounding talk over version of Take Warning from Billy Dyce, who incidentally features on the B side with a cover of a Fats Domino number, Be My Guest.

PM-801 What A Woman - Bill Jentles 1970
Produced by: Bunny Lee
An up-tempo beat from Bill Jentles *(Gentles)* on What A Woman, the well known impressionist sounding very much like Desmond Dekker.

PM-707 The Message - Alton Ellis 1968
Produced by: Alton Ellis
Alton with a message using the rhythm he used for his 1971 Merry, Merry Christmas credited to Alton Ellis & The Lipsticks and released on his Jamaican All Tone label.

PM-710 Bang Bang Lulu - Lloyd Terrel 1968
Produced by: Lynford Anderson
Lloyd Terrell - AKA Charmers or Tyrell with cheeky vocals and late rocksteady at its very best. The track was used for the title as well as the opening track on the 1969 album Bang Bang Lulu PMLP 4 curiously issued with three different colour sleeves. Another oddity is the Prefix for the single was PMB-710.

PM-844 Shake It Loose - Ken Parker 1972
Produced by: Duke Reid
AKA Help Me Make It Through The Night.

PM-792 Birth Control - Lloyd Terrell 1970

Produced by: Lloyd Terrell

Birth Control from Lloyd Terrell was the precursor for the album of the same title issued on SECO 32. Lloyd Terrell AKA Lloyd Charmers et al also recorded a version released by Trojan on the album Censored under the name of Lloydie & The Lowbites, but the Pama one is by far and away the best and always a firm favourite at the school disco.

PM-853 Big Seven - Charlie & Fay 1972

Produced by: Charlie Ace

A much ruder version than Judge Dread's carrying an infectious hypnotic beat punctuated with explicit lyrics, so no chance of air play for Big Seven. The track was originally released in Jamaica as Punnany on the Scorpion label. The duo are better known as Charlie Ace and Fay Bennett.

PM-848(2) Our High School Dance - Stranger Cole 1972

Produced by: Bunny Lee

A fine example of solid reggae and first rate vocals from Stranger Cole and Hortense Ellis. Odd why it was only ever issued as a B side. The track features on Straighten Up Volume 4.

PMB-711 Heart Beat - Ernest Ranglin 1968

Produced by: Clancy Eccles

A first-rate instrumental from the Jamaican guitarist and composer Ernest Ranglin who established an illustrious career working as a session guitarist with various labels including Studio One. Ernest was recruited to compose music for the 1962 Jamaican based James Bond film Dr No.

PM-818 Mary's Boy Child - Laurel Aitken 1970

Produced by: Laurel Aitken

A good seasonal offering from Laurel.

PM-863 Big Eight - Lloyd Terrell 1973

Produced by: Lloyd Charmers

Another slice of rude reggae as Lloyd Terrell uses Ernie Smith's tune Pitta Patta for his Big Eight, although the record comes with some ambiguity as there were three different pressings issued under the same prefix. The first Featured Lloyd Terrell C/W Auntie Lu Lu - Junior Byles. The second by Winston Reed C/W Instrumental Version Of Big Eight - Ranny Williams Allstars with The Classics. The third credits Big Eight to Lloyd Terrell C/W Lighting Stick - Lloyd Terrell.

PM-721 Say What You Say - Monty Morris 1968

Produced by: Clancy Eccles

Sweet vocals over a chugging organ influenced late rocksteady beat from Eric 'Monty' Morris who was the original vocalist for the Skatalites. Monty had several hits during the early 60s back in Jamaica including Humpty Dumpty and Oil In My Lamp. Say What You Say was a big seller for Pama.

PM-722 C.N. Express (Part One) - Clancy's All Stars 1968

Produced by: Clancy Eccles

Classic emerging boss sounds from Clancy Eccles using the same rhythm lifted from Monty Morris Say What You Say.

PM-719 The Champ - The Mohawks 1968 (Soul)

Produced by: Alan Hawkshaw - Jeff Palmer

The Mohawks were a session group led by Alan Hawkshaw.

At the time of launch it was described as the best ever soul instrumental however despite the track selling well and receiving air-play it failed to enter the national chart. The song is based on a 1967 song Tramp with Champ sung rather than Tramp. It has through time become the most sampled record.

PM-701 What Will Your Mama Say - Clancy Eccles 1968

Produced by: Clancy Eccles

Clancy had been singing since the early 60s working with the likes of Coxsone Dodd and this is rock steady at its best. One of the first where he not only performs but also wears the producers hat. That combination proved a great success for Clancy. Harry Palmer offered the recording to Island who showed little interest so he published independently on PM-701. What Will Your Mama Say was given the strings treatment by Norton York and re issued on PS-332 in 1971.

CLANCY ECCLES
ARTIST / PRODUCER

Clancy Eccles spent his early years in the Parish of Saint Mary in Jamaica, the son of a tailor and builder. He was influenced by spiritual music in church and grew to love singing. Clancy's musical career began with a stint working on the north coast hotel circuit, eventually moving to Ocho Rios. Leaving the north coast behind for Kingston gave him his musical break when he took part in a talent show organized by Coxsone Dodd. Clancy's early success featured several ska hits including River Jordon and Sammy No Dead.

In the mid 60s he launched a series of talent shows of his own and began to organise concerts including among many The Wailers. He left behind the music industry in 1965 for a short stint following his fathers profession as a tailor before returning to the music business in 1967. This time saw Clancy producing his own recordings as well as other artists.

Clancy was influential during the period of the hardening of rocksteady into reggae and has been credited as being the originator of the word reggae, derived from streggae, a word used in Kingston to describe a woman of the streets. The claim is emphasized in Bag A Boo - Don't You Brag And Don't You Boast.

However before Bag A Boo his first hit in the UK was What Will Your Mama Say released on PM-701 in 1968. Much of his production work found favour with the skinheads, including Herbman Shuffle from the legendary DJ King Stitt, pronounced Stitch.

Clancy Eccles Artist and Producer on Pama

PM-701 What Will Your Mama Say / Darling Don't Do That - Clancy Eccles 1967
Produced by: Clancy Eccles / Clancy Eccles
PM-703 Western Organ / Mothers Advice - The Clancy Set 1967
Produced by: Clancy Eccles / Clancy Eccles
PM-712 The Fight / Great - Clancy Eccles 1968
Produced by: Ernest Ranglin / Ernest Ranglin
PM-722 C.N. Express (Part One) / CN Express (Part 2) - Clancy's All Stars 1968
Produced by: Clancy Eccles / Clancy Eccles
PM-704 Bad Mind People - Miss Jane / My Heart Is Aching - Trials 1968
Produced by: Clancy Eccles / Clancy Eccles
PM-711Heart Beat - Ernest Ranglin / Birds of The Air - The Coolers 1968
Produced by: Clancy Eccles / Clancy Eccles
PM-720(2) Please Stay - Tommy McKenzie Orchestra 1968
Produced by: Clancy Eccles
PM-721 Say What You Say / Tears In Your Eyes - Monty Morris 1968
Produced by: Clancy Eccles / Clancy Eccles
PM-729(2) Two Of A Kind - The Termites 1968
Produced by: Clancy Eccles

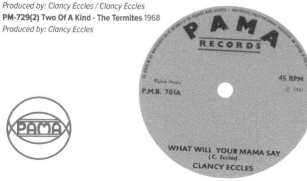

The Jamaican imprint of the Pama label

PAMA SUPREME

PAMA SUPREME one of the last three labels to be set up in 1970 was seen as the commercial arm working with established UK based artists, rivalling Trojan with lots of strings and things courtesy of Norton York. He was Pama's own version of Trojan's Johnny Arthey. The bulk of production came from Ranny Williams and Lloyd Charmers. The labels biggest sellers were undoubtedly Max Romeo's Let The Power Fall PS-306, Densil Dennis with his take on South Of The Border PS-350 and Cynthia Richards energetic Mr. Postman issued on PS-366. It was around this time Trojan were issuing reggae versions of pop hits recorded in Jamaica and Pama would often issue a cover version albeit far less commercial than their rivals. Towards the end production seemed to be coming from Jamaican rather than UK based.

PAMA SUPREME DISCOGRAPHY 1970 - 1974 Prefix PS

PS-297 What's The World Coming To / Live As One - **King Chubby** 1970
Produced by: Lee Perry / Lee Perry
PS-298 Do What You Go To Do / Crying Won't Help - **Pat Rhoden** 1970
Produced by: Ranny Williams / Ranny Williams
PS-299 I Am In Love Again - Owen Gray / Version II - **Ranny Williams Band** 1970
Produced by: Ranny Williams / Ranny Williams
PS-300 Why Can't I Touch You / Can't Turn Your Back On Me - **Laurel Aitken** 1970
Produced by: Laurel Aitken - N Bell / Laurel Aitken - N Bell
PS-301 My Way - D. Dennis / Happy Days - D.D. Dennis 1970
Produced by: Laurel Aitken / Derrick Morgan
PS-302 Candida / When Will I Find My Way - **Owen Gray** 1971
Produced by: Sydney Crooks / Sydney Crooks
PS-303 Don't Let The Tears Fall / Another Saturday Night - **Eugene Paul** 1971
Produced by: Sydney Crooks / Sydney Crooks
PS-304 Painful Situation / Nothing Has Changed - **D.D. Dennis** 1971
Produced by: Sydney Crooks / Sydney Crooks
PS-305 I Found A Man / So Many Things - **Eugene Paul** 1971
Produced by: Sydney Crooks / Sydney Crooks
PS-306 Let The Power Fall / The Raid - **Max Romeo** 1971
Produced by: Derrick Morgan / Derrick Morgan
PS-307 (Not Used)
PS-308 Crackling Rose - Lloyd Jackson / Little Deeds Of Kindness - Lloyd Jackson & The Scorpions 1971
Produced by: Derrick Morgan / Derrick Morgan
PS-309 "Cheer Me Up" / The Clock - **The Mohawks** 1971 (SOUL)
Produced by: Don Lawson / Don Lawson
PS-310 You Gonna Miss Me / I Hear You Knocking - **Owen Gray** 1971
Produced by: Sydney Crooks / Sydney Crooks
PS-311 (Promo Only)
PS-312 - PS-316 (Not Used)
PS-317 Farewell My Darling / Whole Lot Of Woman - **Eugene Paul** 1971
Produced by: Sydney Crooks / H Palmer

PS-318 Don't You Weep / Weeping (Version) - **Max Romeo** 1971
Produced by: Derrick Morgan / Derrick Morgan
PS-319 (Promo Only)
PS-320 (Not Used)
PS-321 John Crow Skank / Give Thanks - **Derrick Morgan** 1971
Produced by: Derrick Morgan / Derrick Morgan
PS-322 (Not Used)
PS-323 Free The People / Not Now - **Winston Groovy** 1971
Produced by: Winston Tucker / Winston Tucker
PS-324 Then You Can Tell Me Goodbye / Up And Down The Highway - **The Mohawks** 1971
Produced by: Harry Palmer / Harry Palmer
PS-325 Summer Sand / Something To Remind Me - **Owen Gray** 1971
Produced by: Derrick Morgan / Harry Palmer
PS-326 (Not Used)
PS-327 Eastern Promise / Fiddle Sticks - **Tommy McKenzie & His Orchestra** 1971
Produced by: Palmer Brothers / Palmer Brothers
PS-328 Ginal Ship - Max Romeo / Version 2 - The Upsetters 1971
Produced by: Lee Perry / Lee Perry
PS-329 Somebody's Changing My Sweet Baby's Mind / Hard Minded Neighbour - **Eugene Paul** 1971
Produced by: Ranny Williams / Ranny Williams
PS-330 I Am A Believer / I'll Make The Way Easy - **D.D. Dennis** 1971
Produced by: Ranny Williams / Ranny Williams
PS-331 Peace Of My Heart / Right On The Tip Of My Tongue - **Mahalia Saunders** 1971
Produced by: Lee Perry / Lee Perry
PS-332 What Will Your Mama Say - Clancy Eccles / United We Stand - Tiger 1971
Produced by: Clancy Eccles - Norton York / Laurel Aitken
PS-333 Owen Gray Greatest Hits (Part 1) / Owen Gray Greatest Hits (Part 2) - **Owen Gray** 1971
Produced by: Lloyd Charmers / Lloyd Charmers
PS-334 Send Me Some Loving / I Am Lost - **Slim Smith** 1971
Produced by: Lloyd Charmers / Bunny Lee
PS-335 Daddy Love (Vocal) / Daddy Love (Instru.) - **Gi Gi** 1971 (SOUL)
Produced by: Charles Hodges / Charles Hodges
PS-336 (Not Used)
PS-337 I Stayed Away Too Long / Country Boy - **Manley Patterson** 1971
Produced by: Manley Patterson / Manley Patterson
PS-338 Rock Steady / Be My Baby - **The Marvels** 1971
Produced by: Lloyd Charmers / Lloyd Charmers
PS-339 Shaft / Harry's Mood - **Lloyd Charmers** 1971
Produced by: Lloyd
PS-340 Red Head Duck / Jingle Jangle - **Lloyd Terrell** 1971
Produced by: Lloyd Charmers / Lloyd Charmers
PS-341 -PS-344 (Not Issued)
PS-345 Pray for Me / Pray For Me (Version) - **Max Romeo** 1972
Produced by: Sonia Pottinger / Sonia Pottinger
PS-346 Show Business - Lloyd Charmers / Gloria - Debby And Lloyd 1972
Produced by: Lloyd Charmers / Lloyd Charmers
PS-347 Moon River / I Can't Find Out - **Alton Ellis** 1972
Produced by: Alton Ellis / Alton Ellis
PS-348 What A Hurricane / If You Love Her - **The Marvels** 1972
Produced by: Norton York / Dimple Hinds
PS-349 What You Gonna Do / Why Did You Leave - **Winston Groovy** 1972
Produced by: Winston Tucker / Winston Tucker
PS-350 South Of The Border - Densil Dennis / Long Island - Graham 1972
Produced by: Ranny Williams / Graham Hawk
PS-351 Time - Owen Gray / Harlesden High Street- Graham 1972
Produced by: Ranny Williams / Ranny Williams
PS-352 Rock Me Mr. Pingwing / Breakdown Rock - **The Harlesden Monks** 1972
Produced by: Ian Smith / Ian Smith
PS-353 I'm Gonna Give Her All The Love I've Got - Pat Kelly / As Long As You Love Me - The Maytones 1972
Produced by: Ranny Williams / Alvin Ranglin
PS-354 That Wonderful Sound / I Wasn't Born Yesterday - **Dobby Dobson** 1972
Produced by: Rupie Edwards / Rupie Edwards
PS-355 Desiderata - Lloyd Charmers / Desiderata Music - Now Generation 1972
Produced by: Lloyd Charmers / Lloyd Charmers

PS-356 Throw Away Your Gun - Busty Brown And The Warners / Sad Song - Twinkle Brothers 1972
Produced by: Sid Bucknor / Sid Bucknor

PS-357 I'll Take You There - Eugene Paul / Lovey Dovey - Eugene Paul & Ranny 1972
Produced by: Ranny Williams / Ranny Williams

PS-358 Hail The Man / I'll Follow You - **Owen Gray** 1972
Produced by: Ranny Williams / Ranny Williams

PS-359 Are You Sure - Max Romeo / Va-Va-Voom - Carl Masters 1972
Produced by: Rupie Edwards / Rupie Edwards - Glen Brown

PS-360 Amazing Grace - Graham Hawk & Owen Gray / Don't Stay Out Too Late - Sketto Rich 1972
Produced by: Ranny Williams / Derrick Morgan

PS-361 Working On A Groovy Thing - Alton Ellis / Groovy Thing (instr.) - Harlesden Skankers 1972
Produced by: Alton Ellis / Alton Ellis

PS-362 And I Love Her / Storm - **The Mohawks** 1972
Produced by: The Mohawks / The Mohawks

PS-363 (Not Used)

PS-364 Sylvia's Mother / Here Is My Heart - **Winston Groovy** 1972
Produced by: Winston Tucker / Laurel Aitken

PS-365 Breakfast In Bed - Winston Reed / Guitar Shuffle - Ranny Williams Allstars 1972
Produced by: Ranny Williams / Ranny Williams

PS-366 Mr. Postman - Cynthia Richards / Postman Version - Skin Flesh and Bone 1972
Produced by: Cynthia Richards / Cynthia Richards

PS-367 Save The Last Dance - Heptones / Dance Version - Joe Gibbs Allstars with Heptones 1972
Produced by: Joe Gibbs / Joe Gibbs

PS-368 (Not Used)

PS-369 Look What You Done To Me - Ken Booth / Version - Lloyd Charmers 1972
Produced by: Lloyd Charmers / Lloyd Charmers

PS-370 - PS-373 (Not Used)

PS-374 Sweet Caroline / Ellena Rigby - **B.B. Seaton** 1972
Produced by: Lloyd Charmers / Lloyd Charmers

PS-375 Mama We're All Crazee Now - Denzil Dennis / A Lady Is A Mans Best Friend - Roy Shirley 1973
Produced by: Derrick Morgan / Ranny Williams

PS- 376 Cherry Pink / The Champ - **The Mohawks** 1973
Produced by: Graham Hawk / Harry Palmer

PS-377 (Not Used)

PS-378 Out Of Time / Put A Little Rain Into My Life - **Pat Rhoden** 1973
Produced by: Ranny Williams / Ranny Williams

PS-379 Twelfth Of Never - Pat Kelly / 5000 Watts - Jerry Lewis 1973
Produced by: Bunny Lee / Bunny Lee

PS-380 You're Mine / What A Guy - **Beverley Simmonds** 1973
Produced by: Harry Palmer / Harry Palmer

PS-381 Garden Party - Junior English / Keep The Faith - Derrick Morgan 1973
Produced by: Ranny Williams / Bunny Lee

PS-382 Power To All Our Friends - Eugene Paul / Wicked & Dreadfull - Ranny Williams Allstars 1973
Produced by: Ranny Williams / Ranny Williams

PS-383 Hide Away - Max Romeo / Sweet And Gentle - Soul Syndicate 1973
Produced by: Victor Chin / Victor Chin

PS-384 I Wish It Could Rain - Pat Kelly / Hallelujah - Pat Kelly Singers 1973
Produced by: Phil Pratt / Phil Pratt

PS-385 Every Man Aught To Know / Version - **Max Romeo** 1973
Produced by: Keith Chin / Keith Chin

PS-386 (Not Used)

PS-387 I'll Never Give Up / I Who Have Nothing - **Derrick Morgan** 1973
Produced by: Bunny Lee / Bunny Lee

PS-388 (Not Used)

PS-389 (Not Used)

PS-390 Thanks We Get / Oppression - **Heptones** 1974
Produced by: P Morrison / P Morrison

PS-391 Woman & Money - D.D. Dennis / 10 Cent Skank - Upsetters 1974
Produced by: P Morrison / P Morrison

63

BOSS SOUNDS FROM
PAMA SUPREME

Boss Sounds from PAMA SUPREME brings some of the highlights from the labels production between 1970 and 1974.

PS-350 South Of The Border - Densil Dennis 1972
Produced by: Ranny Williams

This was big a seller for Pama at the time with a cover version of the popular song describing a trip to Mexico and the title track for the 1936 film of the same name. Densil's vocals flow seamlessly through the chugging beat. The record had an outing on Straighten Up Volume 3.

PS-366 Mr. Postman - Cynthia Richards 1972
Produced by: Cynthia Richards

There seemed to be a raft of boss sounds produced around the time of this release and this self produced Jamaican tune from Cynthia Richards is certainly one of them. Top vocals over another hypnotic chugging beat. It was a sound Pama remained faithful to at a time when the original skinheads were becoming disillusioned that the raw unpretentious sounds were becoming too watered down.

PS-367 Save The Last Dance - Heptones 1972
C/W **Dance Version - Joe Gibbs Allstars with Heptones**
Produced by: Joe Gibbs

A worthy cover of The Drifters Save The Last Dance For Me first recorded in 1960 with lead vocals from Ben E King. This version from the Jamaican trio of Leroy Sibbles, Barry Llewellyn and Earl Morgan is an excellent cover. The B side is well worth a spin as the vocals fade to reveal the true extent of the hypnotic beat.

PS-332 What Will Your Mama Say - Clancy Eccles 1971
Produced by: Clancy Eccles - Norton York

Clancy's vocal talents shine through over a strong rocksteady beat with the influence of Norton York brought in by Pama to sweeten things following the success Johnny Arthey was having at Trojan. First released in 1967 on Pama PM-701 What Will Your Mama Say with an over-dub of strings works well giving the record a new lease of life.

PS-379 Twelfth Of Never - Pat Kelly 1973
Produced by: Bunny Lee

Pat Kelly finally gets the credit for his overdubbed 1968 rocksteady cover of the classic Twelfth Of Never credited to Max Romeo on the Unity release in 1969. The song was first recorded by Johnny Mathis in 1957. The Pama re-issue coincided with chart success for Donny Osmond.

PS-328 Ginal Ship - Max Romeo 1971
C/W **Version 2 - The Upsetters**
Produced by: Lee Perry

A classic from the original rude boy showcasing his lyrical talents. Max had become aware of social injustices and the gulf between the rich and poor in Jamaica and it was reflected in his music. -The cops are afraid of the thieves - The thieves are afraid of the cops-. Version 2 on the B side from The Upsetters is worthy of an A side in its own right. A boss sound.

PS-353 I'm Gonna Give Her All The Love I've Got - Pat Kelly 1972
Produced by: Ranny Williams

C/W **As Long As You Love Me - The Maytones**
Produced by: Alvin Ranglin

A boss tune from Pat Kelly with a cover of a 1967 Jimmy Ruffin song. The B side is another infectious sound from the duo of Vernon Buckley and Gladstone Grant perhaps better known as The Maytones, produced of course by Alvin Ranglin who had formed the GG label in 1970. The Maytones issued a dozen tracks on the various Pama labels between 1969 and 1973 including their Black And White Unite CA-47 influencing the Straighten Up series.

PS-302 Candida - Owen Gray 1971
Produced by: Sydney Crooks

The label was set up for the release of covers of pop hits and this is a prime example from Owen Gray with his soulful voice negotiating the lyrics of the first single released by the American group Dawn, with vocals by Tony Orlando a year earlier.

PS-321 John Crow Skank - Derrick Morgan 1971
Produced by: Derrick Morgan
Derrick Morgan lets his vocal talent loose over the Cherry Oh Baby rhythm. In case you're wondering John Crow is a Jamaican vulture.

PS-376 B The Champ - The Mohawks 1973
Produced by: Graham Hawk
A reggae styled remake of the dance-floor classic from the band that slows down the main organ theme and places it over a bass-heavy rhythm. This time it comes backed with a re rework on the classic Marvels Rock Steady.

PS-365 Breakfast In Bed - Winston Reed 1972
Produced by: Ranny Williams
This version of the Lorna Bennett classic is slightly different but none the less a hot number from a very young Winston (Reedy) who joined forces with the session band The Cimarons when they migrated to London from Jamaica in 1967.

PS-327 Eastern Promise - Tommy McKenzie & His Orchestra 1970
C/W **Fiddle Sticks - Tommy McKenzie & His Orchestra**
Produced by: Palmer Brothers
The instrumental Eastern Promise is reminiscent of My Girl from The Technique issued on Treasure Isle. The B side Fiddle Sticks could well have been the A side as indeed it was when issued on Pama PM-720 in 1968. Fiddle Sticks is a cracking rock steady tune and justifiably features on the Pama albums Ready Steady Go Rock Steady PLMP 3 SP from 1968, Reggae Spectacular With Strings PMP 2001 from 1971 and even had an outing on the 1969 album Ska Ska Ska From Jamaica issued in The Netherlands.

PS-338 Rock Steady - The Marvels 1971
Produced by: Lloyd Charmers
C/W **Be My Baby - The Marvels**
Alex and Cornell Hinds along with Eddie Smith specialised in Doo-wop harmonies and the A side is a cover of Aretha Franklin's Rock Steady issued the same year. The track, although carrying the same title, should not be confused with Alton Ellis & The Flames who were accompanied by Tommy McCook and The Supersonics Band on the outstanding Jamaican release Rock Steady from 1966, issued in the UK on Treasure Isle the following year. Be My Baby on the flip side is an excellent reggae cover of the Ronetts classic hit released on London Records in 1963.

PUNCH

PUNCH DISCOGRAPHY 1969 - 1975 Prefix PH

PH-1 The Burner /Juckie Juckie - **The Dynamics** 1969
Produced by: Lloyd Daley / Lloyd Daley
PH-2 Mix Up Girl / Qua Kue Shut - **The Creations** 1969
Produced by: Lloyd Daley / Lloyd Daley
PH-3 Jump In A Fire / Give To Get - **The Voiceroys** 1969
Produced by: Lloyd Daley / Lloyd Daley
PH-4 Strange / Your New Love - **Bobby Dobson** 1969
Produced by: Rupie Edwards / Rupie Edwards
PH-5 Too Experienced - Winston Francis / Mule Jerk - Jackie Minto 1969
Produced by: Coxson Dodd / Coxson Dodd
PH-6 I Can't Take It Any More - David Isaacs / Anyway - Lloyd Douglas 1969
Produced by: Lee Perry / Lee Perry
PH-7 (Promo Only)
PH-8 History / Just Be Alone - **Harry and Radcliffe** 1969
Produced by: H Robinson / H Robinson
PH-9 Hello Dolly - Pat Satchmo / Never Get Away - Eric Donaldson 1969
Produced by: Lee Perry / Lee Perry
PH-10 A Broken Heart / Tribute To A King - **Busty Brown** 1969
Produced by: Lee Perry / Lee Perry
PH-11 Oh Happy Day / Spinning - **Norman Washington** 1969
Produced by: Harry Palmer / Harry Palmer
PH-12 Masquerade Is Over / Love For Ambition - **Dobby Dobson** 1969
Produced by: Rupie Edwards / Rupie Edwards
PH-13 The Bigger Way - Winston Blake / Chaty Chaty - Itals 1969
Produced by: Rupie Edwards / Rupie Edwards
PH-14 Love Is The Key - Lloyd and Devon / High Tide - The Virtues 1969
Produced by: Rupie Edwards / Rupie Edwards
PH-15 Herbert Splifington - Winston Blake / Oh Lord Why Lord - Itals 1969
Produced by: Rupie Edwards / Rupie Edwards
PH-16 (Promo Only)
PH-17 (Promo Only)
PH-18 Return Of The Ugly / I've Caught You - **The Upsetters** 1969
Produced by: Lee Perry / Lee Perry
PH-19 Dry Acid - The Upsetters / Selassie - The Reggae Boys 1969
Produced by: Lee Perry / Lee Perry
PH-20 Prisoner Of Love - Dave Barker / Soul Juice - The Upsetters 1969
Produced by: Lee Perry / Lee Perry
PH-21 Clint Eastwood - The Upsetters / Lennox Mood - Lennox Brown 1969
Produced by: Lee Perry / Lee Perry
PH-22 You Betray Me / Will You Still Love Me - **Dave Barker** 1969
Produced by: Lee Perry / Lee Perry
PH-23 Ram You Hard - John Lennon and The Bleechers / Soul Stew - Mediators 1969
Produced by: Lee Perry / Lee Perry
H-24 Wonderfull World - Pat Satchmo / Purple Mast - The Mediators 1969
Produced by: Rupie Edwards / Rupie Edwards
PH-25 Shock Of Might / Shock Of Might (Hit Me Back) - **Dave Barker** 1969
Produced by: Lee Perry / Lee Perry
PH-26 Sweeter Than Honey / 1,000 Pearls - **Norman T. Washington** 1969
Produced by: Harry Palmer / Harry Palmer
PH-27 The Result / Feel The Spirit - **The Upsetters** 1970
Produced by: Lee Perry / Lee Perry
PH-28 In The Mood - Peter Western And His Band / Slide Mongoose - Aston Barrett 1970
Produced by: Pete Western / Aston Barrett
PH-29 I'm Proud Of You - Victor Griffiths / Version Of Proud - King Victor Allstars 1970
Produced by: Victor Griffiths / Victor Griffiths
PH-30 Artibella - Ken Boothe / Version Of Artebella - Pratt Allstars 1970
Produced by: Phil Pratt / Phil Pratt
PH-31 Last Good-Bye / Mothers Love - **Norman T. Washington** 1970
Produced by: Harry Palmer / Harry Palmer
PF-32 Smile / Musical I.D. - **Ranny Williams** 1970
Produced by: Ranny Williams / Ranny Williams
PH-33 Morning / Morning (Version) - **Ken Boothe** 1970
Produced by: Phil Pratt / Phil Pratt

PUNCH. If you want to make a bold statement of intent and appeal to the skinhead then what better way than to launch a label called Punch. Now a label doesn't make a record great but in the case of Punch it gave a clearly defined image with a fist smashing through a Melody Maker 1969 top 20 chart.

The label quickly became an iconic symbol and a firm skinhead favourite with the early releases from Lee 'Scratch' Perry concentrating on skinhead reggae. Clint Eastwood was the official follow up to the Upsetters UK hit Return Of Django issued on PH-21. Despite its popularity with the skinheads the record narrowly failed to chart due it was said to poor distribution, a decision that Perry later admitted he'd made a mistake leasing the track to Pama. Perry produced several strong selling singles notably Return Of The Ugly PH-18 and Dry Acid PH-19, both were bought in great numbers by the West Indian community and the growing number of skinheads. PH-25 Dave Barker's Shock Of Might was another of the numerous tracks undoubtedly licensed to both companies with the Trojan release titled Shocks Of Mighty (Hit Me Back). The track written by Ranny Williams was originally titled I Got A Heart

Other notable singles include Cherrio Baby by The Classics PH-79 with a change of pace from Eric Donaldson's falsetto led original and a slight change of title. The Byron Lee produced Johnny (Too) Bad by The Slicker, a group often wrongly attributed to be a pseudonym of The Pioneers, on PH-59 was also issued on Trojan's Dynamic label which may well have held it back in terms of chart sales returns. The hits were plentiful with classics including Hold The Ghost from Herman AKA To The Fields and admirable toasting on Masquito I attributed to El Passo and Ball Of Confusion to B Smith with a with a boss tune Butter Cup from Winston Scotland on PH-100. One perplexing issue was why there was never an album of Punch's greatest hits released.

PH-34 Scandal / Son Of The Wise - **Hugh Roy** 1970
Produced by: Lloyd Daley / Lloyd Daley

PH-35 Serious Love - The Maytones / Musical Combination - Kealin Beckford 1970
Produced by: Alvin Ranglin / Alvin Ranglin

PH-36 Oh My Darlin' - A Royn / Ball Of Confusion - B Smith 1970
Produced by: Keith Hudson / Keith Hudson

PH-37 Mr. Car Man / Chiney Man - **Eli Reynolds** 1970
Produced by: Eli Reynolds / Eli Reynolds

PH-38 Greatest Love / I Love You Madly - **Busty Brown** 1970
Produced by: Lloyd Charmers / Lloyd Charmers

PH-39 Roll On - Roland Alphanso & The Upsetters / True Love - Carl Dawkins 1970
Produced by: Lee Perry / Lee Perry

PH-40 (Promo Only)

PH-41 The Ark - Trevor and Keith / False Reador - Minna Boys 1970
Produced by: A Ranglin / A Ranglin

PH-42 Reggae Meeting - Dave Barker / Soul Bone - Martin Allstars 1970
Produced by: Martin Riley / Martin Riley

PH-43 Death In The Arena - Rupie Martin / Julia Ceasar - Man Cometh 1970
Produced by: R Jackson / Charley Ace

PH-44 For Our Desire - Hugh Roy / Version I I - Winston Wright 1970
Produced by: Byron Smith / Byron Smith

PH-45 Bye Bye Happyness / Sufferation We Must Bear - **The Modifies** 1970
Produced by: Fud Christian / Fud Christian

PH-46 Sons Of Thunder / Only If You Understand - **The Punchers** 1970
Produced by: Lee Perry / Lee Perry

PH-47 (Not Used)

PH-48 My Heart Is Gone - John Holt / Version I I - Pratt Allstars 1970
Produced by: Phil Pratt / Phil Pratt

PH-49 Silver And Gold - Charlie Ace / Bump And Bore - Phill Pratt Allstars 1970
Produced by: Phill Pratt / Phill Pratt

PH-50 Heart Made Of Stone - Jackey Robinson / I May Never See My Baby Anymore - Bob Taylor 1970
Produced by: Phill Pratt / Phill Pratt

PH-51 (Not Used)

PH-52 (Not Used)

PH-53 Book Of Books - Charlie Ace / Musical Dove - Winston Harris 1970
Produced by: Phill Pratt / Phill Pratt

PH-54 Fight The Good Fight / Fight Beat - **Bill Gentles** 1970
Produced by: Bill Gentles / Bill Gentles

PH-55 Hold The Ghost - Herman / Duppy Dance - Aquarious Soul Band 1971
Produced by: Herman Chin-Loy / Herman Chin-Loy

PH-56 What Do You Fall In Love For - The Agros / Two Much - The Slicker 1971
Produced by: Sydney Crooks / Sydney Crooks

PH-57 (Not Used)

PH-58 Listen To the Beat / Sounds Only - **Herman** 1970
Produced by: Herman Chin-Loy / Herman Chin-Loy

PH-59 Johnny (Too) Bad / Too Bad - The Slicker 1971
Produced by: Byron Lee / Byron Lee

PH-60 Strange Thing - John Holt / Want Money - Winston Wright 1971
Produced by: Phil Pratt / Alvin Ranglin

PH-61 Masquito I / Out The Light Baby - **El Passo** 1971
Produced by: Byron Smith / Byron Smith

PH-62 Love I Madly - Lloyd Terrell / Especially For You - Matador All Stars 1971
Produced by: Lloyd Terrell / Lloyd Daley

PH-63 Iron Bird / Cat Hop - **Top Cat** 1971
Produced by: Les Foster / Les Foster

PH-64 (Not Used)

PH-65 Cholera - The Justins / Blackbird - Lloyd's All Stars 1971
Produced by: Lloyd Daley / Lloyd Daley

PH-66 Come Ethiopians - The Robinsons / Zion Gate - The Matadors 1971
Produced by: Lloyd Daley / Lloyd Daley

PH-67 Do Something - Charlie Ace / Run Babylon - The Maytones 1971
Produced by: Alvin Ranglin / Alvin Ranglin

PH-68 (Not Used)

PH-69 What A Confusion - Dave Barker / Small Axe - Bob Marley 1971
Produced by: Lee Perry / Lee Perry

PH-70 Stop Your Crying - Ken Boothe / Suffering Through The Nation - The Conscious Minds 1971
Produced by: Ken Boothe / BB Seaton

PH- 71 Put Your Sweet Lips - Raphel Stewart & The Hot Tops / Stand by Me - The Justins 1971
Produced by: Raphel Stewart / Lloyd Daley

PH-72 You Inspire Me / Inspire Version - **Busy Brown** 1971
Produced by: Lee Perry / Lee Perry

PH-73 Chie Chie Bud / (Bud Version) - **Max Romeo** 1971
Produced by: Victor Chinn / Victor Chinn

PH-74 Goodnight My love / There Is A Land - **Winston And Errol** 1971
Produced by: Claudious Perara / Claudious Perara

PH-75 Hard Fighter - Little Roy / Back To Africa (Version) - Count Ossie 1971
Produced by: Lloyd Daley / Lloyd Daley

PH-76 Don't Say - James Brown / Version - Trans Am All Stars 1971
Produced by: James Brown / James Brown

PH-77 Down Presser - The Wailers / Got The Tip - Junior Byles 1971
Produced by: Lee Perry / Lee Perry

PH-78 (Not Used)

PH-79 Cherrio Baby / Civilization - **The Classics** 1971
Produced by: Lee Perry / Lee Perry

PH-80 (Not Used)

PH-81 Fussing And Fighting / The Man I Should Be - **The Slickers** 1971
Produced by: Sid Bucknor / Sid Bucknor

PH-82 Don't Give Up - Paul Freeman / Give Up (Version) - The Upsetters 1971
Produced by: Lee Perry / Lee Perry

PH-83 Where Love Goes - Donald Smythe / You Can Run - The Hurricanes 1971
Produced by: Lee Perry / Lee Perry

PH-84 You'll Be Sorry / Knock Three Times - **David Isaacs** 1971
Produced by: Lee Perry / Lee Perry

PH-85 (Not Used)

PH-86 (Not Used)

PH-87 Sincerely / Hold On I'm Coming - **Owen Gray** 1971
Produced by: Lord Koos / Lord Koos

PH- 88 Soulful Love - Pat Kelly / One For All (3 In One) - John Holt 1971
Produced by: Phil Pratt / Lloyd Daley

PH-89 Lonely World - Afro / Put It On - Alton Ellis All Stars 1971
Produced by: Alton Ellis / Alton Ellis

PH-90 (Not Used)

PH-91 Rudies Medley - 3rd And 4th Generation / Rude Boy Version - Jogibs And The Soulmates 1971
Produced by: Joe Gibbs / Joe Gibbs

PH-92 (Not Used)

PH-93 Christmas Message / Cool It Girl - **D.D. Dennis** 1971
Produced by: Noel Blake / Noel Blake

PH-94 Winey Winey / There is A Place - **Phil Pratt Allstars** 1971
Produced by: Phil Pratt / Phil Pratt

JOHNNY (TOO) BAD
The SLICKER

PH-95 **Royal Cord** / Soul Beat - **The Jaylads** 1972
Produced by: BB Seaton / Lloyd Charmers

PH-96 **Solid As A Rock** / Rock (Version) - **Rupie Edwards All Stars** 1972
Produced by: Rupie Edwards / Rupie Edwards

PH-97 **Paul, Marcus & Norman** / Version - **The Conscious Mind** 1972
Produced by: B.B. Seaton / B.B. Seaton

PH-98 **Nobody Told Me - Carl Lewin** / Don't Play That Song (inst.) - Wing 1972
Produced by: Ranny Williams / Dimple Hinds

PH-99 **1 2 3 A B C** / Zee - **Combinations** 1972
Produced by: Ranny Williams / Ranny Williams

PH-100 **Butter Cup - Winston Scotland** / I Care - Ronald Wilson 1972
Produced by: Tony Robinson / Tony Robinson

PH-101 **Screw Face** / Face Man - **Bob Marley and The Wailers** 1972
Produced by: Tuff Gong / Tuff Gong

PH-102 **Lively Up Yourself - Bob Marley And The Wailers** / Live - Tommy McCook 1972
Produced by: Tuff Gong / Tuff Gong

PH-103 **Don't Be A Loser** / Jamaican Girl - **Roy Shirley** 1972
Produced by: Roy Shirley / Roy Shirley

PH-104 **Nanyscrank - Hugh Roy** / Skank Version - Pitts Burg Allstars 1972
Produced by: Karl Pitterson / Karl Pitterson

PH-105 **Darling Oohwe - Errol Dunkley And Hugh Roy** / Black Magic Woman - Dennis Brown 1972
Produced by: Rupie Edwards / Phil Pratt

PH-106 **Dungeon - Glen Miller** / Kiss Me Honey - Nora Dean 1972
Produced by: Ranny Williams / Ranny Williams

PH-107 **Forward March** / Plenty Of One - **Derrick Morgan** 1972
Produced by: Derrick Morgan / Derrick Morgan

PH-108 **A Sugar - Roy Shirley** / Part 2 Sugar - Alytman Reid 1972
Produced by: Roy Shirley / Roy Shirley

PH-109 **Pharoah Hiding - Junior Byles** / Hail To Power - The Upsetters 1972
Produced by: Lee Perry / Lee Perry

PH-110 **Have You Seen Her - Lloydie & Ken** / Have You Seen Her - Ken Boothe 1972
Produced by: Lloyd Charmers / Lloyd Charmers

PH-111 **Round And Round - The Melodians** / Round Version - Upsetters 1972
Produced by: Lee Perry / Lee Perry

PH-112 **People Like People - Gerry Meggie** / Softie - Max Romeo 1972
Produced by: Clancy Eccles / Lloyd Charmers

PH-113 **Trying To Wreck My Life - Leroy Samuel** / Pride And Joy - John Holt 1972
Produced by: Bunny Lee / Bunny Lee

PH-114 **You Should Have Known Better** / Known Better - **Tuff Gong Allstars** 1972
Produced by: Tuff Gong / Tuff Gong

PH-115 / PH-120 (Not Used)

PH-121 **Fattie Bum Bum** / Fattie Bum Dub - **Laurel Aitken** 1975
Produced by: Laurel Aitken / Laurel Aitken

BOSS SOUNDS FROM
PUNCH

Boss Sounds from PUNCH brings a selection of some of the highlights from the iconic label's productions between the years 1968 and 1972 with one final roll of the dice coming in 1975.

PH-1 The Burner - The Dynamics 1969
Produced by: Lloyd Daley
The label launched with a boss sound hotter than scorcher with The Burner from The Dynamics who were Tommy McCook and Carl Bryan.

PH-2 Mix Up Girl - The Creations 1969
Produced by: Lloyd Daley
The second release maintains the boss skinhead reggae sound. The Creations AKA Barry York and Ossie Henry sounding very reminiscent of The Pioneers.

PH-18 Return Of The Ugly - The Upsetters 1969
C/W I've Caught You - The Upsetters
Produced by: Lee Perry
Trade mark boss sounds from Lee Perry.
Both tracks featured on the album
Clint Eastwood issued on
PSP 1014 in 1970.

PH-21 Clint Eastwood - The Upsetters 1969
Produced by: Lee Perry
The official follow up to the chart hit Return Of Django / Dollar In The Teeth, another Lee Perry trait and the title track on the album of the same name.

PH-23 Ram You Hard - John Lennon and The Bleechers 1969
Produced by: Lee Perry
A first rate infectious tune with wonderful risqué harmonies from the Jamaican duo of Leo Graham and Wesley Martin plus Sammy. Quite who the accredited John Lennon is remains a mystery.

PH-56 What Do You Fall In Love For - The Agros 1971
C/W Two Much - The Slicker
Produced by: Sydney Crooks

An underrated single from The Agros, a tune that borrows on the rhythm from Chariot Coming with impressive vocals. Tucked away as a B side and definably not a filler is an hypnotic boss sound from The Slickers, credited as The Slicker on Pama releases.

PH-36(2) Ball Of Confusion - B Smith 1970
Produced by: Keith Hudson

Admirable toasting from B Smith who is of course better known as Dennis Alcapone.

PH-41 The Ark - Trevor and Keith 1970
Produced by: A Ranglin

Another much underrated single from the time. An Alvin Ranglin production with a delightful vocal offering over an infectious beat from Trevor Lloyd and Keith.

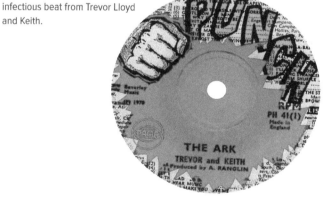

PH-61 Masquito I - El Passo 1971
Produced by: Byron Smith

Toasting doesn't get much better. A boss tune from El Passo AKA Dennis Alcapone toasting over Nora Dean's Barbed Wire. Talking over an old song was the domain of U.Roy and at first many believed Dennis was, but it became apparent that Alcapone's voice was clearer and more distinct.

PH-73 Chie Chie Bud - Max Romeo 1971
Produced by: Victor Chinn

Exceptional outing for Max on Punch with an awesome rhythm with the vocals a take on a Jamaican folk song about birds. The boss rhythm is sampled from Lee Perry's I Am The Upsetter. Chie Chie Bud featured on Max's 1971 album Let The Power Fall issued on PMP 2010.

PH-35 Serious Love - The Maytones 1970
Produced by: Alvin Ranglin
Sweet harmonies from The Maytones.

PH-55 Hold The Ghost - Herman 1971
Produced by: Herman Chin-Loy

Herman was in fact Herman Chin-Loy, co-owner of the Aquarius Record Store in Kingston Jamaica with Lloyd Chin-Loy. Herman also dabbled at production and came up with the boss instrumental with slight toasting on Hold The Ghost, perhaps better known as To The Fields.

PH-66 Come Ethiopians - The Robinsons 1971
Produced by: Lloyd Daley

This is actually The Melodians with an hypnotic song issued on Summit as Come Ethiopians Come and accredited as a Leslie Kong production.

PH-100 Butter Cup - Winston Scotland 1972
C/W I Care - Ronald Wilson
Produced by: Tony Robinson

A pulsating track from Winston Scotland who incidentally was U.Roy's brother in law sampling You Don't Care from Lloyd Parks and This A Butter from Dennis Alcapone as he toasts in Boss style on Butter Cup, which features on Hot Numbers Volume 2. The B side is well worth of a spin, a version with intermittent horns from Ronald Wilson.

PH-31 Last Good-Bye - Norman T. Washington 1970
Produced by: Harry Palmer

A melodic chugging beat with impressive vocals. Norman's other singles issued on Punch were Oh Happy Day PH-11 and Sweeter Than Honey PH-26, both produced by Harry Palmer.

PH-77 Down Presser - The Wailers 1971
Produced by: Lee Perry

Lee 'Scratch' Perry comes up trumps again on this track with great vocals from Peter Tosh and inspired harmonies from The Wailers. As with early recordings referred to as Peter Touch.

PH-48 My Heart Is Gone - John Holt 1970
Produced by: Phil Pratt

Reggae was moving on from the raw sounds that emerged from rocksteady in '68 with the pace a little slower. The former Paragon who'd become one of the biggest stars of reggae delivers a tale of heartbreak with his usual aplomb and the slower pace suits the mood.

LEE PERRY

SCRATCH - THE UPSETTER

Rainford Hugh Perry AKA Lee 'Scratch' Perry was born on the 20th March 1936 in Kendal, a small town close to the centre of Jamaica. One of the major influential figures in the emerging world of reggae producer 'Scratch' is best known as The Upsetter. His musical career began in 1959 when he formed an association with Clement 'Coxsone' Dodd's sound system, initially as a record seller.

He soon progressed to supervising auditions at Dodd's shop on Orange Street in Kingston, although his relationship with Dodd was described as sometimes turbulent. As the situation with Dodd worsened due to personal and financial problems he moved to Joe Gibbs Amalgamated Records. Perry continued recording but problems soon surfaced again and he left Gibbs to form his own Upsetter label.

His first single, People Funny Boy, credited to Lee 'King' Perry released on Doctor Bird was aimed as an insult to Gibbs, selling a remarkable 60,000 copies in Jamaica. The record carried what was described as a fast chugging beat, a change from the slower rocksteady, a beat that soon became identifiable as reggae. The record was popular with the emerging skinheads who'd bought previous Lee Perry recordings from 1968 including David Isaacs Place In The Sun and The Untouchables Tighten Up.

From '68 through to '72 Perry continued to release numerous recordings on several labels including Camel and Punch with the latter perhaps his most identifiable brand. His idiosyncratic approach to music-making saw him become a firm favourite among the skinhead with his classic skinhead reggae Clint Eastwood PH-21, the official follow up to his massive hit Return Of Django. Bob Marley And The Wailers had Down Presser produced by Lee Perry issued on PH-77 with lead vocals from Peter Tosh.

During 1970 'Scratch' produced two Upsetters albums for Pama. Clint Eastwood PSP 1014 and Many Moods Of The Upsetters issued on SECO 24.

THE UPSETTERS

The Upsetters were Perry's House Band, the name coming from a nickname he earned after releasing I Am The Upsetter in reference to his former boss 'Coxsone' Dodd. The band saw many changes to its line-up over the years initially starting out as Gladdy's All Stars led by pianist, keyboard player and singer Gladstone 'Gladdy' Anderson.

When The Pioneers and The Upsetters arrived in London in November 1969 to do a six week tour on the back of the success of Long Shot Kick De Bucket and Return Of Django respectively other commitments prevented the All Stars from leaving Jamaica so The Hippy Boys were recruited to do the tour. That line up of Glen Adams, Alva Lewis, Carlton Barrett and Aston 'Family Man' Barrett remained the studio band 'till eventually the latter two formed the core of The Wailers. In 1972 Boris Gardiner, Sly Dunbar and Winston Wright became the next generation of The Upsetters.

ROY SHIRLEY

ARTIST / PRODUCER

Roy Shirley was born on the 18th July 1944 in Kingston's Trench Town where he spent his developing years. His early attempts at recording were never released so he joined Leslie Kong with his first record co-arranged with his close friend Jimmy Cliff. After a spell with Ken Boothe he joined the original Uniques. In 1966 he recorded Hold Them said to be the first record to slow down the infectious ska beat, therefore creating rocksteady. The story goes that the song just wouldn't work with ska so Joe Gibbs suggested he slowed down the rhythm, a move that inadvertently created a massive hit in Jamaica.

Roy then had a stint with Bunny Lee before setting up his own Public label in 1968 releasing Flying Reggae and Prophecy Fulfilling. A Jamaican hit came in 1971 with A Sugar. Roy wrote the song asking a deejay Altyman Reid to sing it, but there was a problem with some of the vocals so Lloyd Charmers asked Roy to sing it again. The record was released in the UK in 1972 on Punch PH-108. The original Jamaican pressing credits Roy and Altyman Reid.

DAVE BARKER

Dave Barker AKA David Crooks and one half of the most famous duo of the boss reggae years. After a difficult childhood he began singing in his teens inspired by James Brown and Otis Redding. His rise to fame began with a stint singing with The Two Tones which he formed with friends. He then had a spell with Winston Riley's Techniques as well as working at the pressing plant at Studio One. He was introduced to Lee Perry who came up with the stage name Barker and encouraged toasting to compliment his high tenor voice.

He scored with Shock Of Might PH-25 and toasted over Bob Marley's Small Axe on Shocks '71. It was his renewed partnership with Winston Riley and joining forces with Ansil Collins that really saw him hit the top spot.

ECONOMY / PUNCH   STEREO   SECO-24

MANY MOODS OF "THE UPSETTERS"

MANY MOODS OF THE UPSETTERS   UPSETTERS
PAMA SECO 24   1970

Side 1
1. EXRAY VISION   2. CAN'T TAKE IT ANY MORE
3. SOUL STEW   4. LOW LIGHTS   5. CLOUD NINE   6. BEWARE

Side 2
1. SERIOUS JOKE   2. GOOSY   3. PROVE IT   4. BOSS SOCIETY
5. MEAN AND DANGEROUS   6. GAMES PEOPLE PLAY

Many Moods of "THE UPSETTERS"   SECO 24

THE UPSETTERS, the group of Musicians and singers who in their native JAMAICA have been known to appear individually both on records and for stage work, in various groups - THE HIPPY BOYS, THE GAY BOYS, THE REGGAE BOYS, THE UPSETTERS, PAMA ALL STARS, UNITY ALL STARS, BUNNY LEE'S ALL STARS, LLOYD CHARMERS BAND, etc. They have made many, many hits in reggae form under their various groups and have been known to score high in the British charts under the name THE UPSETTERS with a tune entitled "RETURN OF DJANGO".

Harry Palmer went to Jamaica in August 1969, and whilst there took the opportunity (with the consent of their previous producers - Lee Perry, Bunny Lee, Lloyd Charmers, Ronnie Williams), to produce a brand new album under the title "Many Moods of The Upsetters". He has featured on the cover the man whom they all nicknamed "Upsetter" Mr Lee Perry in the company of some very delicious looking girls and also showing the organist from The Upsetters, Mr Glen Adams himself shaking hands with the Upsetter whilst he lay on top of his suped up motor car. All the pictures were taken at 4-30 to 5-30 on a Sunday morning when Harry was awakened from his hotel bedroom and sped at 80 miles per hour along the sea coast to witness the lovely sceneries at so early in the morning. Needless to say The Upsetter was the one who woke him up by tempting him with the "Beauties in Bikinis".

Sure The Upsetters sing as well as they play and they have done themselves proud on this album. Great arrangements and great productions when an English promoter Harry Palmer, met up with the real Jamaican thing in the form of Reggae. The Upsetters and Lee Perry, Bunny Lee, Lloyd Charmers, Glen Adams, Ronnie Williams, Alva Lewis, Aston Barrett (family man), Carlton Barrett and a slick studio owner and engineer Randy Chin of North Parade, and man what a session they had, the end product of which can be heard on this album, "Many Moods". So it's Reggae, Reggae, Reggae all the way with the Pama/Punch productions and the wonderful, fantastic, incredible, marvellous, "UPSETTERS".

Get going then boys and here you shall have you very first Chart Busting L.P. THE UPSETTERS.

Donald Lee

Produced in Jamaica by PAMA/ PUNCH PRODUCTIONS

PAMA RECORDS LIMITED 78 Craven Park Road London N.W.10 England

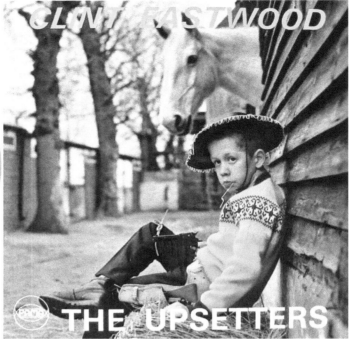

CLINT EASTWOOD THE UPSETTERS   PAMA PSP 1014 1970

Side 1
1. RETURN OF THE UGLY 2. FOR A FEW DOLLARS MORE 3. PRISONER OF LOVE
4. DRY ACID 5. RIGHTFUL RULER 6. CLINT EASTWOOD

Side 2
1. TASTE OF KILLING 2. SELASSIE 3. WHAT IS THIS
4. AIN'T NO LOVE 5. MY MOB 6. I'VE CAUGHT YOU

THE SLICKERS

JOHNNY (TOO) BAD

The Slickers are one of the mysteries of Jamaican music. Its members at various stages included brothers Sydney and Derrick Crooks who formed the group along with George Agard and Winston Bailey. Derrick was the only constant member with Abraham Green joining and taking lead vocals at the time of the release of their classic Jamaican rude-boy song, Johnny (Too) Bad. The song was written by Derrick, Winston, Roy Beckford and Trevor Wilson, who were also members for a time. although some sources revel that Trevor may have wrote the lyrics and also been the central character for the rude-boy song. A tour of the UK followed on the back of the success of Johnny (Too) Bad.

The Slickers history is rife in rumour and contradiction and have often been assumed to be an alias of The Pioneers due to their similar vocal styles. The connection is fuelled by one of their early releases Nana, rumoured to be The Pioneers recording as Johnny Melody & The Slickers.

The original version of Johnny (Too) Bad is one of the most celebrated tracks ever recorded in Jamaica, elevated to cult status with its inclusion on the soundtrack of The Harder They Come.

The Slicker on PUNCH

PH-56(2) Two Much 1971
Produced by: Sydney Crooks
An infectious fast moving beat with delightful harmonies, a boss tune.

PH-59 Johnny (Too) Bad 1971
C/W **Too Bad**
Produced by: Byron Lee
The awesome classic rude-boy song will have you running down the road. The B side features an instrumental version with intermittent vocals. Boss reggae doesn't get any better.

PH-81 Fussing And Fighting 1971
Produced by: Sid Bucknor
A change of Slicker pace with this vocal led request to stop fussing and fighting.

SUCCESS

BOSS SOUNDS FROM
SUCCESS

RE-901 Look Who A Bust Style - The Mediators 1969
C/W **Look Who A Bust Style (Verion 3) - Rupie Edwards All Stars**
Produced by: Rupie Edwards

An infectious up-tempo early reggae sound and good harmonies with a slight take on Them A laugh And A Ki Ki. Version 3 on the B side is well worth a spin.

SUCCESS was set up in 1969 to issue Rupie Edwards production from his Jamaican imprint of the same name launched a year earlier. Only thirteen single were issued between '69 and '70.

SUCCESS DISCOGRAPHY 1969 - 1970 Prefix RE *(Rupie Edwards)*

RE-901 Look Who A Bust Style - The Mediators / Look Who A Bust Style (Verion 3) - Rupie Edwards All Stars 1969
Produced by: Rupie Edwards / Rupie Edwards
RE-902 Grandfathers Clock - Rupie Edwards All Stars /
Promoters Grouse - **Rupie Edwards** 1969
Produced by: Rupie Edwards / Rupie Edwards
RE-903 Fat Girl, Sexy Girl / Man And Woman - **John Holt** 1970
Produced by: Rupie Edwards / Rupie Edwards
RE-904 Don't Let Me Suffer / Red Sun Rise - **The Concords** 1970
Produced by: Rupie Edwards / Rupie Edwards
RE-905 Handicap / If You Can't Beat Them - **Rupie Edwards** 1970
Produced by: Rupie Edwards / Rupie Edwards
RE-906 Crazy - Dobby Dobson / Your New Love -
Rupie Edwards All Stars 1970
Produced by: Rupie Edwards / Rupie Edwards
RE-907 Conjunction - Neville Hinds / Love Is A Wonderful Wicked Thing -
Rupie Edwards 1970
Produced by: Rupie Edwards / Rupie Edwards
RE-908 (Promo Only)
RE-909 Pop Hi - Rupie Edwards All Stars / High Tide -
Val Bennett And The Bunny Lee All Stars 1970
Produced by: Rupie Edwards / Rupie Edwards
RE-910 Return Of Herbert Splifinton - Rupie And Sidy /
Young Gifted And Black (Instr) - Rupie Edwards All Stars 1970
Produced by: Rupie Edwards / Rupie Edwards
RE-911 Census Taker / Souling Way Out - **Rupie Edwards All Stars** 1970
Produced by: Rupie Edwards / Rupie Edwards
RE-912 Cry A Little Cry - Dobby Dobson / Revenge Version 11 - Rupie Edwards All Stars 1970
Produced by: Rupie Edwards / Rupie Edwards
RE-913 That Wonderful Sound / Don't Make Me Over -
Dobby Dobson 1970
Produced by: Rupie Edwards / Rupie Edwards
RE-914 Too Late - Gregory Isaacs / Can't Wine - The Kingstonians 1970
Produced by: Rupie Edwards / Rupie Edwards

RE-904 Don't Let Me Suffer - The Concords 1970
Produced by: Rupie Edwards

Similar rhythm track to Look Who A Bust Style but this time from The Concords featuring the vocal talents of Gregory Isaacs. He teamed up with two other artists to form the trio for a short while before leaving to launch his own solo career.

RE-910 Return Of Herbert Splifinton - Rupie And Sidy 1970
C/W **Young Gifted And Black (Instr) - Rupie Edwards All Stars**
Produced by: Rupie Edwards

A real humdinger of a tune from Rupie and Sidy with eerie or should that be Irie vocals over a mix of the rhythm from Young Gifted And Black. The B side instrumental version is absorbing. The Return Of Herbert Splifinton and RE-901 Look Who A Bust Style feature on the album African Melody PMP 2004 released in 1971.

Jamaican imprint of Rupie Edwards' Success label

DOBBY DOBSON

Highland Dobby Dobson earned his nick-name from the 1967 rocksteady classic track I Am A Loving Pauper. In the early 60s after a stint performing in a duo he became a solo artist recording for Sonia Pottinger. He worked with Coxsone Dodd and recorded I Am A Loving Pauper while he was with Duke Reid.

He recorded an album That Wonderful Sound for Rupie Edwards which sold over 40,000 copies in Jamaica. The album was issued in the UK on Pama in 1970, licensed from Rupie Edwards Jamaican Success label, under the title Strange. The album was also licensed to Trojan who released the album for a limited time as That Wonderful Sound.

STRANGE   DOBBY DOBSON   PAMA SECO 33 1970

Side1	Side 2
1. STRANGE 2. CRAZY	1. BABY MAKE IT SOON
3. MASQUERADE IS OVER	2. WHAT LOVE HAS JOINED TOGETHER
4. THAT WONDERFUL SOUND	3. I WASN'T BORN YESTERDAY
5. DON'T MAKE ME OVER	4. CRY A LITTLE CRY 5. YOUR NEW LOVE

ECONOMY   STEREO   SECO 33

STRANGE
DOBBY DOBSON

"Strange how you stopped loving me when he came along..."

The voice filled with simplicity and yet as appealing as any heartbroken voice can be. A voice singing of the end of the world and the beginning of loneliness. A voice warm as the Caribbean sun tells the tragedy of untrue love, unfrequented love and love lost forever.
The voice sad with the knowledge that "She has finally found herself a new love" and a little glad that at last "The Masquerade is over."
This is the voice of Dobby Dobson as only Dobby Dobson can be...stealing into the heart of every person who ever loved and lost.

Marcia Carnegie

PRODUCED BY RUPIE EDWARDS FOR PAMA/SUCCESS RECORDS

PAMA RECORDS LIMITED 78, Craven Park Road London, NW10 England

SUPREME

SUP-213 **Musical Attack** / Music Alone - **Rupie Edwards Allstars** 1970
Produced by: Rupie Edwards / Rupie Edwards
 SUP-214 **You Must Believe Me - Niney** / Funk The Funk - Rupie Edward's Allstars 1970
Produced by: Rupie Edwards / Rupie Edwards
SUP-215 **Burning Fire - Joe Higgs** / Push And Push - Rupie Edwards Allstars 1971
Produced by: Rupie Edwards / Rupie Edwards
SUP-216 **I Like It Like This - Bob Marley** / Am Sorry - Bunny Gale 1971
Produced by: Perry Marvin / Perry Marvin
SUP-217 **Mount Zion - The Rightious Soles** / All Over - Eccle & Nevil 1971
Produced by: Perry Marvin / Perry Marvin
SUP-218 **Every Night** / Ethiopia - **Ruddy & Sketto Rich** 1970
Produced by: Laurel Aitken / Laurel Aitken
SUP-219 **Stay** / You're My Everything - **Slim Smith** 1971
Produced by: Slim Smith / Slim Smith
SUP-220 **Just My Imagination** / I've Gotta Get A Message To You - **The Charmers** 1971
Produced by: Lloyd Terrell / Lloyd Terrell
SUP-221 **Love Bug** / Sound Of Our Forefathers - **The Ethiopians** 1971
Produced by: Alvin Ranglin / Alvin Ranglin
SUP-222 (Not Used)
SUP-223 **Go Back** / Go Back (Version 2) - **Impact** 1971
Produced by: Victor Chin / Victor Chin
SUP-224 **Don't Get Weary - Tony Brevett** / Weary (Version) - Brevitt All-Stars 1971
Produced by: The Gaylads / The Gaylads
SUP-225 **Let It Fall - Eugene & Burst** / Can't Change - Denzil & Burst 1971
Produced by: Sydney Crooks / Sydney Crooks
SUP-226 **Starvation - The Ethiopians** / Jordon River - Maxie & Glen 1971
Produced by: Alvin Ranglin / Alvin Ranglin
SUP-227 **My Application - Stranger & Gladdy** / Oh No My Baby - Taddy & The Diamonds 1971
Produced by: Stranger Cole / Stranger Cole
SUP-228 **Double Heavy** / Johnny Dollar - **Dave Barker** 1971
Produced by: Martin Riley - Ranny Williams / Martin Riley - Ranny Williams
SUP- 229 **Not You Baby -The Upsetting Brothers** / Baby (Version) - Dreadlock All-Stars 1971
Produced by: Dreadlock / Dreadlock

SUPREME was launched in 1970 with some doubt surrounding the inaugural release. There appears somewhat of an anomaly as What's The World Coming To by King Chubby launched the Pama Supreme label the same year using the same prefix 297. No doubt over the next three releases as they were trade-mark 'Coxsone' Dodd productions with Time To Pray from Lloyd Robinson, credited to Mr. Foundation, an instrumental More Games, sampling the track Games People Play, which worked well from Sound Dimension, and the third, Work It Up, all excellent sounds.

Only thirty singles were issued on the label which ceased production a year later. However during the labels short reign it issued several well received tracks including The Mohawks cover of Let It Be on SUP-204, Bob Marley's I Like It Like This on SUP-216, Stay from Slim Smith on SUP-219 and Go Back from Impact with a Version on the B side of SUP-223. Ruddy & Sketto Rich also have an outing on SUP-218 with an updated cover of the classic track Every Night.

SUPREME DISCOGRAPHY 1970 - 1971 Prefix SUP

SUP-297 **What's The World Coming To** / Live As One - King Chubby 1970
Produced by: Lee Perry / Lee Perry
SUP-201 **Time To Pray** / Young Budd - **Mr. Foundation** 1969
Produced by: C.S. Dodd / C.S. Dodd
SUP-202 **More Games - Sound Dimention** / Maga Dog - Mr. Foundation 1970
Produced by: C.S. Dodd / C.S. Dodd
SUP-203 **Work It Up** / Chatty Chatty - **Jack and The Bean-Stalks** 1969
Produced by: C.S. Dodd / C.S. Dodd
SUP-204 **Let It Be** / Looking Back - **The Mohawks** 1970
Produced by: Graham Hawks / Graham Hawks
SUP-205 **For Our Liberty** / Wicked Lady - **The Mohawks** 1970
Produced by: Graham Hawks / Graham Hawks
SUP-206 **Surfin** / All The Love - **Owen Gray** 1970
Produced by: Ranny Williams / Ranny Williams
SUP-207 **Give Me Some** / Give Me Some (Inst) - **The Mohawks** 1970
Produced by: Graham Hawks / Graham Hawks
SUP-208 **Funky Funky** / Funky Funky (Inst.) - **The Mohawks** 1970
Produced by: Graham Hawks / Graham Hawks
SUP-209 **Halleluiah - The Emotions** / Boat Of Joy - Matador Allstars 1970
Produced by: Lloyd Daley / Lloyd Daley
SUP-210 **When You Go To A Party - The Mediations** / Stop The Party - Rupie Edwards Allstars 1970
Produced by: Rupie Edwards / Rupie Edwards
SUP-211 **Double Attack - Hugh Roy** / Puzzle - Murphy Allstars 1970
Produced by: G Murphy / G Murphy
SUP-212 **Share My Rest - John Holt** / Allways - Al Brown 1970
Produced by: Keith Hudson / Keith Hudson

BOSS SOUNDS FROM SUPREME

Boss Sounds from SUPREME brings a selection of highlights from the labels brief stint with production between the years '70 and '71.

SUP-201 Time To Pray - Mr. Foundation 1969
C/W Young Budd - Mr. Foundation
Produced by: C.S. Dodd

Both tracks on this the numerical first on the label from Mr. Foundation are good chugging reggae sounds from 'Coxsone' Dodd's Studio One. The A side is in fact by Lloyd Robinson and the B side features The Ethiopians.

SUP-211 Double Attack - Hugh Roy 1970
Produced by: G Murphy

Hugh Roy toasting over The Tennors 1968 Jamaican release World Is A Stage.

SUP-203 Work It Up - Jack and The Bean-Stalks 1969
C/W / Chatty Chatty - Jack and The Bean-Stalks
Produced by: C.S. Dodd

An infectious tune from Jack and The Bean-Stalks, although there is some doubt to the actual artists, with Work It Up. The B side is definitely not a filler, another driving hypnotic beat with swift lyrics making for another great tune from the boss producer 'Coxsone' whose album Boss Reggae was issued on SECO 17 in 1969.

SUP-204 Let It Be - The Mohawks 1970
Produced by: Graham Hawks

An excellent cover version of The Beatles 1970 number one hit, vocals are stand out over a hypnotic beat.

SUP-221 Love Bug - The Ethiopians 1971
Produced by: R Ranglin

Another boss tune from The Ethiopians produced by Alvin Ranglin.

SUP-218 Every Night - Ruddy & Sketto Rich 1970
Produced by: Laurel Aitken

An update from Ruddy & Sketto Rich of the 1966 evocative track from Joe White & Chuck with The Baba Brooks Band of Every Night. The single was re-issued on Camel in 1975.

SUP-202 More Games - Sound Dimention Mr. Foundation 1970
C/W Maga Dog - Mr. Foundation
Produced by: C.S. Dodd

The third from producer 'Coxsone' with both sides good boss sounds. More Games is an instrumental sampling Games People Play. Maga Dog, credited to Mr. Foundation, is believed to be The Invaders. It differers to Peter Tosh's celebrated single but is still a cracking hypnotic tune in itself with impressive vocals and guaranteed to get the feet moving.

COXSONE DODD

STUDIO ONE - PRODUCER

Coxsone or Coxone? His nick-name came about at school due to his talents as a cricketer with many comparing him with the Yorkshire cricketer Alec Coxon.

Clement Seymour Dodd opened his legendary Studio One on Brentford Road, Kingston, Jamaica in 1963 and it was where he auditioned Bob Marley who was singing as part of the Wailers. He produced a plethora of ska hits for artists like The Maytals, The Gaylads and Skatalites. It was Dodd who first recorded the renowned song You're Wondering Now in 1964 by Andy & Joey. He produced the twelve tracks featured on the exclusive and sought-after album BOSS REGGAE issued on SECO 17 in 1970 which is featured next.

ECONOMY - STEREO - SECO 17

BOSS REGGAE

BOSS REGGAE Various Artistes   PAMA SECO 17 1969

Side 1
1. POOR MI ISRAELITES - Winston Jarette 2. SCARE HIM - The Flames
3. GIVE ME TRUE LOVE - The Mediators 4. HELP - The Helpers
5. NIGHT DOCTOR - Jackie Mitto 6. RUN FOR RESCUE - Lloyd Robinson

Side 2
1. TOMORROW WHEN YOU'RE GONE - The Mediators 2. TOO MANY MILES - W Wellington
3. DOUBLE CROSSER - Lloyd Robinson 4. SWEET TALKING - The Heptones
5. JUST CAN'T SATISFY - W Jarette 6. JANE - The Gladiators

ECONOMY   STEREO   SECO 17

BOSS REGGAE
VARIOUS ARTISTES

As the man says, its Reggae time with BOSS REGGAE from the Coxone Studio, Brentford Road, Kingston, Jamaica, West Indies.
On this album, the first of a series from Coxone's Mr Dodd to be released on the Supreme's label deal with Pama/Economy, you will find Stereo Reggae of the highest quality both from the production and selection angles and we do trust you will enjoy this. So queue in anticipation for all the others in this series which promises to be of greatest value to your collection.

BARRY BROWN

Produced by: C.S. DODD AT COXONE STUDIO KINGSTON JAMAICA
Distributed by: PAMA RECORDS LIMITED LONDON ENGLAND

Poor Mi Israelites is a boss reggae Jamaican cut of Desmond's massive hit by Winston Jarette who was also a member of The Flames who are up next with **Scare Him**. The Mediators keep the studio sounds rolling with **Give Me True love.** The Helpers come in with **Help** followed by Jackie Mitto's **Night Doctor**, a catchy organ led tune, one to get you on the dance-floor. Side one concludes with **Run For Rescue** from Lloyd Robinson, the man who brought us the Worm.

Side two has another track from The Mediators with **Tomorrow When Your'e Gone** followed by **Too Many Miles** from W Wellington.

Track three comes from Lloyd Robinson with **Double Crosser** getting the Boss sounds running again. The Heptones pitch in with **Sweet Talking**. Winston Jarette is back with the penultimate offering from Studio One with **Just Can't Satisfy**, good vocals with a catchy beat. The album concludes with **Jane** from The Gladiators.

Contrary to the sleeve notes promising further albums in the series this was the only Studio One album released on Pama. Nevertheless as most of the tracks are rarities and never released as 45s it contributes greatly to the albums appeal.

UNITY

UNITY. Harry Palmer wanted to establish a solid link with Jamaica to ensure a constant supply of records for the UK market, tunes that had already hit the charts back in Jamaica and a mix of new recordings. The man for the job had already produced several top tracks during the rocksteady era, he was of course Bunny Lee who was licensing work to Island so the venture gave 'Striker' a label in the UK .

When Lee came to London the Palmer Brothers met up to negotiate a long term agreement which saw him flying back to Jamaica with an advance from Pama to produce singles for release in the UK and Jamaica. Unity was chosen as the moniker for the new joint venture with the Palmer Brothers paying for the records to be recorded in Jamaica and made available both in the UK and Jamaica on Lee's Jamaican Unity imprint.

Last Flight To Reggie City was the labels inaugural release in 1968. Along with the same batch of recordings was Bangarang issued on UN-502 by Stranger Cole and Lester Sterling, trialling a new sound having a jerky organ line cited by many as the first authentic reggae record. The label soon became synonymous with Bunny Lee productions. The third official release on the label brought chart success for Pama in the form of Max Romeo's legendary risqué Wet Dream issued on UN-503.

UN-500 (Promo Only)
UN-501 Last Flight To Reggie City - Tommy McCook & Stranger Cole / Watch Dem Go - Junior 1968
Produced by: Bunny Lee / Roy Smith
UN-502 Bangarang - Lester Sterling & Stranger Cole / If We Should Ever Meet - Stranger Cole 1968
Produced by: Bunny Lee / Stranger Cole
UN-503 Wet Dream / She's But A Little Girl - **Max Romeo** 1968
Produced by: H Robinson / J Smith
UN-504 Everybody Needs Love - Slim Smith / Come Back Girl - Junior Smith 1968
Produced by: Bunny Lee / Roy Smith
UN-505 Reggie On Broadway - Lester Sterling / "Love Can Be Wonderful" - The Clique 1969
Produced by: Derrick Morgan / J Smith
UN-506 The Avengers - Tommy McCook / Donkey Man - Laurel Aitken 1969
Produced by: Bunny Lee / Laurel Aitken
UN-507 Belly Woman - Max Romeo / Please Stay - Paulette & The Lovers 1969
Produced by: H Robinson / D Robinson
UN-508 For Once In My Life / Burning Desire - **Slim Smith** 1969
Produced by: Bunny Lee / Bunny Lee
UN-509 Spoogy - Lester Sterlin / Monkey Fiddle - Tommy McCook 1969
Produced by: Derrick Morgan / Derrick Morgan
UN-510 Zip-A-Di-Do-Da / On Broadway - **Slim Smith** 1969
Produced by: Bunny Lee / Bunny Lee
UN-511 Twelfth Of Never - Max Romeo / Solid As A Rock - The Tartons 1969
Produced by: D T Leigh / Ken Lack
UN-512 (Promo Only)
UN-513 Let It Be Me / Love Makes Me Do Foolish Things - **Slim Smith & Paulette** 1969
Produced by: Bunny Lee / Bunny Lee
UN-514 When I Get My Freedom / Life Can Be Beautiful - **Stranger Cole** 1969
Produced by: Stranger Cole / Bunny Lee
UN-515 Somebody To Love / Confusion - **Slim Smith** 1969
Produced by: Bunny Lee / Bunny Lee
UN-516 Wine Her Goosie - Max Romeo / Fire Ball - King Cannon 1969
Produced by: Derrick Morgan / Bunny Lee
UN-517 (Promo Only)
UN-518 (Not Used)
UN-519 Peyton Place / Red Gal Ring - **D. Tony Lee** 1969
Produced by: Bunny Lee / Bunny Lee
UN-520 Slipaway / Spanish Harlem - **Slim Smith** 1969
Produced by: Bunny Lee / Bunny Lee
UN-521 (Promo Only)
UN-522 30 Pieces Of Silver / Everybody Ska - **Prince Buster** 1969
Produced by: Cat Campbell / Cat Campbell
UN-523 (Promo Only)
UN-524 Sunny Side Of The Sea / Place In The Sun - **Slim Smith** 1969
Produced by: Bunny Lee / Bunny Lee
UN-525 The Return Of Al Capone - Peter Tosh / Q Club - Lenex Brown 1969
Produced by: Bunny Lee / Bunny Lee
UN-526 Pepper Seed / Ambitious Begger - **Ranny Williams** 1969
Produced by: Winston Holness / Winston Holness
UN-527 (Promo Only)
UN-528 Dreams To Remember / Peace Maker - **The Hippy Boys** 1969
Produced by: Lloyd Charmers / Lloyd Charmers
UN-529 Sun Valley - Peter Touch / Drums Of Fu-Manchu - Headley Bennett 1969
Produced by: Bunny Lee / Bunny Lee
UN-530 What You Gonna Do - Reggae Boys / Hot Coffee - Headley Bennett 1969
Produced by: Bunny Lee / Bunny Lee
UN-531 Lonesome Feeling / Bright As A Rose - **Lester Sterling** 1969
Produced by: Bunny Lee / Bunny Lee
UN-532 Mini-Skirt Vision / Far Far Away - **Max Romeo** 1969
Produced by: Derrick Morgan / Ranny Williams

The album Unity's Greatest Hits was issued on ECO 7 in 1969.

UN-533 Hook Up / Full Up - **Bunny Lee Allstars** 1969
Produced by: Keith Chin / Keith Chin
UN-534 Dream Boat / Tommy's Dream - **Tommy McCook** 1969
Produced by: Bunny Lee / Bunny Lee
UN-535 Peanut Vendor / 100,000 Tons Of Rock - **Tommy McCook** 1969
Produced by: Bunny Lee / Bunny Lee
UN-536 No Matter What / Walk Through This World - **Doreen Shafer** 1969
Produced by: Bunny Lee / Bunny Lee
UN-537 Keep That Light Shining On Me / Build My World Around You - **Slim Smith** 1969
Produced by: Bunny Lee / Bunny Lee
UN-538 How Much Is That Dogy In The Window / As Long As He Needs Me -
Doreen Shaffer 1969
Produced by: Bunny Lee / Bunny Lee
UN-539 (Promo Only)
UN-540 Derrick-Top The Pop - Derrick Morgan / Capones Revenge - Glen Adams 1969
Produced by: Derrick Morgan / Glen Adams
UN-541 Day Dream / Joy Ride - **Bunny Lee Allstars** 1969
Produced by: Bunny Lee / Bunny Lee
UN-542 Honey / There Is A Light - **Slim Smith** 1969
Produced by: Bunny Lee / Bunny Lee
UN-543 Ivan Itler The Conqueror - Bunny Lee Allstars / The Splice -
Bunny Lee Allstars (featuring Lloyd Willis) 1969
Produced by: Bunny Lee / Bunny Lee
UN544 Melting Pot - Max Romeo and The Hippy Boys / Death Rides A Horse -
The Hippy Boys 1970
Produced by: Keith Chin / Keith Chin
UN-545 Clap - Clap - Max Romeo and The Hippy Boys / You've Got Your Troubles -
Max Romeo 1970
Produced by: Keith Chin / Keith Chin
UN-546 Return Of Jack Slade / Fat Man - **Derrick Morgan** 1970
Produced by: Derrick Morgan /Derrick Morgan
UN-547 What A Cute Man / Buy You A Rainbow - **Max Romeo** 1970
Produced by: Bunny Lee / Bunny Lee
UN-548 Sometimes - John Holt / Lash-La-Rue - Bunny Lee Allstars 1970
Produced by: Bunny Lee / Winston Holness
UN-549 Sea Cruise - John Holt / Niney's Hop - Bunny Lee Allstars 1970
Produced by: Bunny Lee / Winston Holness
UN-550 (Not Used)
UN-551 Why Did My Little Girl Cry - Little Freddy / Change Partners - Peter Austin 1970
Produced by: Bunny Lee / Bunny Lee
UN-552 Walking Along - John Holt / Ware Fare - Bunny Lee Allstars 1970
Produced by: Bunny Lee / Bunny Lee
UN-553 When You Were Mine - Ken Parker / The Angles - The Clarendonians 1970
Produced by: Bunny Lee / Bunny Lee
UN-554 My Special Prayer / Never Hurt The One You Love - **Errol Dunkley** 1970
Produced by: Bunny Lee / Bunny Lee
UN-555 Ten Cent - The Soul Mates / Stay With Me Forever - Doreen Shaffer 1970
Produced by: Bunny Lee / Bunny Lee
UN-556 Give Her All The Love - John Holt / Nobody But You - Busty Brown 1970
Produced by: Bunny Lee / Bunny Lee
UN-557 Do It My Way / Where In The World (Are You Going) - **Monty Morris** 1970
Produced by: Bunny Lee / Bunny Lee
UN-558 Goodnight My Love / Lover Girl - The Corsairs 1970
Produced by: Bunny Lee / Bunny Lee
UN-559 Drink Wine Everybody - Delroy Wilson / Someone To Call My Own -
Joe White 1970
Produced by: Bunny Lee / Bunny Lee
UN-560 Fish In The Pot / Feel It - **Max Romeo** 1970
Produced by: Derrick Morgan / Derrick Morgan
UN-561 No Love / A Little Tear - **Little John** 1970
Produced by: Bunny Lee / Bunny Lee
UN-562 Slip Up - Lester Sterling / On Broadway - **Dave Barker** 1970
Produced by: Bunny Lee / Bunny Lee
UN-563 Skan Kee - Niney And The Allstars / Version II - Niney Allstars 1970
Produced by: Bunny Lee / Bunny Lee

UN-564 Love Makes The World Go Round / Love (Version Inst.) - **Ernest Wilson** 1970
Produced by: Ernest Wilson / Ernest Wilson
UN-565 More Balls - Mark Anthony & The Jets / Bum Ball (Chapter II) - Tony King 1970
Produced by: Errol Thompson / Errol Thompson
UN-566 Peace And Love / Peace And Love (Version) - **The Third Dimension** 1970
Produced by: Bunny Lee / Bunny Lee
UN-567 Blessed Are The Meek - Slim Smith & Dave Barker / People's Voice -
The Whip 1970
Produced by: Bunny Lee / Bunny Lee
UN-568 1,000 Tons Of Version - Jeff Barnes / Wake The nation -
Jeff Barnes & Hugh Roy 1970
Produced by: Bunny Lee / Bunny Lee
UN-569 The Conqueror / Bedweight - **Derrick** 1970
Produced by: Derrick Morgan / Derrick Morgan
UN-570 Jenny / The Race - **Slim Smith** 1970
Produced by: Slim Smith / Slim Smith
UN-571 Macabee Version - Max Romeo / Music Book - Soul Syndicate 1971
Produced by: Willie Francis / Willie Francis
UN-572 Rent Crisis / Version - **Max Romeo** 1973
Produced by: Winston Holness / Winston Holness
UN-573 Big Haire - Dirty Harry / Skank In Skank - Young Doug 1973
Produced by: Cat Campbell / Cat Campbell

BOSS SOUNDS FROM
UNITY

Boss Sounds from UNITY brings a selection of some of the highlights from the label most associated with Bunny Lee productions between the years 1968 and 1970 with the labels final three releases coming between 1971 and 1973.

UN-501 Last Flight To Reggie City - Tommy McCook & Stranger Cole 1968

Produced by: Bunny Lee

This first official release on the label combines the theatrical vocals from Stranger Cole and Tommy McCook's versatility on the flute. A chugging very early reggae sound from the stable of Bunny Lee and a reworking of Stranger & Gladys Just Like A River. Last Flight To Reggie City featured on Unity's Greatest Hits and Reggae Hits 69.

UN-506 The Avengers - Tommy McCook 1969

Produced by: Bunny Lee

Another outing from Tommy McCook this time with an instrumental adaptation of Bangarang. The Jamaican saxophonist was a founding member of the Skatalites and recorded with the foremost artists of the era. He also worked alongside Bunny Lee and his house band.

UN-547 What A Cute Man - Max Romeo 1970

Produced by: Bunny Lee

How could this have not been another chart hit for Pama? The recognisable rhythm is of course Monkey Man with Max's versatile voice negotiating the lyrics. Has this seen the light of day since 1970? It has now, with the digital re issue of Reggae For Days album from 1969, although the Unity single label dates release as 1970.

UN-563 Skan Kee - Niney And The Allstars 1970

Produced by: Lee Perry

A very hypnotic beat toasted over by Niney (Winston Holness) with brilliant vocal skills complementing the boss tune. Skanking originated in Jamaica during the ska era.

UN-530 What You Gonna Do - Reggae Boys 1969

Produced by: Bunny Lee

The Hold You Jack backing track gets its third outing on the label with a vocal rendition from The Reggae Boys with What You Gonna Do. The melodic rhythm stays spot on and true to the original Wet Dream. The lyrics are understood to be 'Striker' taking a swipe at Joe Gibbs. A boss sound that has been hidden away for far too long.

UN-569 The Conqueror - Derrick Morgan 1970

Produced by: Derrick Morgan

A fine re-worked version of Derrick's original 1968 track issued on Island.

UN-511 Twelfth Of Never - Max Romeo *(Actually Pat Kelly)* **1969**

Produced by: D T Leigh

The Johnny Mathis song was recorded during the rocksteady era by Pat Kelly and Bunny Lee updated the rhythm track to a reggae beat to produce this single issued on the back of Max's success, although at the time it was well known to be Pat Kelly. It did however produced a vivacious boss sound and one guaranteed to get the skinhead on the dance-floor.

UN-572 Rent Crisis - Max Romeo 1973

Produced by: Winston Holness

- A who dat a knock so early -
Wonderful pacey vocals from Max over a rocking beat.
- A me Nine Finger the renti -

UN-515 Somebody To Love - Slim Smith 1969

Produced by: Bunny Lee

A chugging reggae interpretation of Solomon Burke's 1964 song Everybody Needs Somebody To Love from one of Jamaica's greatest vocalist Slim Smith. The song was used as the opening track for his album of the same name issued on ECO 9 the same year.

UN-568 1,000 Tons Of Version - Jeff Barnes 1970

Produced by: Bunny Lee

- Here comes the boss with a 1,000 tons of version - A real scorcher from Jeff Barnes.

UN-532 Mini-Skirt Vision - Max Romeo 1969

Produced by: Derrick Morgan

How can you follow perfection? Max would never eclipse Wet Dream but the risqué lyrics described as having a captivating rhythm soon saw the record banned by the BBC. The album cut of Mini-Skirt Vision has a slight change of pace, feels much cleaner and comes under the title The Horn, with no horns masking any lyrics.

UN-540 Derrick-Top The Pop - Derrick Morgan 1969

Produced by: Derrick Morgan

May be there is a twist to the story as this sounds like Pop A Top 2 from Andy Capp with a touch of Fat Man and saxophone but nevertheless still a boss tune.

UN-503 Wet Dream - Max Romeo 1968

Produced by: H Robinson

This one needs no introduction but needless to say one that found favour with the skinhead with its risqué lyrics and strong melody. Always the first to be requested at a stomp. Strange as it may be the record was banned from airplay in Jamaica and only released as a promo copy on the island at the time.

UN-507 Belly Woman - Max Romeo *(Actually Derrick Morgan)* **1969**

Produced by: H Robinson

C/W **Please Stay - Paulette & The Lovers**

Produced by: D Robinson

Belly Woman was released in Jamaica in 1969 and credited to Derrick Morgan which a cursory listen will confirm as the artist. The UK release on Unity credits Max Romeo, could this be due his new found celebrity status or just a 'misprint'. The song dealing with infidelity has an infectious beat. The B side features Paulette & The Lovers with a boss sound and definitely not a B side filler.

UN-524 Sunny Side Of The Sea - Slim Smith 1969

C/W **Place In The Sun - Slim Smith**

Produced by: Bunny Lee

A beautiful song with a chugging reggae beat treated with Slim's unique style.

The B side features a version of David Isaacs' reggae treatment of the classic track Place In The Sun which was itself a cover of Stevie Wonder's 1966 hit.

UN-538 How Much Is That Dogy In The Window - Doreen Shaffer 1969

Produced by: Bunny Lee

Doreen was a founding member of the Skatalites and became known as the Queen of Ska. When the Sakatalites disbanded in '65 she joined forces with Bunny Lee to launch her solo career. A collection of her recordings were issued on the album First Lady Of Reggae SECO 31 in 1970.

UN-516 Wine Her Goosie - Max Romeo 1969

Produced by: Derrick Morgan

More rude reggae that made it onto the album A Dream.

BUNNY LEE

<u>STRIKER - THE PRODUCER</u>

Bunny was born on 23rd August 1941 and was the eldest of six children who were brought up in the Greenwich Farm district of Kingston. He was a man of great self-belief with a determination to make it, forcing his way into the music business initially with a stint as a radio plugger for 'Coxsone' Dodd, Duke Reid and Leslie Kong's Beverley's. Impressed with Bunny Duke Reid offered him some recording time at his legendary Treasure Isle studios and so began his unparalleled career as an influential producer.

Bunny met Island's Dave Betteridge in Jamaica prior to the setting up of Trojan and during Bunny's first visit to England in '68 to see Dave he had a chance meeting with the Palmer brothers brought about by Dandy who had been given money by the brothers to record an album for Pama. Bunny became good friends with Dandy and took him to Trojan who persuaded Dandy to sell the album to them, which had been made with Pama's money. The album Dandy Returns became one of the first issued by Trojan and sold very well.

The Palmers Brothers paid Bunny a visit who was staying in East London with the chance meeting eventually leading to a deal being struck with Bunny receiving £700 to produce singles in Jamaica and send over to England. They decided on a label featuring a black and a white hand shaking over a mountain, calling it Unity. Bunny returned to Jamaica and utilised the money as Harry Palmer had asked and produced the legendary Bangarang, the start of a partnership which saw Bunny introduced his friend Lee Perry to Pama.

Striker - so named due to his talent for producing a hit record - was instrumental in upping the tempo of the slowed down rocksteady rhythm to reggae with the famous organ shuffle coming to the fore on Bangarang which means woman don't want no problem, anyone don't want no problem.

Everything changed with Max Romeo's Wet Dream based on a bawdy conversation Lee had overheard. Originally sent over as a B side the record became a hit with the burgeoning skinheads, spending six months in the charts, partly thanks to being banned by the BBC although it nearly never got recorded. Bunny had booked studio time at Dodd's Studio One and when Max started to sing Dodd stopped the tape asking Bunny "where you get them fool artiste and fool lyrics"? After some debate the record was cut in one take.

The Jamaican imprint of the Pama Unity label

UNITY'S GREATEST HITS Various Artistes   PAMA ECO 7 1969

Side 1
1. BANGARANG - Stranger Cole & Lester Sterlin
2. LAST FLIGHT TO REGGAE CITY - Tommy McCook & Stranger Cole
3. LET IT BE ME - Slim Smith & Paulette 4. EVERYBODY NEEDS LOVE - Slim Smith
5. REGGAE ON BROADWAY - Lester Sterlin 6. TWELFTH OF NEVER - Max Romeo

Side 2
1. SPOOGY - Lester Sterlin 2. FOR ONCE IN MY LIFE - Slim Smith
3. IF WE SHOULD EVER MEET - Stranger Cole 4. THE AVENGER - Tommy McCook
5. ON BROADAWAY - Slim Smith 6. BRIGHT AS A ROSE - Lester Sterlin

The album carried comprehensive linear notes, from the great man Derrick Morgan.

ECONOMY   MONO   ECO 7

UNITY'S GREATEST HITS
VARIOUS ARTISTES (Volume One)

On entering any record shop during December '68 one could hardly help noticing that a new record label called "Unity" was dominating the "Blue Beat" scene. Unity had its first three releases during that month and each of them was a hit on its own. Let's begin with the first to be released on this label, a tune entitled "Last Flight To Reggae City" on Unity 501. If you remember The Pyramids "Flight To Rainbow City" you will understand what I mean when I say this tune was quite its superior although they were built on the same lines, the only difference being - one was in Ska and the other in Reggae. Thus The Last Flight To Reggae City became the first flight up the R.& B. charts for Unity and its first release. Following hot on the heels of this number was another Hit "BANGARANG" this was also by the same Artistes - Stranger Cole, Lester Sterlin and Tommy McCook three of Jamaica's top Artistes teaming together to make these fantastic tunes.

The next in line for release in December could not be released as it was Banned. This was a tune entitled "Wet Dream" sung by Max Romeo which later went on to hit the National British and world wide charts in a very big way. So Unity released "Everybody Needs Love" by a new young man Slim Smith, which sure enough followed suit behind its two predecessors and became one of Unity's biggest hits. (An album is now on release by Slim Smith entitled - " Everybody Needs Love").

The label has never looked back since and on this album you can find tunes like - "Let It Be Me" performed by Slim Smith & Paulette in reggae, "Twelfth Of Never" by Max Romeo, "Spoogy" by Lester Sterlin, "If We Should Ever Meet" by Stranger Cole and a lot of other top tunes which have been hits on the great great Unity label.

Do enjoy yourselves and remember the slogan - Unity is strength.

Derrick Morgan

A Pama /Unity Records Production - London, England and Kingston, Jamaica

Distributed by:- PAMA RECORDS 78 CRAVEN PARK ROAD LONDON NW10 ENGLAND

MAX ROMEO

Maxwell Livingstone Smith AKA Max Romeo was born in the parish of St Anne, on the north coast of Jamaica in 1944. After enduring hardship in his early years he moved to Kingston at the age of ten, before leaving home four years later to live on the streets. His first introduction to the record industry came after a spell cleaning out irrigation ditches on a sugar plantation finding himself delivering records, always singing as he went. The potential was soon spotted prompting his return to Kingston in search of fame and fortune.

His first recording was released in 1967 titled I'll Buy You A Rainbow with a group called The Emotions with Max as the lead singer making number two in Jamaica and established him as a star. A move that eventually brought worldwide fame for Max was an introduction to Derrick Morgan's brother in law, producer Bunny Lee, who was trialling with the new sound evolving as reggae. Bunny 'Striker' Lee persuaded Max to go solo.

The name Romeo came about when Max was spending time with a girl. The story goes that he was talking to the girl at eight in the morning when her father left for work. Max returned later in the day a short time before her father returned from his work. Thinking they'd been there all day, stood in the same spot, the father said "You must be Romeo". Bunny Lee heard the story and suggested Max should change his stage name to Max Romeo.

Max began writing lyrics and Bunny came to him with a suggestion for doing a rude song, a theme that was becoming popular with some of the other artists at the time. He penned Wet Dream but didn't want to perform it. Lee initially wanted Derrick Morgan to record the song who'd previously released Hold You Jack also penned by Romeo using the same rhythm. Derrick flatly refused so Bunny, after rejections by others including John Holt and Slim Smith, persuaded Max to voice the lyrics. As has been mentioned the recording session was booked at Studio One but when Romeo started to sing Dodd stopped the tape asking Bunny Lee "where you get them fool artiste and fool lyrics?"

Max has always insisted he was forced to do that song by Bunny Lee, claiming on many occasions he was threatened if he didn't do the song he couldn't stay around. The song was banned from airplay in Jamaica and never released at the time. It was however sent over to England with a batch of other recordings to Harry Palmer who subsequently released it on the Unity label in 1968 and the rest as they say is history!

The record managed an airing or two courtesy of Emperor Rosko on Radio One before the hierarchy got wind of the patois content. Max claimed that the song was telling the story of his leaking roof, he was asking his girlfriend to get out of the way as he tried to push a broom up in the hole to stop the leak. The BBC were having none of it, describing it as bawdy, and immediately censored the record. - *Give the crumpet to Big Foot Joe - Give the fanny to me* - probably didn't help the cause. The ban did however serve to make it more popular with the new skinheads and record buying public at large with one theory the youth reacted to an injunction, inhibiting their freedom of choice, thus enhancing sales.

Wet Dream took the charts by storm in May 1969 despite having no further air play on the BBC. The record was always referred to as - a record by Max Romeo - during a run-down of the charts. It eventually made it into the top thirty reaching number 10 in August 1969 and was reported to have sold over 250,000 copies, and spending a very respectable twenty five weeks in the charts. The chart speaks for itself in highlighting what a massive contrast Wet Dream was in comparison to the rest of the top ten, and how the skinheads would have warmed to the incessant, melodic rhythm, a sound they claimed for their own, along that was with their new West Indian friends.

CHARTBUSTER!
- At the top of the chart on 16th August 1969 were The Rolling Stones with Max reaching number 10 -

PAMA   STEREO   PMLP- II
"DREAM" WITH MAX ROMEO

The recipe for a hit, nowadays, seems to be the collection of words that have suggestive meaning against a very rhythmic background, punctuated with heavy breathing. As the theory goes such a record will be banned and the permissive record buying public will react against this injunction that inhibits their freedom of choice, hence a high sales turnover is certain.

MAX ROMEO'S "WET DREAM" falls into this category. Max, twenty-five years old, from Jamaica, made a tremendous impact on the scene recently when "WD", his resounding hit, disrupted the British Charts for more than twenty weeks and was the subject of much controversy. However, that Max is a very talented singer is not a subject for debate. This becomes obvious when one realises the rate at which his fans are growing each day. At the Caribbean Music Festival at Wembley recently, Max received a double standing ovation from the ten thousand capacity crowd. As well as being a fabulous entertainer, Max proved he was truly a top exponent of the Reggae idiom. Due to the general misunderstanding surrounding his chart success, Max is now in the unfortunate position of trying to live down an image which is at variance with the genuine warmth and sincerity of Max the person. This long-awaited album is filled with Romeo's versatility, here Max is caught doing his own thing - whatever he is singing or writing, Max is always immaculate. This album is a must for all Reggae-lovers. Well done Max.

SIDE ONE
1. WET DREAM (Electronically Rebalanced) - (M ROMEO)
2. A NO FE ME PICKNEY - (M ROMEO)
3. FAR FAR AWAY - (M ROMEO)
4. THE HORN - (M ROMEO)
5. HEAR MY PLEA - (M ROMEO)
6. LOVE - (M ROMEO)

SIDE TWO
1. I DON'T WANT TO LOSE YOUR LOVE - (M ROMEO)
2. WOOD UNDER CELLAR - (M ROMEO)
3. WINE HER GOOSIE - (H DEE)
4. CLUB RAID - (M ROMEO)
5. YOU CAN'T STOP ME - (M ROMEO)

Musical Arrangements by: Randy Williams and Derrick Morgan Musical Backing: The Rudies The Hippy Boys
Cover Design: Jeff and Carl Palmer   Produced by: H. LEE / B. LEE / D. MORGAN

A PAMA / UNITY RECORD PRODUCTION

Distributed by - PAMA RECORDS LIMITED, 78 CRAVEN PARK ROAD, LONDON, N.W. 10, ENGLAND

BRITAIN'S TOP 50

RECORD RETAILER   AUGUST 16, 1969

THIS WEEK	LAST WEEK			
1	(1)	Honkey Tonk Woman	The Rolling St	
2	(3)	Saved By The Bell	Robin	
3	(7)	Make Me An Island	Joe	
4	(2)	Give Peace A Chance	Plastic On	
5	(6)	My Cherie Amour	Stevie W	
6	(4)	Goodnight Tonight	Clodagh Rod	
7	(8)	Conversations	Cilla Bla	
8	(17)	Early In The Morning	Vanity Fare	
9	(13)	Bring Back The Good Times	Love Affair	
10	(30)	Wet Dream	Max Romeo	Unity
11	(5)	In The Ghetto	Elvis Presley	RCA
12	(32)	Too Busy Thinking 'Bout My Baby	Marvin Gaye	Tamla Motown
13	(21)	In The Year 2525	Zager And Evans	RCA
14	(14)	Goo Goo Barabajagal	Donovan And Jeff Beck	Pye
15	(15)	I Can Sing A Rainbow - Love Is Blue	The Dells	Chess
16	(11)	That's The Way God Planned It	Billy Preston	Apple
17	(23)	When Two Worlds Collide	Jim Reeves	RCA
18	(9)	Baby Make It Soon	Marmalade	CBS
19	(19)	Curley	The Move	RegalZonophone

The 1970 single Fish In The Pot UN-560 was a take on Derrick Morgan's 1967 rock steady track Kill Me Dead issued on Pyramid. The B side featured Feel It, a very rhythmic explicit song from Max believed to be the missing track twelve from the album.

A DREAM MAX ROMEO   PAMA PMLP 11 1969

Side 1
1. WET DREAM (Electronically Rebalanced) 2. A NO FEE ME PICKNEY
3. FAR FAR AWAY 4. THE HORN 5. HEAR MY PLEA 6. LOVE

Side 2
1. I DON'T WANT TO LOOSE YOUR LOVE 2. WOOD UNDER CELLAR
3. WHINE HER GOOSIE 4. CLUB RAID 5. YOU CAN'T STOP ME

PAMA   STEREO   PMLP - 11

"DREAM" WITH MAX ROMEO

The recipe for a hit, nowadays seems to be the collection of words that have suggestive meaning against a very rhythmic background, punctuated with heavy breathing. As the theory goes such a record will be banned and the permissive record buying public will react against this injunction that inhibits their freedom of choice, hence a high sales turnover is certain.

MAX ROMEO'S "WET DREAM" falls into this category. Max twenty-five years old, from Jamaica, made a tremendous impact on the scene recently when "WD", his resounding hit disrupted the British charts for more than twenty weeks and was the subject of much controversy. However, that Max is a very talented singer is not a subject for debate. This becomes obvious when one realises the rate at which his fans are growing each day. At the Caribbean Music Festival at Wembley recently Max received a double standing ovation from the ten thousand capacity crowd. As well as being a fabulous entertainer, Max proved he was truly a top exponent of the Reggae idiom.

Due to the general misunderstanding surrounding his chart success, he is now in the unfortunate position of trying to live down an image which is at variance with the genuine warmth and sincerity of Max the person. this long-awaited album is filled with Romeo's versatility, here Max is caught doin' his own thin' - Whatever it is he is singing or writing, Max is always immaculate. This album is a must for all reggae-lovers. Well done Max.

Ornette Denardo

Musical Arrangements: Ranny Williams and Derrick Morgan Musical Backing: The Rudies The Hippy Boys

Cover Design: Jeff and Carl Palmer *Produced By:* H. Lee / B. Lee / D. Morgan

A PAMA / UNITY RECORDS PRODUCTION

Distributed by - PAMA RECORDS LTD 78, CRAVEN PARK ROAD, LONDON, N.W.10 ENGLAND

LET THE POWER FALL   PAMA PMP 2010   1971

The album carried comprehensive sleeve notes, full of praise for Max and Derrick Morgan

Side 1
1. MISSING YOU 2. PUPPET ON A STRING 3. CRACKLIN ROSE 4. CHIE CHIE BUD
5. BLACK EQUALITY 6. LET THE POWER FALL

Side 2
1. DON'T YOU WEEP 2. MOTHER OH MOTHER 3. CHICKEN THIEF 4. GINALSHIP
5. MACABEE VERSION 6. BATCHELOR BOY

PAMA / MEDIUM   MONO   PMP 2010

LET THE POWER FALL

Overdue, that's what they say. This new Max Romeo Album is very much overdue. Sure they are right, nobody is arguing but when you have a perfectionist like Maxie to deal with you just can't rush things. Yes, he himself makes sure that his fans are going to be satisfied by putting every little extra that may be possible into composition of his songs, the production of each track, the mixing of the masters and the cutting of the metric. He is a perfectionist our Maxie is, and I am sure you will be pleased with the result of this power packed Album "LET THE POWER FALL" named after his latest world wide "Hit". That track is also included on this album, together with such great numbers as "Puppet On A String", "Macabee Version", "Bachelor Boy", Neil Diamond's "Cracklin Rose" also Maxie's latest release "Mother Oh Mother". Altogether you have twelve tracks in this package which are bound to keep you life members of the Max Romeo's fan club.

We must give a timely word of praise to the man who co-produced this record with Maxie, Derrick Morgan. Maxie owes Derrick a lot for piloting him to stardom and guiding him in the selection of numbers to record.

Max Romeo's last album "Dream" was of course a resounding success and although it was released in 1969, still sells in good quantities today. That surely is the mark of perfection which Max Romeo is all about.

PAMA RECORDS LIMITED 78 Craven Park Road London N.W.10 England

Let The Power Fall produced by Bunny Lee in 1971 highlighted a complete change of style for Max who became increasingly aware of social injustices in Jamaica and the huge gulf between the rich and the poor, now reflecting the restlessness in his homeland within his music. The shift was further highlighted with the release of Are You Sure PS-359 the following year and Pray For Me on PS-345.

Those releases represented the way forward for Max, who has spent much of his career trying to live down the rude image. Notwithstanding that statement Hole Under Cratches was issued in 1973 credited to Henry & Liza, actually Max Romeo & Fay Bennett with their own humorous take on the traditional song There's A Hole In My Bucket.

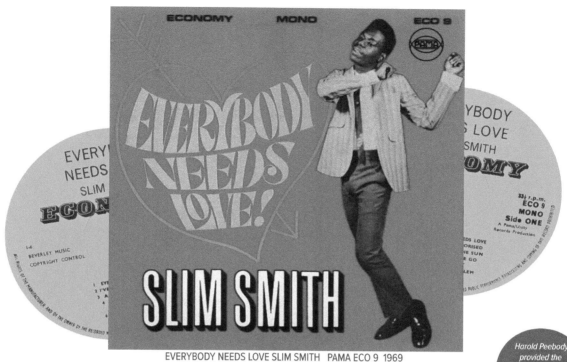

EVERYBODY NEEDS LOVE SLIM SMITH PAMA ECO 9 1969

Side 1

1. EVERYBODY NEEDS LOVE 2. I'VE BEEN TERRORISED 3. A PLACE IN THE SUN 4. NEVER LET ME GO
5. SLIP AWAY 6. SPANISH HARLEM

Side 2

1. SOMEBODY TO LOVE 2. STRANGER ON THE SHORE 3. BURNING DESIRE 4. ON BROADWAY
5. ZIP-PA-DE-DO-DA 6. TOO PROUD TO BEG

Harold Peebody provided the comprehensive sleeve notes and was a great fan of Slim.

ECONOMY   MONO   ECO 9

everybody needs love
Slim Smith

The romantic Slim Smith is in his elements on this album - his very first to be exact and what an album it is too, with every track a winner beginning with the title track "Everybody Needs Love" - which pretty well scored an international hit for him and won him thousands of fans throughout the world.

Slim, the former lead singer of the famous Jamaican group the Uniques, branched out on his own and with his first single release on the Unity label he was hailed as the greatest singer to come out of sunny Jamaica since Harry Belafonte - Now that's saying something as Jamaica is famous for producing hordes of very good and talented singers.

The album "Everybody Needs Love" caters for the young at heart and lovers in general no matter what nationality you may be. As they say 'Music speaks a Universal Language' and songs performed with young Smith in control are sure to break down all possible barriers and leave young lovers more in love than ever before. Tracks like - "SOMEBODY TO LOVE", "SLIPAWAY", and "TOO PROUD TO BEG" are sure to leave you completely wrapped in your lovers arms

Slim Smith is himself a young man of twenty who began his singing career at a school's talent contest when he literally walked off with the first prize and I am told with his teacher's beautiful daughter as well (which must have been the prize of his choosing). From the type of numbers he sings one can tell he is a true born lover. It is said that he has a magnet for attracting members of the opposite sex wherever he goes, so boys beware and keep on the alert when Slim is in Town. However please do not get the idea that he is a *Bird Snatcher* - but he just can't help it if the girls keep falling in love with him - and with talent, looks and charm like he's got - who can blame them.

The other side of Slim is a more serious character, calm and studious with an amiable disposition. he is a man who would never dream of going to his bed at night before first going down on his knees for a talk with his maker. He takes an occasional cigarette but never a drink. Plays cricket and loves sport of every type especially boxing and has been known to take a few punches himself. Slim has made a resolution to be one of the world's greatest singers by the time he is 25 years old and heading in the direction he is - he is sure to make that goal. All the efforts that he has put into his singing have not been in vain although at times things have been extremely hard. You know what it is when one does singing as a living and has to depend on gigs to eat bread and pay for their lodging. As the pop columnist said when reviewing Slims' single "Somebody To Love" - A new star has now been born' - so please join with me in cheering him to the winning post.

Best of luck Slim Smith.

HAROLD PEEBODY

 Distributed by: PAMA RECORDS LIMITED, 78, CRAVEN PARK ROAD,LONDON,N.W.10. ENGLAND

ECONOMY   Stereo   SECO-31

DOREEN SHAFFER

THE FIRST LADY OF REGGAE DOREEN SHAFFER PAMA SECO 31 1969

Side 1
1. WALK THROUGH THIS WORLD 2. EVERYBODY NEEDS LOVE
3. NO MATTER WHAT 4. TRY TO REMEMBER
5. HOW LONG 6. IF IT DON'T WORK OUT
Side 2
1. AS LONG AS HE NEEDS ME 2. DOGGIE IN THE WINDOW
3. I FALL IN LOVE EVERYDAY 4. ONE OF US WILL WEEP
5. JUNE NIGHT 6. LOVE ME WITH ALL YOUR HEART.

ECONOMY   STEREO   SECO 31

THE FIRST LADY OF REGGAE
DOREEN SHAFFER

After a rip-roaring journey through London, in search of the elusive SECO 31 album, Jeff palmer and I decided to go to Pye Studios itself to obtain a copy of this - Doreen Shaffer's first album release. After collection it was back to PAMA'S H.Q. (through red traffic lights, like no-ones business, I may add) to listen to the finished product.

There we were seated in the listening room; recovering from our escapade, as the record began to revolve on the turntable... Believe me, listening to Doreen is a feast to ones ears. The sound beaming through the big speakers put life back into us - so much in fact Jeff found it impossible to keep his feet still.

Like Aretha Franklin is to soul and Ella is to jazz, Doreen and reggae are a perfect combination. Together with her producer - Bunny Lee - Doreen has combined songs old and new, and given them that increasingly popular reggae treatment. Songs like "If It Don't Work Out" or even wait for it "How Much Is That Doggie In The Window", prove just how well this lady handles a song.

Doreen is a 23 year old Jamaican, who has had years of experience in the cabaret field and each one of her performances has proved to be unforgettable. Of course on this album one can rectify the odd 'dud track' - but you tell me: What is good without bad? Anyway ladies and gentlemen, here for you is the "First Lady Of Reggae" - Doreen Shaffer.

REX GOMES.

Produced by BUNNY LEE   PAMA / UNITY RECORDS LIMITED

PAMA RECORDS LIMITED, 78 Craven Park Road, London, N.W.10, England

Vinyl label credits Lester Sterlin & Co.

BANGARANG LESTER STERLIN   PAMA SECO 15 1969

Side 1
1. BANGARANG 2. REGGAE IN THE WIND 3. SPOOGY 4. 1,000,000 TONS OF T.N.T.
5. MAN AT THE DOOR 6. MAN ABOUT TOWN

Side 2
1. REGGAE ON BROADWAY 2. DOCTOR SATAN 3. DANGER MAN 4. BRIGHT AS A ROSE
5. REGINA 6. MAN AT WORK

Mr. Reggae provides the enlightening linear notes this time out and does so again on the Reggae Hits '69 albums covers.

ECONOMY   STEREO   SECO 15

"BANGARANG"

By Lester Sterlin

Bang Bang Bangarang, Ma Ma Ma Mama. What a Bangarang. The Album, the titles, the tunes are nothing if not a compilation of the greatest recordings put together for the enjoyment of Reggae lovers who like quality, music, rhythm and soul.

In December 1968 a new sound hit the music scene and this sound was called Reggae. Among the most outstanding in this new field of music, was a tune entitled BANGARANG, performed by Lester Sterlin with narration and singing by the sophisticated "Stranger Cole". This number was *Reggae Number One "Hit"* for quite a few months and still is quite a favourite. The great Joe Loss Band wasted no time in including this number in their repertoire and feature it quite a lot, to the thrill and enthusiasm of their thousands of followers. As the song goes "Mama No Want Bangarang", but retailers repeatedly report that it's the Mothers as much as the Teenagers and Grans who really go for - and buy this record in such great quantities.

Enough is enough and I have rattled on about this fantastic tune enough, so it's about time I gave you a chance to play it for yourself and also listen to the other eleven great tracks on this album, all of which are performed by Lester (Mr. Versatile) Sterlin. So put on your dancing shoes, pin back your lug holes and grab a belly full of Mr. Sterlin, playing for you such great creations as:-

"Reggae In The Wind", "Spoogy", yes Spoogy is spoogy, "1,000,000 Tons Of T.N.T", powerful eh, "Man At The Door", well let him in because he is a "Man About Town" doing the "Reggae On Broadway", in the show called "Doctor Satan", but he is a real "Danger Man", whose smile is as "Bright As A Rose", when he sees "Regina", talking to the "Man At Work". Ah me yes, de same one who writes up the *Reggae Hit's '69* album covers.

Palpitation Mr. Reggae

A PAMA/UNITY RECORD PRODUCTION - London, England and Kingston, Jamaica

The girl in the picture on the front cover is Miss Unity Records Eunice Cook and the boy, Mr. Sounsville himself youg Harry Harrison

Distributed by: PAMA RECORDS LIMITED, 78, CRAVEN PARK ROAD,LONDON,N.W.10. ENGLAND

SLIM SMITH

Ken Smith AKA Slim Smith was one of the most soulful of Jamaica's singers during the rocksteady early reggae era. He was born in Jamaica in 1948. His break came with producer 'Coxsone' Dodd where he performed solo as well as a member of The Techniques. His powerful falsetto voice had music lovers comparing him to the great Sam Cooke. He soon took centre stage as lead singer with The Techniques but a move away saw him revive his solo career. In 1967 he formed a new version of The Uniques teaming up with Jimmy Riley and Lloyd Charmers and there began his fruitful association with Bunny Lee. They topped the Jamaican hit parade with Let Me Go Girl, but after recording one album, Absolutely The Uniques, he left the group, staying with Lee to concentrate once again on a solo career. Slim released many great tracks a mix of soul covers and original material. He had a hit with Everybody Needs Love and an album of the same name was issued on ECO 9 in 1969 which presented opportunity for more successful hits.

By 1972 he had succumbed to personal problems and was detained at a sanatorium in Jamaica. The following year he was unable to gain entry to his parents' house so he broke a window, badly cutting his arm. He bled to death before he could receive medical treatment. His death at the time stunned the world of reggae and he is still to this day regarded as one of Jamaica's finest vocalists.

Slim Smith singles issued on Unity.

UN-504 Everybody Needs Love 1968
Produced by: Bunny Lee
Slim is ably accompanied by Glen Adams on organ for his version of the popular song produced by Bunny Lee.

UN-508 For Once In My Life / Burning Desire 1969
Produced by: Bunny Lee / Bunny Lee

UN-510 Zip-A-Di-Do-Da / On Broadway 1969
Produced by: Bunny Lee / Bunny Lee

UN-513 Let It Be Me / Love Makes Me Do Foolish Things -
Slim Smith & Paulette 1969
Produced by: Bunny Lee / Bunny Lee

UN-515 Somebody To Love / Confusion 1969
Produced by: Bunny Lee / Bunny Lee
A rhythmic reggae beat and Slim' soulful vocals on a cover of Solomon Burke's 1964 release.

UN-520 Slipaway / Spanish Harlem 1969
Produced by: Bunny Lee / Bunny Lee
Re-issued on Camel CA-81 in 1971 with the A and B sides reversed.

UN-524 Sunny Side Of The Sea / Place In The Sun 1969
Produced by: Bunny Lee / Bunny Lee

UN-537 Keep That Light Shining On Me / Build My World Around You 1969
Produced by: Bunny Lee / Bunny Lee
The B side is a rocksteady rhythm revival from 1968 actually by The Uniques with Slim on lead vocal, but now credited to Just Slim. A cover of a Motown hit from 1967.

UN-542 Honey / There Is A Light 1969
Produced by: Bunny Lee / Bunny Lee
The unique sounding Honey was also issued on Trojan's Pressure Beat label as No Money, No Honey with the credit going to Niney And The Destroyers.

UN-567 Blessed Are The Meek - *Slim Smith & Dave Barker* 1970
Produced by: Bunny Lee / Bunny Lee

UN-570 Jenny / The Race 1970
Produced by: Slim Smith / Slim Smith

Too Proud To Beg from The Uniques who included Slim Smith was issued on GAS 117. The Jamaican releases was titled Ain't Too Proud To Beg by Slim Smith.

LESTER STERLING

ALTO SAXOPHONE PLAYER / ARRANGER

Lester Sterling learnt his trade as many Jamaican musicians have done at the Alpha Boys school founded in 1880 run by The Sisters Of Mercy. His early musical encounter was playing trumpet and cornet and it wasn't until his twenties he decided he wanted to play Alto Saxophone. In the early sixties he played studio musician with the original Skatalites and was a founder member of the band along with Doreen Shaffer. When they disbanded in '65 he joined Byron Lee And The Dragonaires. He recorded several singles for London based Clancy Collins. It was his association with Bunny Lee that led to perhaps one of the most famous reggae tracks to come out of Jamaica, Bangarang.

I was very honoured to interview Bunny in 2016 who was a true gentleman and this extract surrounds Bangarang.

"Rocksteady was a beautiful music. Up to now, you still have the rocksteady. But you see, the reggae - you know what 'reggae' is? reggae is the organ shuffle in the rocksteady. It carries up back the beat a little. Carry up back the beat and make it in-between. Because you take out the organ shuffle out of the reggae... you take the organ shuffle out a de business. It was started by us in '68 upstairs in Duke Reid studio - Bunny begins to sing - Woman No Want Bangarang..............................".

Lester Sterling singles issued on Unity.

UN-502 Bangarang - Lester Sterling & Stranger Cole 1968
Produced by: Bunny Lee
UN-505 Reggie On Broadway - Lester Sterling 1969
Produced by: Derrick Morgan
UN-509 Spoogy - Lester Sterlin 1969
Produced by: Derrick Morgan
UN-531 Lonesome Feeling / Bright As A Rose - **Lester Sterling** 1969
Produced by: Bunny Lee / Bunny Lee
UN-562 Slip Up - Lester Sterling 1970
Produced by: Bunny Lee

Pama albums.
BANGARANG Lester Sterlin SECO 15 1969

ALBUMS

19'11

15'6

PAMA ALBUM Discography 1969 -1975

(Missing catalogue numbers are Not Used - Not Established)

Traditionally Jamaican music, ska and rocksteady, found success in the singles market with albums seen as luxury items. The vinyl 45 was named after its play speed with the first single produced in 1949 by RCA in America. The format soon took off with the young record buying public preferring the smaller and cheaper 45 (single) to the more expensive 12 inch Long Player (LP). In Britain the sales of records increased providing competition for the USA but at the time it was a tiny Island in the Caribbean that was witnessing a new revolution.

The sound system operators in Jamaica had started turning their hand to record production, replacing the imported American R&B previously the only source of music on the island. Ken Khouri opened the first recording studio in Jamaica, recording mento music with the islands first record label Federal Records launched by Khouri in 1954. Coxsone Dodd and Duke Reid soon followed suit. The music produced was a fusion of Caribbean and rhythm and blues. As things progressed the bass evolved as a much more prominent feature and ska was born, the forerunner of rocksteady and reggae.

Pama and Trojan began putting out compilation budget priced reggae albums in 1969, Trojan with their Tighten Up series retailing at 14/6 and Pama with their greatest hits from the subsidiary labels, featuring a collection of hits from the previous year, a format that gave wider access to the music retailing at just 15/6.

The art work for Trojan featured scantily clad young ladies but Pama who'd traditionally used shots of singers and club scenes on their album covers went a step further with sleeves often more explicit than Trojan. The first Straighten Up from Pama was issued in 1971.

The Economy Series ECO (Mono) SECO (Stereo) (1969 -1970) was launched with the recording celebrating the Investiture of The Prince of Wales from Hammersmith Welsh Male Choir SECO 1.

ECO 2 **Crab Biggest Hits**
Various Artistes 1969
ECO 3 **Reggae Hits '69 Volume 1**
Various Artistes 1969
ECO 4 **Gas Greatest Hits**
Various Artistes 1969
SECO 5 **Butlin's Red Coat Review**
The Butlin's Red Coats 1969
ECO 6 **Nu-Beat's Greatest Hits**
Various Artistes 1969
ECO 7 **Unity's Greatest Hits**
Various Artistes 1969
ECO 8 **Scandal In A Brixton Market**
Laurel Aitken & Girlie 1969
ECO 9 **Everybody Needs Love**
Slim Smith 1969
ECO 10 **Derrick Morgan In London**
Derrick Morgan 1969
ECO 11 **Reggae Hits '69 Volume 2**
Various Artistes 1969
SECO 12 **Rudy Mills Reggae Hits**
Rudy Mills 1969
SECO 13 **Derrick Harriott Sings Jamaican Reggae**
Derrick Harriott 1969
ECO 14 **Rico In Reggae Land**
Rico Rodriguez 1969
SECO 15 **Bangarang**
Lester Sterling 1969
SECO 17 **Boss Reggae**
Various Artistes 1969
SECO 18 **The Best Of Camel**
Various Artistes 1970
SECO 19 **Bullet A World Of Reggae**
Various Artistes 1970
SECO 20 **A Gift From Pama**
Various Artistes 1970
SECO 24 **Many Moods Of The Upsetters**
The Upsetters 1970
SECO 25 **House In Session**
Lloyd Charmers And The Hippy Boys 1970
SECO 31 **First Lady Of Reggae**
Doreen Shaffer 1970
SECO 32 **Birth Control**
Various Artistes 1970
SECO 33 **Strange**
Dobby Dobson 1970
ECO 34 **Reggae For Days**
Various Artistes 1970
ECO 35 **Young Gifted And Black**
Various Artistes 1970

PMLP Series (1968 - 1969)

PMLP 1 **Remember Otis**
Beverley Simmons 1968
PMLP 3 **Ready Steady Go - Rock Steady**
Various Artistes 1968
PMLP 4 **Bang Bang Lulu**
Various Artistes 1969 *(Issued with the option of orange, red or black sleeve)*
PMLP 5 **The Champ**
The Mohawks 1969
PMLP 6 **Made Of Gold**
The Crowns 1968
PMLP SP 7 **Rocksteady Cool**
Various Artistes 1969
PMLP SP 8 **Soul Sauce From Pama**
Various Artistes 1969
PMLP SP 9 **Remember Otis**
Beverley Simmons 1969 *(Re issue)*
PMLP 11 **A Dream**
Max Romeo 1969
PMLP 12 **Pat Kelly Sings**
Pat Kelly 1969

PMP Series (1971 - 1973)

PMP 2001 **Reggae Spectacular With Strings**
Various Artistes 1971
PMP 2002 **Straighten Up**
Various Artistes 1971
PMP 2003 **Something Sweet The Lady**
Various Artistes 1971
PMP 2004 **African Melody**
Various Artistes 1971
PMP 2005 **This Is Reggae Volume 2**
Various Artistes 1971
PMP 2006 **Hot Numbers Volume 1**
Various Artistes 1971
PMP 2007 **Straighten Up Volume 2**
Various Artistes 1971
PMP 2008 **This Is Reggae Volume 3**
Various Artistes 1971
PMP 2009 **Hot Numbers Volume 2**
Various Artistes 1972
PMP 2010 **Let The Power Fall**
Max Romeo 1972
PMP 2011 **Free The People**
Winston Groovy 1972
PMP 2012 **Reggae To Reggae**
Various Artistes 1972
PMP 2014 **Straighten Up Volume 3**
Various Artistes 1972
PMP 2015 **Sixteen Dynamic Reggae Hits**
Various Artistes 1972
PMP 2016 **This Is Reggae Volume 4**
Various Artistes 1972
PMP 2017 **Straighten Up Volume 4**
Various Artistes 1973

PSP Series (1969 - 1970)

PSP 1001 **The Lovely Dozen**
Various Artistes 1969
PSP 1002 **Hey Boy, Hey Girl**
Various Artistes 1969

PSP 1003 **This Is Reggae Volume 1**
Various Artistes 1970
PSP 1004 **Reggae To UK With Love**
Various Artistes 1970
PSP 1006 **Moon Hop**
Derrick Morgan 1970
PSP 1007 **Live At The Cumberland**
Mood Reaction 1970
PSP 1012 **The High Priest Of Reggae**
Laurel Aitken 1970
PSP 1014 **Clint Eastwood**
The Upsetters 1970

PTP Series (1975)

PTP 1001 **Reggae Hit The Town**
Various Artistes 1975

STRAIGHTEN UP!

The Straighten Up series launched in 1971 some two years after Trojan had released the inaugural Tighten Up album although Pama had been issuing compilation albums since 1968 with Ready Steady Go - Rock Steady and Gas Greatest Hits et al from '69. The Straighten Up albums were an admirable collection of well received singles that had peaked in terms of sales, giving the record buying public, and in particular the skinhead, a chance to own a dozen tracks for just 15/6 (78p). Not a bad deal when a single cost about 7 /- (35p).

The Pama singles were always far more difficult to get hold of down to distribution so having the opportunity of a dozen tracks on one album was always going to be a winner. The series ran to four volumes with the final volume released in 1973 holding the distinction of being the final album to be be issued by Pama between the glory years of 1968 and 1973.

STRAIGHTEN UP!

STRAIGHTEN UP Various Artistes   PAMA PMP 2002 1971

Side 1
1. LET IT BE - The Mohawks   2. LAST GOODBYE - Norman T Washington
3. WITHOUT MY LOVE - Little Roy 4. GOT TO GET YOU OFF MY MIND - Shel Alterman
5. CHARIOT COMING - The Viceroys 6. STRAIGHTEN UP - The Maytones

Side 2
1. GIVE HER ALL THE LOVE I'VE GOT - John Holt 2. BRING BACK YOUR LOVE - Owen Grey
3. YELLOW BIRD - Winston Groovy 4. SOMEDAY WE'LL BE TOGETHER - The Marvels
5. TOO EXPERIENCED - Winston Francis 6. PICK YOUR POCKET - The Versatiles

No comprehensive sleeve notes to kick off the Straighten Up series.

The cover version of **Let It Be** issued on Supreme SUP-204 in 1970 kicks off the Straighten Up series and is performed admirably by The Mohawks in true skinhead reggae style. The Beatles hit number two with the song in March 1970 the same week Young Gifted And Black and Elizabethan Reggae were in the top 30. Little Roy comes in with a cracking tune and superb vocals on **Without My Love**. **Last Goodbye** is another vocal led tune over a captivating hypnotic beat from Norman T Washington. Shel Alterman comes up with a good cover of a Solomon Burke number **Got To Get You Off My Mind**. **Chariot Coming** by The Viceroys was released on Bullet in 1970 and has another outing on the excellent Sixteen Dynamic Reggae Hits album. Side one concludes with the sound that gave the series its title, **Straighten Up** from The Maytones. The single with a prominent bass line was released in 1970 on Camel CA-47 but under the title Black And White Unite.

John Holt gets the proceedings back under-way on side two with **Give Her All The Love I've Got** making use of the Upsetters Shocks Of Mighty rhythm. **Bring Back Your Love** from Owen Gray also gets an outing. **Yellow Bird** was originally released on the re-branded New Beat label NB-055 in 1970, a some-what traditional offering from Winston Groovy. **Someday We'll Be Together** is a vocal outing from The Marvels with backing from The Mohawks. The single was issued on Gas GAS-139 in 1970. The group Alex and Cornell Hinds and Eddie Smith specialised in Doo-wop harmonies. Perhaps one of their most endearing hits came later during 1972 with their version of Then He Kissed Me, plugged as a Christmas hit along with Big Seven by Trojan. Winston Francis comes in with a rocking sound on **Too Experienced** issued on Punch PH-5 in 1969. The Versatiles continued their tradition concluding the album with a classic skinhead reggae sounds on **Pick My Pocket** released on Nu Beat NB-060, one of the last few to appear on the Nu Beat label before the complete transition to New Beat.

STRAIGHTEN UP VOLUME 2 Various Artistes   PAMA PMP 2007 1971

Side 1
1. GUILTY Tiger 2. JUST MY IMAGINATION - Dave Barker
3. FAREWELL MY DARLING - Eugene Paul 4. DON'T YOU WEEP - Max Romeo
5. JOHN CROW SKANK - Derrick Morgan 6. FREE THE PEOPLE - Winston Groovy 7. MY GIRL - Slim Smith
Side 2
1. MONKEY SPANNER - Larry And Lloyd 2. LOVE AND EMOTION - The Righteous Flames
3. PUT YOUR SWEET LIPS - Raphael Stewart 4. I WANNA BE LOVED - Winston Groovy
5. CHEERIO BABY - The Classics 6. SAMETHING FOR BREAKFAST - Winston & Pat
7. EVERY NIGHT - Rudy & Sketto

PAMA MEDIUM

Straighten Up Volume 2 was the only one in the series to feature any sleeve notes.

STEREO PMP 2007
(Electronically Rebalanced)

The first volume of STRAIGHTEN UP has been such a phenomenal success, bringing numerous requests for a second volume that it was very easy to decide to release volume two. However, to follow a success story a lot of thought, planning and practical application is needed, all of which, believe me, has been put into this action-packed volume of STRAIGHTEN UP.

We have selected just about the very best Reggae numbers available today, bearing in mind your favourite artistes, adding two extra numbers for bonus and giving you a dish of old Jamaica's grass skirted damsels on the front cover.

Enjoy volume two won't you and we look forward to hearing from you with your favourite comments and ideas for volume three.

STRAIGHTEN UP!
Volume Two
A PAMA GROUP RECORDS PRODUCTION
PAMA RECORDS 78 CRAVEN PARK ROAD LONDON NW10 ENGLAND

Volume two gets off in great style with **Guilty** by Tiger AKA Laurel Aitken. Dave Barker, the vocal part of the famous duo, is up next with Lloyd Charmers Jamaican single **Just My Imagination**. Eugene Paul then gives a good rendition over a catchy rhythm with **Farewell My Darling**. Derrick Morgan delivers on **John Crow Skank** admirably, although a change of direction for him with the track utilising the rhythm from Cherry Oh Baby. **My Girl** from Slim Smith completes side one, a catchy number from the man heralded as the greatest vocalist of the early reggae era. A cover of **Monkey Spanner** was always going to be difficult for Larry & Lloyd to pull off with their release on New Beat. The single was poles apart from Dave & Ansel Collins. They did though keep the original single format with an instrumental Version 2 on the B side.

Love And Emotion from The Righteous Flames and **I Wanna Be Loved** from Winston Groovy are up next, the latter a recognisable Winston Groovy sound. The skinhead reggae sound is back with **Cherrio Baby** from The Classics, who were in fact The Wailing Souls from Jamaica and also recorded under the name of The Little Roys. This one differs from the tight Eric Donaldson version where his fine acrobatic voice skilfully negotiated the lyrics, nevertheless a cracking sound. **Samething For Breakfast** from Winston & Pat who are better known as Winston Groovy and Pat Rhoden was issued as the B side to Sweeter Than Honey from Winston Groovy but is equally as good. The album concludes with an excellent revived number from Ruddy & Sketto with **Every Night**, the track produced by Laurel Aitken.

PMP 2014

STEREO
(electronically rebalanced)

STRAIGHTEN UP (VOL. 3)
Various Artistes

SIDE ONE
TITLE
1. Rum Rhythm
2. South Of The Border
3. Nanny Scank
4. Bend Down Low
5. Owen Gray Greatest Hits
6. Rock Steady
7. A Sugar

SIDE TWO
1. Pray For Me
2. Linger A While
3. Aily and Ailaloo
4. Searching So Long
5. Way Down South
6. Nothing Can Separate Us
7. Plenty Of One

ARTISTE
Shirley & Charmers
Denzil Dennis
Hugh Roy
The Groovers
Owen Gray
The Marvels
Roy Shirley

Max Romeo
John Holt
Niney & Max
Derrick Morgan
Hugh Roy
Owen Gray
Derrick Morgan

PMP 2002 PMP 2006

PMP 2006 PMP 2007 PMP 2011

GROUP RECORD PRODUCTION
CORDS LTD., 78 Craven Park Road, London NW10 4AE

STRAIGHTEN UP VOLUME 3 Various Artistes   PAMA PMP 2014 1972

Side 1

1. RUM RHYTHM - Shirley & Charmers 2. SOUTH OF THE BORDER - Denzil Dennis
3. NANNY SKANK - Hugh Roy 4. BEND DOWN LOW - The Groovers
5. OWEN GRAY GREATEST HITS - Owen Gray 6. ROCK STEADY - The Marvels 7. A SUGAR - Roy Shirley

Side 2

1. PRAY FOR ME - Max Romeo 2. LINGER A WHILE - John Holt
3. AILY AND AILALOO - Niney & Max 4. SEARCHING SO LONG - Derrick Morgan
5. WAY DOWN SOUTH - Hugh Roy 6. NOTHING CAN SEPARATE US - Owen Gray
7. PLENTY OF ONE - Derrick Morgan

STRAIGHTEN UP!

Kicking off volume three is **Rum Rhythm** from Shirley & Charmers, better known as Roy Shirley and Lloyd Charmers, released on Bullet BU-502 in 1972. The Jamaican release was titled Mucking Fuch by The Muckers. **South Of The Border** is a well travelled song from a film dating way back to 1939 describing a road trip to Mexico. Probably easier to list who hasn't released the song than who has. This excellent version, issued on Pama Supreme PS-350, is performed admirably by Denzil Dennis who was the other half with Jennifer on the re-issued Escort release of Young Gifted And Black. Hugh Roy or U. Roy is up next with **Nanny Skank** although the single issued on Punch PH-104 reads Nannyscrank, presumably a take on Larry Marshalls Nanny Goat. Next up is a cover version by The Groovers of **Bend Down Low** issued on Escort ERT-863. The original Bob Marley & The Wailers single issued in Jamaica in 1966 is still perhaps the best.

Owen Gray Greatest Hits gives an outing for Owen Gray with a compilation single of his greatest hits, not always a favourable option up against the singles in their original form. **Rock Steady** from The Marvels is next then side one concludes with the well documented **A Sugar** from Roy Shirley and Altyman Reid, issued on both Trojan's Green Door label, GD-4026(2) and the Pama Punch label PH-108 in 1972.

Side two opens with Max Romeo, this time in a completely different mood with **Pray For Me,** highlighting a change in style with politically motivated influences showing that his musical talent went far beyond risqué lyrics. John Holt comes up with a scorcher on Camel CM-78 with **Linger A While** in true boss reggae fashion. A change of pace with **Aily And Ailaloo** from Niney And Max issued on Bullet BU-503. Max is of course Max Romeo and Niney is Winston 'Niney' Holness. **Searching So Long** is a track composed, produced and sung by Derrick Morgan issued on Crab CRAB-67 in 1970, having the distinction of the ultimate record issued on the Crab label.

Hugh Roy is back with **Way Down South**, a resounding talk over version of the first-rate Take Warning from Billy Dyce issued on Trojan's GG label. Hugh Roy's true reggae classic was issued on the main Pama label PM-835 in 1972. To keep it in the family The B side features Be My Guest by Billy Dyce. Duplications of recordings were not uncommon as often Jamaican producers would license the same record to both companies and a release on Trojan's GG label highlights this having the A side of GG-4532 as Be My Guest and the B side Way Down South.

Nothing Can Separate Us comes from Owen Gray, refreshing to listen to an original single issued on Camel CA-73 in 1971. Derrick Morgan concludes the last Straighten Up of 1972 with **Plenty Of One** issued on Punch PH-107, produced and preformed by Derrick. Alas another of those compilations, this time of Derrick's earlier recordings kicking off with Tougher Than Tough, a track previously issued on Pyramid PYR-610 in 1967.

STRAIGHTEN UP VOLUME 4 Various Artistes   PAMA PMP 2017 1973

Side 1
1. SOUL SISTER - The Groovers 2. THE GODFATHER - Jerry Lewis
3. LEAN ON ME - B.B. Seaton 4. BREAKFAST IN BED - Winston Reed 5. MY CONFESION - Cornell Campbell
6. HERE COME THE HEARTACHES - Delroy Wilson 7. BLACK HEART - U.Roy

Side 2
1. HIJACK PLANE - The Avengers 2. I WANT JUSTICE - B.B. Seaton
3. OUR HIGH SCHOOL DANCE - Stranger Cole 4. FEVER - Junior Byles
5. GOOD HEARTED WOMAN - Clarendonians 6. I HEAR YOU KNOCKING - Owen Gray
7. I DON'T WANT TO DIE - Junior English

The final volume of Straighten Up was released in 1973. A time when the raw unpretentious boss sounds had eased with political unrest surrounding the 1972 election in Jamaica having paved the way to the more conscious lyrics, and the emergence of early roots reggae. The Groovers get thing going with **Soul Sister**, conscious lyrics over a chugging reggae beat. Jerry Lewis talks us through the **Godfather** using the same rhythm as Slim Smith's The Time has Come. B.B. Seaton a former member of The Gaylads slows it down with a cover of **Lean On Me**. The pace picks up with a young Winston Reed and his version of Lorna Bennett's classic **Breakfast In Bed**. Cornell Campbell comes up with **My Confession,** his smooth vocals over a chugging beat are complimented with a wonderful guitar riff midway. Delroy Wilson declares **Here Come The Heartaches** with his convincing vocals over some impressive drum work. **Life And All Its Dreams** from The Avengers is followed by **Black Heart** from U.Roy in his inimitable style.

The Avengers **Hijack Plane** sets side two in motion followed by another from B. B. Seaton, this time with conscious lyrics requesting **I Want Justice.** Stranger Cole gets a chugging unhurried reggae beat up and running with **Our High School Dance** ably accompanied by Hortense Ellis. Ansel Collins on organ with Les Foster's vocals deliver **The Man In Your Life**. The vocal offering of **Fever** from Junior Byles is ahead of its time. The Clarendonians get the raw sounds of reggae back on board with **Good Hearted Woman.** Owen Gray and Junior Byles complete the Straighten Up series with **I Hear You Knocking** and **I Don't Want To Die** respectively.

STRAIGHTEN UP!

REGGAE HITS 69 Volume One   Various Artistes   PAMA ECO 3 1969

Side 1
1. CHILDREN GET READY - The Versatiles
2. BANGARANG - Stranger Cole & Lester Sterling
3. HEY BOY, HEY GIRL - Derrick & Patsy 4. RHYTHM HIPS - Ronald Russell
5. RIVER TO THE BANK - Derrick Morgan 6. REGGAE HIT THE TOWN - The Eathiopians

Side 2
1. THE HORSE - Eric Barnett 2. I LOVE YOU - Derrick Morgan
3. REGGAE IN THE WIND - Lester Sterling & The Soul Mates
4. LETS HAVE SOME FUN - Devon & The Tartons 5. PUSH PUSH - The Termites
6. LAST FLIGHT TO REGGAE CITY - Stranger Cole & Lester Sterling

ECONOMY   MONO   ECO 3

REGGAE HITS 69 (VOLUME ONE)
VARIOUS ARTISTES

Children Get Ready surely one of the best in modern reggae beat very good backing along with good singing and fine lyrics. The Versatiles - a group of young Jamaicans first began singing together at school but soon graduated to the professional field. This is their first release and after listening we feel sure there is plenty more good stuff where that came from. Best of luck boys. **Last Flight To Reggae City** a combination of great talent here which has gone into the making of this entertaining record. The spoken comedy of Stranger Cole coupled with the fine flute work of Mr. Lester Sterling has put Flight To Reggae City into the ska charts without any fuss whatsoever - and just listen to that beat - keep dancing. **Bangarang** like the song says mama no want Bangarang and who would with such authentic rhythm to dance to. Stranger Cole and company again, and this time Bangarang went straight to number one in the Jamaican charts and stayed there for several weeks, while in England and the USA it created havoc over Christmas and was the most popular ska record for many weeks. **The Horse**, now here is a surprise hit. Some time ago a gentleman called Cliff Noble made an instrumental and called it The Horse round about the same time a gentleman called Mr. Eric Barnett in another part of the world made another instrumental and he too called his The Horse as a follow up to a local hit, The Donkey. Both discs were issued in England and both were hits, one a R&B the other a ska hit, great eh! **Rhythm Hips** on release was voted discotheque record of the week by a well known disc columnist The Swinger. Ronald Russell the artiste tells a story all men love to hear, about the young mini-skirted girls who when they walk are living poetry in motion. Good story, good record.

Reggae In The Wind. Why not? if you feel you should, then go on Reggae In The Wind. A great beaty number dished up by those hit-makers Lester Sterling & The Soulmates, great fun. **River To The Bank**. Derrick Morgan and friends have served us with an old Jamaican ring play song. River To The Bank brings back memories of great fun, thoroughly enjoyable so join in and sing. **Push Push**, the ruder variety of ska music but very subtle and the children will not be able to detect any rudeness at all in this song. Well composed and very well performed indeed by those stalwarts of ska, The Termites. **Hey Boy, Hey Girl**. This song is very well known in the United Kingdom, played quite often over the radio and a discotheque hit. The mums and dads as well as the teenagers go for this one in a very big way, nice to find it on an album with so many other good numbers. Artistes Patsy and Derrick, both no strangers to the scene and it's the same Derrick Morgan that dishes up **I Love You** another good reggae number that is sure to go down especially among the romantics. **Lets Have Some Fun**. New artistes Devon and The Tartons are surely off to a grand start with their very own composition Lets Have Some Fun. Nice harmony with some good voices, ska music is surely glad to enrol them. **Reggae Hit The Town**. Once again The Ethiopians, higher tenor voices, individual styling and right in rhythm with the great reggae beat when Reggae Hit The Town - and it will with this album.

Happy listening and have lots of fun with this record and mind you - learn the new dance - THE REGGAE

John Jones - from Jamaica

Distributed by:- PAMA RECORDS LIMITED 78 Craven Park Road London N.W.10 England

REGGAE HITS 69 Volume Two   Various Artistes   PAMA ECO 11 1969

Side 1

1. 1,000 TONS OF MEGATON - Roland Alphoso 2. WHO YOU GONNA RUN TO - The Techniques
3. DOWN IN THE PARK - The Inspirations 4. SPREAD YOUR BED - The Versatiles
5. TAKE YOUR HAND FROM MY NECK - The Paragons 6. THROW ME CORN - Winston Shane

Side 2

1. SOUL CALL - The Soul Rhythms 2. WORK IT - The Viceroys
3. RUN GIRL RUN - G.G. Grossett 4. PRIVATE NUMBER - Ernest Wilson
5. SINCE YOU'VE BEEN GONE - Eric Fatter 6. SPOOGY - Lester Sterlin

ECONOMY   MONO   ECO-11

REGGAE HITS '69 VOLUME 2 VARIOUS ARTISTES

As with the predecessor to this album we wish to give you a brief insight to the make-up of each number contained in this album, the second volume of Reggae-Hits Sixty Nine. So we begin at the beginning.

1,000 Tons Of Megaton A very powerful title for a very powerful tune - Instrumental with narration at intervals. This number has become the signature tune for many a Disc Jockey and one Radio Stations J.B.C. has adopted it fully as the introduction tune to all of their pop programmes - The artistes blowing that fantastic saxophone melody on it is the eminent - ROLAND ALPHONSO. **Who You Gonna Run To** Good question me thinks, because after listening to THE TECHNIQUES singing this song to such sophisticated backing, there's just no point in running. A very outstanding number, excellently performed. **Down In The Park** "Down in the Park we go, it isn't quite dark we know" sings THE INSPIRATORS, a new group with great harmony, could be compared to the Temptations and other greats in this field. An excellent number by a promising young group. **Spread Your Bed** On our first volume we had this group THE VERSATILES doing their thing with a number called "Children Get Ready", now we have them following up quite nicely with "Spread Your Bed". As the first was a biggie, this one is a greatie. How's that? judge for yourself. **Take Your Hands From My Neck** THE PARAGONS are an established group who came off the scene some two years ago because one member of the group left to go to University in the States. He is now back and if this is the result of his studies, well I'm going to college again. Very good. **Throw Me Corn** Every year in the Blue-Beat field a really big one comes out, last year it was Ride Your Donkey by THE TENNORS, this year for your pleasure *Mr Winston Shane* has provided us with "Throw Me Corn". Very unusual backing, very unusual singing, great lyrics and an entirely great number.

Soul Call The Soul Rhythms are quite new to me but by their performance on this number one can tell they are here to stay. "Soul Call" is a very outstanding instrumental which is being compared to numbers like "The Champ" by the Mohawks and "Green Onions" by Booker T. & The M.G.S. A very good blending of horns to a very good rhythm. **Work It** We are all lazy I know, sometimes even too lazy to eat, but with this tune laziness is totally abolished and a vigorous working activity is compelled by a great driving beat and a well arranged number with good lyrics and good singing by THE VICEROYS. **Run Girl Run** This song is in the same vein as "Work It" although produced in different camps. Radio Disc Jockey Mike Raven praised this number as one of the best Reggaes he has ever heard and forecast great success for it. He was right - this was a huge Blue Beat Hit for the singer/arranger - G.G. Grossett - Mr. Treble G. **Private Number** Remember a great chart record performed in soul by Judy Clay and William Bell? Now here is a new Reggae version, performed by Ernest Wilson the youth and former lead singer of the Clarendonians. An excellent recording. **Since You've Been Gone** Last October a brilliant new producer turned out a great record "No More Heartaches", this May he has made another masterpiece called "Since You've Been Gone" and once again it's by another new discovery of his, this time "Eric Fatter". Well done chaps. **Spoogy** LESTER STERLIN is not a new name to us, neither is he new to Reggae Hits - because of his success on volume one - "Reggae In The Wind" an "Bangarang". Lester is on his own this time with a live performance at the *National Stadium, Jamaica,* and on this recording you can hear him being cheered on by the packed crowd of very appreciative reggae lovers - So Reggae on SPOOGY.

In as much as you enjoyed volume one (ECO 3) of Reggae Hits 69, we are sure you are going to be proud of this new recording and your friends will be tempted to borrow it - but be wise, don't lend them, let them buy their own.

Once again - Johnny Jones from J.A.

 Distributed by:- PAMA RECORDS LIMITED 78 Craven Park Road London N.W.10 England

ROCK STEADY FROM PAMA

READY STEADY GO ROCK STEADY   Various Artistes   PAMA PMLP 3 SP 1968

Side 1
1. SOUL FOOD - Lynn Tait And The Jets 2. MY TIME IS THE RIGHT TIME - Alton Ellis
3. C.N. EXPRESS - Clancy's All Stars 4. WHERE IN THIS WORLD - Carlton Alponso
5. EASTERN PROMISE - Earl St. Joseph 6. YOU WERE MEANT FOR ME - The Groovers
7. WHAT WILL YOUR MAMA SAY - Clancy Eccles

Side 2
1. FIDDLESTICKS - Tommy McKenzie & His Orchestra
2. SAY WHAT YOUR SAYING - Monty Morris 3. THE FIGHT - Clancy Eccles
4. HEART BEAT - Ernest Ranglin 5. THE MESSAGE - Alton Ellis
6. THEY WASH - Joyce Bond Show 7. BANG BANG LULU - Lloyd Terrel

READY STEADY GO - ROCK STEADY   PMLP-3 SP

VARIOUS ARTISTES

The album is packed with fourteen tracks of SKA and ROCKSTEADY most of which have been in the top ten Ska chart and are now put together to make what to my mind, must be the best Rock Steady or Blue Beat Album ever to be offered to the public at large. If you study the titles and Artistes names listed you will soon be convinced that this is a must for you and like me you will vouch to make SOUL FOOD your very first meal of the day.

Bill Vincent

PAMA RECORDS LIMITED 16 Peterborough Road, Harrow, Middlesex, England

As the brief sleeve notes mentioned from Bill Vincent this is an excellent album. One of the earliest from Pama, note the above address, and possibly very underrated from 1968. It features some of the earliest Pama releases including Clancy Eccles **What Will Your Mama Say**.

Clancy's All Stars feature with the classic boss skinhead favourite **C.N. Express** using the same rhythm from Monty Morris' **Say What Your Saying** which also has an outing on the album. Clancy has another jaunt with **The Fight**, slow-paced rocksteady at its best and very reminiscent of a Prince Buster number.

ROCK STEADY COOL   Various Artistes   PAMA PMLP 7 SP   1969

PAMA SPECIAL   MONO   PMLP 7 SP

ROCK STEADY COOL
FROM JAMAICA

THE BEST OF THE GREAT
ROCK STEADY NUMBERS ON THIS
ONE ALBUM AT THE NEW
LOW PRICE
14/6D

SO SKA - SKA - SKA AND ROCK STEADY

Side 1
1. TRAIN TO VIETNAM - The Rudies
2. HEY BOY, HEY GIRL - Derrick & Patsy
3. BYE BYE LOVE - Alton Ellis
4. YOUNG LOVE - The Imperials
5. ON THE TOWN - Bunny & Buddy
6. SEARCHING - Junior Smith
7. MINI REALLY FIT DEM - Soul Flames

Side 2
1. LA LA MEANS I LOVE YOU - Alton Ellis
2. BLUE SOCKS - Reco
3. COVER ME - Fitz & The Coozers
4. RHYTHM & SOUL - Bobby Kalphat
5. ENGINE 59 - The Rudies
6. MUSIC BE THE FOOD OF LOVE - Derrick Morgan
7. ROCK STEADY COOL - Frederick Bell

Distributed by: PAMA RECORDS 78 CRAVEN PARK ROAD LONDON NW10 ENGLAND

THIS IS REGGAE   Various Artistes   PAMA PSP 1003 1970

Side 1
1. MOON HOP - Derrick Morgan 2. GIRL WHAT YOU DOING TO ME - Owen Grey
3. HOW LONG - Pat Kelly 4. CLINT EASTWOOD - The Upsetters
5. WET DREAM - Max Romeo 6. SENTIMENTAL MAN - Ernest Wilson

Side 2
1. PRETTY COTTAGE - Stranger Cole 2. SENTIMENTAL REASON - The Maytones
3. DERRICK TOP A POP - Derrick Morgan 4. JESSE JAMES - Laurel Aitken
5. HONEY - Slim Smith 6. CAT NIP - Lloyd Charmers

This album is up there with the best, and almost certainly one of the most relevant compilations from Pama as most of the tracks on This Is Reggae are laid down in true boss skinhead manner with the album launched at a time when reggae and the skinheads were truly entwined in a musical love affair.

Derrick Morgan had a huge hit with **Moon Hop** released on CRAB-30 in 1969 reaching number 49 in the UK chart during January 1970. It was written to commemorate the 1969 Apollo moon landing but as has been well documented Skinhead Moonstomp seemed to hold back further chart success for Derrick and Pama. The skinhead reggae beat and the screeching lyrics made for a foot stomping classic and was the catalyst for the Moon Hop album issued on PSP 1006 in 1970. Owen Grey, sometimes spelt Gray, is no stranger to the music scene, he was recording as far back as 1960 in Jamaica and comes up with a dance crashing sound finding his way around the lyrics in falsetto style on **Girl What You Doing To Me,** another favourite with the skinheads released on Camel CA-25 in 1969.

Pay Kelly's well documented **How Long Will It Take** comes next. Another top tune, the record issued on Gas GAS-115 in 1969 is seen by many as his greatest soulful tune. Reggae with strings added was not as common for Pama as it became for Trojan but the record sold well only failing to chart as the sales were predominantly from non chart return stores. Another record that narrowly failed to chart, again due to non chart retailers and perhaps a lack of distribution options was **Clint Eastwood** issued on Punch PH-21 in 1969 by The Upsetters. The track was a take on Yakety Yak over a vibrant Lee Perry rhythm, again another favourite boss reggae sound. Sometimes the term 'needs no introduction' is clichéd but not the case with Max Romeo's risqué **Wet Dream**. If ever there was a skinhead favourite this is it, an up-tempo number with a very strong melody, almost unique at the time. **Sentimental Man** from Ernest Wilson concludes side one, the track issued on Crab CRAB-45 in 1969.

Side two kicks off with **Pretty Cottage**, a vocal led single issued on Escort ES-810 in 1969. The label credits Stranger 'Soul' Cole but is actually accompanied by Gladdy Anderson. Next up comes **Sentimental Reason** reigniting the boss skinhead sounds running right throughout the album. Admirably preformed by The Maytones the captivating boss reggae track was issued on Pama's Camel label CA-27 in 1969.

Derrick-Top The Pop as the title suggests is another classic track credited to Derrick Morgan and issued on Unity UN-540 in 1969. But maybe there is a twist to the story as the track sounds very much like Pop A Top Part 2 from Andy Capp released on Duke DU-71B, with a touch of Fat Man. Lynford Anderson AKA Andy Capp was a studio engineer and producer. He produced this track and the original version titled Popatop issued on Treasure Isle, a release that fashioned quite a shift for the reggae beat. Perhaps his most endearing song was The Law (Part 1) released on Trojan's Duke label during 1970.

A boss sounding album without an offering from Laurel Aitken would be out of character so here he is with a self produced number **Jessie James**, issued on Nu Beat NB-045 in 1969. A chugging infectious beat with intermittent gun fire declaring Jessie James rides again. The penultimate offering is **Honey** from Slim Smith issued on Unity UN-542, always great vocals from Slim but the rhythm track seems a little at odds to the rest of the album. **Cat Nip** issued on Camel CA-29 in 1969 from The Hippie Boys brings the excellent album to a close, another infectious beat this time with organ running through, defiantly one to get those old boots on the dance floor.

No linear notes were written for Pama's This Is Reggae series.

THIS IS REGGAE

VOLUME TWO

THIS IS REGGAE Volume Two   Various Artistes   PAMA PMP 2005 971

PAMA/MEDIUM   STEREO   PMP 2005

THIS IS REGGAE

VOLUME TWO

Side1

1. MY SWEET LORD - Fitzroy Sterling
2. DENVER - Alton Ellis
3. HISTORY OF AFRICA - The Classics
4. FEEL IT - Sister
5. BAND OF GOLD - Joan Ross
6. I'LL NEVER FALL IN LOVE AGAIN - Winston Yearwood

Side 2
1. GROVE ME - Owen Gray
2. KEEP ON TRYING - Little Roy
3. BACK TO AFRICA - Alton Ellis
4. DELIVER US - Alton Ellis
5. HEAVEN HELP US - Winston Groovy
6. MACABEE VERSION - Max Romeo

PUBLISHED BY BEVERLEY MUSIC AND COPYRIGHT CONTROL

A Pama Records Group Production

Would it be fair to say the designer had another appointment to get to on the hurry up. Not even the usual promotion of Pama albums on the sleeve.

THIS IS REGGAE Volume 3   Various Artistes   PAMA PMP 2008 1971

PAMA/MEDIUM   MONO   PMP 2008

THIS IS REGGAE

VOLUME THREE

Side 1

1. PIECE OF MY HEART - Mahalia Saunders 2. WHAT WILL YOUR MAMA SAY - Clancy Eccles
3. HOLD THEM ONE TWO THREE FOUR - Roy Shirley 4. BLACK MAN'S PRIDE - Alton Ellis
5. AFRICAN MUSEUM - Sounds Combine 6. LET IT BE ME - Cariboes

Side 2

1. SEVEN IN ONE - The Gaylads 2. STANDING BY - Derrick Morgan
3. HAVE YOU EVER BEEN HURT - Tiger 4. I WILL NEVER LET YOU DOWN - Laurel Aitken
5. ONE MINUTE TO ZERO - Ken Walker 6. FREEDOM TRAIN - The Gladiators

A PAMA RECORDS GROUP PRODUCTION

PAMA RECORDS LIMITED, 78, Craven Park Road, London, NW10, England

Side one opens with a sweet sounding melodic vocal from Mahalia Saunders AKA Hortense Ellis. Clancy follows with his Norton York sweetened track from 1968 and skinhead favourite **What Will Your Mama Say**. **Hold Them One Two Three Four** from Roy Shirley continues the theme of an update of his 1968 hit Hold Them et al. Alton Ellis comes next with **Black Man's Pride**. Sounds Combine recreated the rhythm from Picture On The Wall with their own instrumental organ version on **African Melody**. A reggae love song completes side one from The Cariboes in romantic style with their gentle chugging organ led cover of an awesome 1960 Everly Brothers hit, **Let It Be Me**.

Side two opens with a medley from The Gaylads, **Seven In One**, including their massive Jamaican hit Stop Making Love. The single issued on Camel CA-79 carries (Part Two) on the B side. Mr Moon Hop Derrick Morgan has a change of pace on **Standing By**. Tiger's up next with a sample of Guilty running through **Have You Ever Been Hurt**. Laurel is grooving on **I Will Never Let You Down,** although a pace away from the boss skinhead sounds. The penultimate tune comes from way back, in fact 1966. The Ken Walker track **One Minute To Zero** was released on the Rymska label so is some-what of an oddity as its ska, ska, ska. The album concludes with **Freedom Train** from The Gladiators who found success as a roots reggae band, although their first taste of success was hitting the top of the Jamaican charts in 1968 with a Coxsone produced number Hey Carol.

THIS IS REGGAE Volume 4   Various Artistes   PAMA PMP 2016 1972

PAMA/MEDIUM   COMPATIBLE STEREO   PMP 2016

THIS IS REGGAE

VOLUME FOUR

Side 1

1. MR. POSTMAN - Cynthia Richards 2. THE TIME HAS COME - Slim Smith 3. I MISS MY SCHOOL DAYS - B.B. Seaton
4. SAD MOVIES - Barbara Jones 5. I AM FEELING LONELY - The Maytones 6. THIS IS MY STORY - The Clarendonians 7. ARE YOU SURE - Max Romeo

Side 2

1. DARLING FOREVER - The Clarendonians 2. HOWDY AND TENKY - Flowers And Alvin 3. YOU HAVE LOST THAT LOVING FEELING - The Heptones
4. THE KING MAN IS BACK - Hofmers Brothers 5. TEN TIMES SWEETER THAN YOU - Tony Gordon 6. JAIL THE MAN - Owen Gray 7. JESERMINE - Junior English

A PAMA RECORDS GROUP PRODUCTION

DISTRIBUTED BY:- PAMA RECORDS LIMITED, 78, Craven Park Road, London, NW10, England

The fourth and last in the series still has the sounds of Jamaica's best with the inspired opening track from Cynthia Richards **Mr. Postman** - bring me a letter make me feel better - foot stomping reggae at its best. Slim Smith sings **The Time Has Come** with so much soul and is backed by a melodic beat with impressive drum work. **I Miss My School Days** declares B B Seaton as he reminisces the past, very nostalgic. Boss tune and vocals from Barbara Jones continues the theme of the album with **Sad Movies**. The Maytones released a plethora of top tunes and **I Am Feeling Lonely** is no exception. The Clarendonians who'd been on the scene since the early ska years are saying **This Is My Story**, a melodic gem with pumping horns. Max concludes side one asking **Are You Sure** - think before you answer are you sure?

The Clarendonians are back with their vocal led **Darling Forever** getting side two underway. Flowers And Alvin come in with a boss tune from Alvin Ranglin sampling Cherry Oh Baby with their **Howdey And Tenky**. The Heptones are next with a cover of the Righteous Brothers hit You've Lost That Lovin' Feelin' from 1964 with **You Have Lost That Loving Feeling.** The **King Man Is Back** so declares Hofmers Brothers. **Ten Times Sweeter Than You** was issued on Camel and credited to Tony Gordon, but the sweet vocal led melodic tune comes from Winston Francis. Owen Gray comes in with **Jail The Man** ahead of the track signing off the series, a Syndney Cooks production from Junior English, **Jesermine**.

HOT NUMBERS

HOT NUMBERS Volume One   Various Artistes   PAMA PMP 2006 1971

PAMA

STEREO
(ELECTRONICALLY REBALANCED)

PMP 2006

HOT NUMBERS
VOLUME ONE

Side1

1. CANDIDA - Owen Gray
2. LET THE POWER FALL - Max Romeo
3. CRACKLIN' ROSE - Lloyd Jackson
4. MY LOVE - Rupie Edwards Allstars
5. ALL COMBINE - The Upsetters
6. KNOCK THREE TIMES - Carl

Side 2

1. I FOUND A MAN - Eugene Paul
2. FIRE FIRE - The Youth
3. NOTHING HAS CHANGED - D.D. Dennis
4. DO SOMETHING - Charlie Ace
5. TALK ABOUT LOVE - Pat Kelly
6. CHOLERA - The Justins

A PAMA RECORDS GROUP PRODUCTION

PAMA RECORDS LIMITED, 78, Craven Park Road, London, NW10, England

No linear notes for Hot Numbers.

Stars are coming out for Hot Numbers Volume one with Owen Gray's excellent vocal rendition of the classic **Candida**. Next up is Max Romeo with **Let The Power Fall**, a powerful blast of gospel reggae. A cover of any Neil Diamond song is always a challenge and one taken up by Lloyd Jackson with **Cracklin' Rose**. **My Love** from Rupie Edwards Allstars BU-462 was produced by Rupie but is in fact the exceptional hypnotic Can't Hide The Feelings sung with heart and soul by The Gaylads, authentic Jamaican reggae at its very best. The Upsetters follow with another boss tune from the great man himself Mr Lee 'Scratch' Perry sampling several rhythms with **All Combine** - see how many you can count. Carl Lewin completes side one with a cover of **Knock Three Times** - Brent Dowe also did an exceptional cover.

Side two has Eugene Paul declaring **I Found a Man** - in my bed. Next is **Fire Fire** from The Youth, a record produced by Harry Palmer. Denzil Dennis contributes with the vocal led **Nothing Has Changed.** Charlie Ace gets some toasting in on his tune **Do Something.** Charlie' classic Ontarious Version was issued while working with Alvin Ranglin and he also performed on Big Seven PM-853 with Fay Bennet. Track five **Talk About Love** is another classic from Pat Kelly.

The first volume concludes with **Cholera** from The Justins with vocals similar to The Pioneers early tunes. The Jamaican release on Syndicate credits the producer as Lloyds Radio and TV Ltd, the Punch release credits Lloyd Daley - one and the same.

HOT NUMBERS Volume Two   Various Artistes   PAMA PMP 2009 1971

PAMA/MEDIUM

STEREO
(ELECTRONICALLY REBALANCED)

PMP 2009

HOT NUMBERS
VOLUME TWO

Side 1	Side 2
1. ONE NIGHT OF SIN - The Stickers	1. BUTTER CUP - Winston Scotland
2. RUDIES MEDLEY - 3rd & 4th Generation	2. YOU'LL BE SORRY - David Isaacs
3. ROYAL CORD - The Gaylads	3. IN THE GHETTO - Rip 'N' Lan
4. MAGA DOG - Peter Tosh	4. THE COMING OF JAH - Max Romeo
5. SINCERELY - Owen Gray	5. DANDY SHANDY VERSION 4 - Impact Allstars
6. RASTA BAND WAGON - Max Romeo	6. WALK A LITTLE PROUDER - Carl Dawkins
7. SOULFUL LOVE - Pat Kelly	7. YOU GONNA MISS ME - Owen Gray

A PAMA RECORDS GROUP PRODUCTION

PAMA RECORDS LIMITED, 78, Craven Park Road, London, NW10, England

The opening track comes from The Stickers who are in fact Jackie Brown and The Gaytones. A boss medley is next, **Rudies Medley** featuring Peter Tosh doing a good impersonation of Desmond Dekker, but no disguising his voice when he sings The Toughest. The Gaylads are credited with **Royal Cord** which is an unusual part talk-over from Lloyd Charmers of It Comes And Goes from The Melodians. Peter Tosh is at his best with the boss version of the song **Maga Dog**. It doesn't come much better than this. Tosh negotiates the vibrant rhythm with his unmistakable voice, just listen to - Me jus' a do wha' me haffi do . Owen Gray's vocal led **Sincerely** is up next. Max is back to his best with a message in **Rasta Band Wagon** a brilliant tune and great vocals with a little bit of toasting from Lee Perry. Side one concludes with Pat Kelly's **Soulful Love**.

The opening track on side two features Winston Scotland who incidentally was U.Roy's brother in law, toasting with **Butter Cup**, a true boss sound issued on Punch sampling You Don't Care and This A Butter. David Isaacs declares in falsetto style **You'll Be Sorry**. Track three is a plausible chugging reggae version of Elvis' pop hit **In The Ghetto** from Rip 'N' Lan. Max is back with a vocal offering and his second outing on the album with **The Coming Of Jah**. **Dandy Shandy Version 4** is a vibrant offering from The Impact Allstars. The boss reggae track is a DJ version of Rice And Peas issued on CA-68 and credited to Dandy & Shandy. The pace slows and changes with Carl Dawkins **Walk A Little Prouder**. Appropriately the last track on the album and series is **You Gonna Miss Me** from Owen Gray. The single issued on Pama Supreme PS-310 carried a credible reggae version of I Hear You Knocking on the B side.

REGGAE FOR DAYS

GREAT ALBUM
FANTASTIC VALUE

VARIOUS ARTISTES

REGGAE FOR DAYS Various Artistes PAMA ECO 34 1970

Side 1
1. SOUL OF AFRICA - Tiger 2. THE WORM - Lloyd Robinson
3. CATCH THIS SOUND - Martin Riley 4. JUMPING DICK - Glorias Allstars
5. SOMTIMES - John Holt 6. LEAVING ON A JET PLANE - Glen Adams

Side 2
1. WHAT A CUTE MAN - Max Romeo 2. BUMPER TO BUMPER - Eric Barnett
3. SINCE YOU LEFT - The Maytones 4. SHOCK OF MIGHT - Dave Barker
5. LONDON BRIDGE - Neville Hinds 6. TAMMY - Pat Kelly

ECONOMY   MONO   ECO 34

REGGAE FOR DAYS
VARIOUS ARTISTES

REGGAE REGGAE REGGAE

GREAT ALBUM FANTASTIC VALUE

A PAMA RECORDS GROUP PRODUCTION

PAMA RECORDS LIMITED, 78, Craven Park Road, London, NW10, England

Reggae For Days featured rockstedy early reggae sounds. The cover depicts an idyllic scene, possibly somewhere on the north coast of Jamaica. All tracks were issued in 1970.

Side one gets underway with a recording from Tiger, AKA Laurel Aitken. The record was also produced by Laurel. **Soul Of Africa** released on New Beat NB-052 was the first of a handful of recordings issued under the name Tiger. **The Worm** is up next from Lloyd Robinson with his version of Queen Of The World and really gets the reggae beat underway issued on Camel CA-41. Another cover track follows with **Catch This Sound**, and organ cut of Watch This Sound release by The Techniques, the Pama offering from Martin Riley who also produced the record was released on Camel CA-53. **Jumping Dick** from Gloria Allstars is an interesting early reggae instrumental released on Camel CA-48. The next artist needs no introduction having been a member of the successful Paragons for many years. **Sometimes** from John Holt issued on Unity UN-548 sound very reminiscent of the later Paragons recordings.

Side two kicks off with a Boss sound and one to get the old skinhead boots stomping. It's Max Romeo singing over the rhythm track to Monkey Man with **What A Cute Man** issued on Unity UN-547. Eric Barnet is next with an instrumental **Bumper To Bumper** a track following up his successful The Horse, both issued on Gas this one on GAS-147. The Maytones are already a successful group with hits such as Sentimental Reason and Black & White Unite on their C.V. and are up next with **Since You Left** issued on Camel CA-49. Dave Barker comes in with **Shock Of Might**, a track with a little notoriety issued on Punch PH-25, a real Boss sound and one to grace any compilation album. Track five is **London Bridge** an instrumental cover from Neville Hinds, produced by Lloyd Daley and issued on Camel CA-44. Pat Kelly the gentlemen of reggae rounds off the album with **Tammy.** His fine soulful voice express' the emotion in the song with a catchy tune from Pama Records Production issued on Gas GAS-144. Maybe the title should read *Reggae For Days and Days and Days. Great Album, Fantastic value.*

SPECIAL   MONO   PSP 1001

THE LOVELY DOZEN
best sellers of
SKA · REGGAE · BLUE BEAT
GREAT DANCE MUSIC ~ GOOD FOR PARTIES

THE LOVELY DOZEN   Various Artistes   PAMA PSP 1001   1969

Side 1

1. REGGAE ON BROADWAY - Lester Sterling 2. PEACE ON EARTH - Premo & Joe
3. REGGAE CITY - Val Bennett 4. REGGAE IN THE WIND - Lester Sterling
5. MR. RHYA - Lloyd Terrell 6. REGGAE HIT THE TOWN - The Eathiopians

Side 2

1. PUSH PUSH - The Termites 2. LULU RETURNS - Lloyd Terrell
3. THE AVENGER - Tommy McCook 4. I LOVE YOU - Derrick Morgan
5. SPREAD YOUR BED - The Versatiles 6. DIANA - Alton Ellis

PAMA SPECIAL   MONO   PSP 1001

THE LOVELY DOZEN
VARIOUS ARTISTES

Twelve of the best for you in this collection of Rock Steady Reggae numbers. this album is made with you and your parties in mind, it's built to give maximum entertainment for you and all the family and quests at all times.

There is nothing very fancy about the sleeve of The Lovely Dozen because we wanted you to be able to afford it no matter what your status in life. After all music forms a great part of modern living and what's the sense of living without music and in these days without the fantastic Ska Reggae music to be found on this BUDGET PRICED ALBUM.

The Lovely Dozen is for your enjoyment so go on, fork out and get what you really deserve - everlasting pleasure.

PAMA PROMOTION DEPARTMENT

A Pama Group Records Production

Distributed by: PAMA RECORDS 78 CRAVEN PARK ROAD LONDON NW10 ENGLAND

It certainly is a classic collection of a dozen early boss reggae tracks, most covered in the Boss Sounds sections. One assured to keep the Christmas party swinging is **Peace On Earth** from Premo & Joe, a boss sound issued on the main Pama label in 1968. **Reggae City** from Val Bennett will keep the dance-floor bulging and the boots stomping. Things get livened up with the risqué **Mr. Rhya** from Lloyd Terrell. **Reggae Hit The Town** needs no introduction, a real boss tune. The risqué theme returns with the subtle **Push Push** from the Termites getting side two under-way. The party seems to be going one way with Lloyd Terrell back with **Bang Bang Lulu**. Tommy McCook switches the mood with his chugging saxophone led instrumental version of Bangarang on **The Avenger.**

Before Wet Dream there was **I Love You** from Derrick Morgan ensuring the party goes with a swing. The boss skinhead sounds continue with the vibrant infectious **Spread Your Bed** from The Versatiles while the album concludes with yet another top tune from Alton Ellis with **Diana**.

SIXTEEN DYNAMIC REGGAE HITS   Various Artistes   PAMA PMP 2015 1972

An unusual album sleeve as the back carries the same image as the front. An album of the same title was issued by Trojan the following year featuring hits from The Dynamic Studios in Jamaica.

Side 1
1. SUGAR PIE - The Hammers 2. SHOCK OF MIGHT - Dave Barker
3. GIRL WHAT YOU DOING TO ME - Owen Gray 4. GUILTY - Tiger
5. CLINT EASTWOOD - The Upsetter 6. LET IT BE - The Mohawks
7. SEVEN LETTERS - Derrick Morgan 8. HOW LONG WILL IT TAKE - Pat Kelly

Side 2
1. EVERYBODY NEEDS LOVE - Slim Smith 2. LET THE POWER FALL - Max Romeo
3. MR. POPCORN - Laurel Aitken 4. THROW ME CORN - Winston Shan
5. BUMPER TO BUMPER - Eric Barnet 6. MAY BE THE NEXT TIME - Pat Rhoden
7. WHO YOU GONNA RUN TO - The Techniques 8. CHARIOT COMING - The Viceroys

Notable outings on the album come from **Shock Of Might** by Dave Barker. The record needs no introduction, released on Punch PH-25. The A side was actually Set Me Free with the B side the well known Hit Me Back, also released on Trojan's Upsetter label which only credits Upsetters. **Girl What You Doing To Me** by Owen Gray was another dynamic sound living up to the album title, the single released on Camel CA-25 in 1969. **Guilty** by Tiger needs little introduction, another classic release from the Camel stable, produced by Laurel Aitken and according to many sources Laurel was indeed Tiger. **Seven Letters** by Derrick Morgan and **How Long Will It Take** from Pat Kelly are also stand out tracks. The Pat Kelly single sold very well but as has already been noted never charted as the sales were predominantly from non chart retailers. **Throw Me Corn** released on Bullet BU-399 in 1969 gives the full credit to Winston Shan & The Shieks, another vibrant skinhead reggae sound.

May Be The Next Time is a very melodic outing from Pat Rhoden, backed amiably by The Mohawks on Pama PM-811. **Where You Gonna Run To** has already had a mention on Reggae Hits 69 Volume 2. Produced by Winston Riley and the inaugural release on Camel CA-10. The vibrant early reggae sound is credited to The Techniques but the artist is believed to be The Shades. The album concludes with **Chariot Coming** by The Viceroys issued on Bullet BU-441 in 1970. As with some singles, including the instrumental version of Bob & Marcia's hit Young Gifted & Black on Trojan's Harry J label, the B side Stackato by Syndey Allstars, is well worth a spin. The record produced by Sydney Crooks soon became a favourable skinhead reggae instrumental track in its own right.

All in all Sixteen Dynamic Reggae Hits really does lives up to its title!

ADULTS ONLY

15'6

Jamaican music has a long history of risqué lyrics dating back to mento and calypso times from Lord Kitchener with tracks like Dr. Kitch. Then came Prince Buster with his Big Five and Wreck A Pum Pum. But for the uninitiated there is a difference between rude reggae and the Rude Boy.

The Rude Boy emerged as ska was slowing to rocksteady. Jamaica was in turmoil after independence and social behaviour declined. Young men moved in droves from the country to seek fame and fortune in Kingston but there was no milk and honey as violence was prevalent - Dem a loot - Dem a shoot - Dem a wail A Shanty Town - The lyrics in the music reflected what was happening as Jamaica was embroiled with poverty, violence and political unrest. The term Rude Boy was derived from the Jamaican slang for mischievous or obscene at about the same time a youth culture revolution was taking place in the UK.

Where did it all begin? Well we need to go back to the early 60s, a time before the hippie movement when the British youths were divided into primarily two groups based on their musical tastes. The mods had formed an allegiance to R&B and British rock bands like The Who and Small Faces; perhaps most significantly they had taken to Jamaican ska. The mods rode scooters and had a tendency toward dressing well. Their rivals the rockers had far more progressive musical taste, rode motorcycles and wore leather jackets.

When the psychedelic 60s hit Britain the mods split into a wide variety of fashions and styles including hippies and the skinhead. This period is where the style of the skinhead was first defined. Skinhead fashion was intended to show a pride in the traditional English working-class look. The hard mod's couldn't empathise with the hippie attitude and style so got harder, and with a little influence from the Jamaican Rude Boys the traditional skinhead was born.

The hair was cropped but not shaven. The dress code included a Ben Sherman shirt or Fred Perry polo with half mast Levi jeans held up with braces about a half inch wide and crossed at the back. The appearance was complete with a pair of boots. Dr. Martens became the preference with the eight-eyelet Cherry Red, known as the 1460 so named as they entered production on 1 April 1960. The Dr. Martens air filled soles were invented by a German doctor, Klaus Martens, in 1947. In 1960 the Griggs company acquired a license to manufacture the air cushioned footwear in the UK, introducing for the first time the distinctive yellow welt stitch, a two-tone grooved sole edge and the unique sole pattern.

The original skinhead was influenced by Jamaican music and the Rude Boy, never regarding politics or racism as central to the subculture. I recall Max Romeo just finished a boss performance at a school in Guilford to an audience of mainly white skinheads. On the way out a white man shouted something like - How you doing Mr Black - Max replies - All right Mr. White - The white guy then spat at Max which prompted the skinheads following Max to turn and beat the white man up.

Back to the rude reggae and the most influential ever has to be Max Romeo's Wet Dream, played a couple of times on Radio One courtesy of Emperor Rosko before the hierarchy got wind of the lyrics and promptly banned the record, despite Max's appeal. My mates mother threw his copy on the dustcart, but he soon got hold of a replacement. Despite its notoriety it failed to make the line-up on Pama's three risqué albums, Bang Bang Lulu from '69 - although the label and sleeve tell different - Birth Control from 1970 and Something Sweet The Lady from 1971, but please remember it's adults only next.

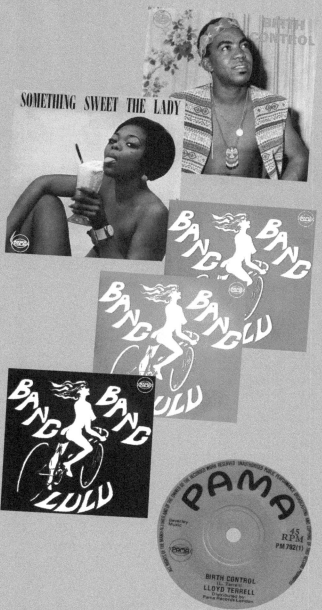

BANG BANG LULU Various artistes PAMA PMLP 4 1969

Side 1
1. BANG BANG LULU - Lloyd Tyrell 2. MR. RYAH - Lloyd Tyrell
3. MAKING LOVE - The Tartons 4. PUSH PUSH - The Termites
5. SIMPLE SIMON - Monty Morris 6. HER I COME - Lloyd Tyrell

Side 2
1. LULU RETURNS - Lloyd Tyrell 2. I LOVE YOU - Derrick Morgan
3. SOUL FOOD - Lynn Tait & The Jets 4. PUSH IT UP - The Termites
5. MONEY GIRL - Larry Marshall 6. RHYTHM HIPS - Eric Barnett

Jamaican music has a long history of risqué lyrics dating back to the days of calypso and continuing with the shift through to rocksteady and reggae where Lloyd Tyrell AKA Lloyd Charmers or Lloyd Terrell gets the album under way with **Bang Bang Lulu**, rock steady at its best with cheeky vocals released on Pama PM-710 in the spring of 1968. Track two is listed as Wet Dream but is in fact **Mr Rhya**, another offering from Lloyd Tyrell with a driving rhythm released on Nu Beat NB-023 in 1969. Devon And The Tartons are up next with **Making Love** issued as a B side on Nu Beat NB-021 the previous year, although lacking a storming instrumental rhythm. **Push Push** by the Termites gets the album back on track so to speak with a vocal inspired recording.

A look to the future will see Judge Dread rule the roost with the rude version of nursery rhymes, but here Eric 'Monty' Morris gives us a Clancy Eccles production **Simple Simon**, another Nu Beat B side issued on NB-011 in 1968 gets a good run out. Lloyd Tyrell opened side one and closes with **How Come**, or does he? the track issued on Pama PM-740 sounds very much like How You Come performed by Lee Perry And The Gaylets.

Lulu Returns opening side two with another risqué offering from Lloyd Tyrell released on Pama PM-752 in 1969. As the title suggests Lulu has returned with good vocals over a hypnotic beat. The melodic rhythm track from **I Love You** issued on Nu Beat NB-16 in 1968 by Derrick Morgan can be described as storming and one to get the DM's moving. Why? well it's the rhythm track Max Romeo utilised for his massive hit. **Soul Food** is an early Pama recording on PM-723 from Lynn Tait & The Jets with a distinctive vocal led track that takes a while for the dance floor to beckon. **Push It Up** from The Termites is another Pama recording issued on PM-729 in 1968, the number produced by Clancy Eccles has a good rock steady early reggae beat. **Money Girl** from Larry Marshall is another of the B sides to feature, issued on Nu Beat NB-022, the A side sported Max Rome's Blowing In The Wind.

The album concludes with **Rhythm Hips** from Ronald Russell, the track is another rock steady early reggae dance crasher produced by Eric Barnet and issued on Nu Beat NB-019 during 1968. If the tune sounds familiar that's because The Horse from Eric Barnett is an instrumental version and the initial release on Gas GS-100 in 1968.

BIRTH CONTROL
Various Artistes
PAMA SECO 32 1971

Side 1
1. BIRTH CONTROL - Lloyd Tyrell
2. THE PILL - Bim, Bam & Clover
3. SOCK IT ONTO I - Max Romeo
4. FEEL IT - Max Romeo
5. RAM YOU HARD - John Lennon
6. BENWOOD DICK - Laurel Aitken

Side 2
1. WINE HER GOOSIE - Max Romeo
2. SATAN GIRL - The Ethiopians
3. ADULTS ONLY - Calypso Joe
4. PUSSY PRICE - Laurel Aitken
5. CAUGHT YOU - King Stick
6. FIRE IN ME WIRE - Girlie and Laurel Aitken

ECONOMY   MONO   SECO 32

BIRTH   CONTROL

REGGAE EXPLOSION

SIDE ONE
1. BIRTH CONTROL   Lloyd Tyrell
2. THE PILL   Bim, Bam & Clover
3. SOCK IT ONTO I   Max Romeo
4. FEEL IT   Max Romeo
5. RAM YOU HARD   John Lennon
6. BEND WOOD DICK   Laurel Aitken
SIDE TWO
7. WINE HER GOOSIE   Max Romeo
8. SATAN GIRL   The Ethiopians
9. ADULTS ONLY   Calypso Joe
10. PUSSY PRICE   Laurel Aitken
11. CAUGHT YOU   King Stick
12. FIRE IN YOUR WIRE   Girlie and Laurel Aitken

REGGAE EXPLOSION

PAMA RECORDS LIMITED, 78, Craven Park Road, London, N.W.10, England

Printed in England by Wass Brothers - Printers - Limited, London, S.W.19

Rude reggae at its best always sounds vibrant, melodic and infectious and this album is no exception. First up is **Birth Control** from Lloyd Tyrell on the album but Terrell on the Pama single. Lloyd also recorded a version as Lloydie & The Lowbites for Trojan but this is by far and away the best. A vibrant rhythm track runs through **The Pill** from Bim, Bam & Clover keeping the risqué theme running. Bim & Bam started out as a comedy duo touring the hotels circuits in Jamaica. Max arrives with a jolly organ led outing declaring **Sock It Onto I**. He's back again with **Feel It** a very rhythmic track with explicit lyrics - was this the missing track twelve from the album A Dream? John Lennon is up next with **Ram You Hard** with an infectious beat and brilliant drum work. Laurel Aitken comes in with his take on the time honoured Trinidad and Tobagao song **Bendwood Dick**.

Side two opens with Max's **Wine Her Goosie** follwed by The Ethiopians **Satan Girl**, a good dose of melodic vocals and a chugging reggae beat. A dash of updated calypso comes from Calypso Joe with **Adults Only**. Laurel is back with a more boss sound on **Pussy Price** in his inimitable style. The penultimate offering comes from King Stick according the sleeve with **Caught You** and Girlie & Laurel complete proceedings with **Fire In Me Wire**.

SOMETHING SWEET THE LADY Various Artistes PAMA PMP 2003 1971

PAMA/MEDIUM   MONO   PMP 2003

SOMETHING SWEET THE LADY
VARIOUS ARTISTES

Side 1
1. SOMETHING SWEET THE LADY - Dora King And Joe Marks
2. NICE GRIND - Rebels
3. IT DON'T SWEET ME - Laurel Aitken
4. BIG HEAD WALKING STICK - Bim And Clover
5. MY DICKIE - Derrick Morgan
6. WHERE IT SORE - King Stitt

Side 2
1. YOU RUN COME - Little Roy
2. EXPOSURE - Lloyd Tyrell
3. FISH IN A POT - Max Romeo
4. WOMAN A LOVE IN A NIGHTTIME - Gloria's All Stars
5. WINEY WINEY FOR 10 CENTS - Soul Tones
6. BLUES DANCE - Girlie And Laurel

A PAMA GROUP RECORD PRODUCTION

Distributed by: PAMA RECORDS 78 CRAVEN PARK ROAD LONDON NW10 ENGLAND

The album gets under-way with an x rated **Something Sweet The Lady** voiced over an infectious beat. A Syndey Crooks production is up next, **Nice Grind**, another very vocal led number that only runs for just over a minute and a half. Laurel is next with a talkative **It Don't Sweet Me**. Bim and Clover have a jolly outing with **Big Head Walking Stick.** Derrick Morgan who refused to voice Wet Dream comes in with **My Dickie** although the Crab single credited The Commentator. **Where It Sore** is a horns cut of Count Sticky's Musical Bop issued on Bullet and is in fact Count Sticky at the mike.

Side two continues the X rated theme with **You Run Come** from Little Roy with a pulsating beat. A boss tune from Lloyd Tyrell is up next with **Exposure** AKA Birth Control with subtle changes. Max had to feature, this time with **Fish In A Pot**. **Woman A Love In A Nighttime** was issued on Escort ERT-839 with the calypso track credited to Lord Spoon and David, although it was produced by Alvin Ranglin. Another jolly tune is delivered this time from Soul Tones with **Winey Winey For 10 Cents.** The album concludes in Laurel Aitken style with **Blues Dance** accompanied by Girlie.

FROM JAMAICA

REGGAE TO UK WITH LOVE
Various Artistes
PAMA PSP 1004 1970

Side 1
1. LIVE ONLY FOR LOVE -
The Progressions
2. SUMMERTIME ROCK -
The Progressions
3. SOLONG, FAREWELL -
Frederick McClean
4. SUNNY SUNDAY MORNING -
Frederick McClean
5. ALL I NEED IS LOVE -
Barry Anthony
6. LOVE YOU MOST OF ALL -
The Emotions

Side 2
1. THIS OLD HOUSE -
The Emotions
2. FAIR DEAL -
The Progressions
3. ARE YOU READY -
The Progressions
4. TEARS WON'T HELP -
Frederick McClean
5. AIN'T THAT CRUDE -
The Progressions
6. THE DUM DUM SONG -
The Progressions

The album sleeve carries a delightful story.

Orchestra conducted by Ranny Williams

PAMA SPECIAL
(AIRBOURNE SERIES)

PSP 1004
(NBP 1001)

REGGAE TO THE UK WITH LOVE
VARIOUS ARTISTES

Dear Brother,

 I am sitting on de beach, the sun high and yellow, the sea blue calm and deep. I have every reason to be happy, so I let my mind wonder, why not, in these happy conditions its bound to settle on some happy spot. So my mind follows a course of its own. I see myself in THIS OLD HOUSE you now call home. The skies outside is grey, not a trace of white or yellow. The sun has long dispelled from de skies, but the world didn't suddenly turn grey. No, the grey followed the fog that had followed the snow. "In short my loved one my mind sees you in the U.K. But as if seas and miles were nothing but a narrow road. I see you walk out of your door on this same SUNDAY MORNING, and like always you shout back to us ARE YOU READY? Yes ready to join the folks on the road doing the SUMMERTIME ROCK.

 You remember how we used to dance in the streets. That was the one time when old and young were one. Yes, stimulated by THE DUM DUM SONG the old would drop their walking sticks, the ill would forget their pains. The grumpy forgot to complain, the toddlers find strength to stand and all would leave their houses for the streets. The love that flowed in this one big family make the sweetest music ever. Then on Mondays, Papa would bring cane back from the plantation. I remember how you'd cry when you felt you weren't getting a FAIR DEAL in the sharing out. I can still see Mama and hear her saying derr words "Chill" TEARS WON'T HELP YOU. By Tuesday you were friends again and we'd spend the week pestering Mama into sickness with our mischief. But we had to make her better by Sunday we'd offer to get a doctor. You remember how she'd say I don't need no medicine, ALL I NEED IS LOVE and quiet. Yes and we'd be quiet until Sundays dancing was done.

 You remember How we did learn all the special bad words to talk, that night when Grandma did near on skin you with her Tambrin Switch when we did use one of those words on her. How she got mad saying de word and asking Grandpa well AIN'T THAT CRUDE? In my day we now know dis kinda word. Next day we were back with Papa. The hills were not a big enough adventure for you, so you hit the streets in a another way. You headed for Kingston 'n the Ships, and again on SUNNY SUNDAY MORNING we all came out into the streets to say goodbye. Yes this time Grandma picked up her walking stick an' came out into the road not to dance but to walk to the ship. How she can mek her granchil go without some last words.

 You remember how she said SOLONG FAREWELL my chil' and remember LIVE ONLY TO LOVE let that be your guide. Yes my brother then you were gone. How when I think of the snowballs, the cane or the mangoes I think of you. When the sun shines or when the clouds burst in the rays an' in the drops I see you. Is true how the people dem say you don't fee the true value of things till it gone. So even though I got a big family here I find each day that I LOVE YOU MOST OF ALL though you're so far away. You've been away so long now all these things seem like a dream. If I could I'd bring them all back again. I'd sing and we'd dance in the street no matter where. In de music shall be de love of one big family and in your dance shall be JAMAICA. No, the water and the miles will be no obstacle to our love. The sea will transport it. The sun radiate it and the clouds will picture it. And so, with it burnin' in our hearts like fire I shall always feel it and remember you. So our message expressed come across by "REGGAE TO THE UK WITH LOVE."

Your loving sister
Jennifer Brow

RONNIE WILLIAMS conducted the musicians
PAMA RECORDS presents: "REGGAE TO THE U.K. WITH LOVE" - A Noel Brown *Production*
Recordings supervised and produced by Timmy George *Cover design and artwork by* Jennifer Brown

Distributed By:-

PAMA RECORDS LIMITED 78, Craven Park Road, London, N.W.10, England

Published By: **AIRBOURNE MUSIC LIMITED** *and* **BEVERLEY MUSIC LIMITED**

SKA - SKA - SKA FROM JAMAICA   PAMA (Netherlands) 1969

Side 1
1. DREAM - Max Romeo 2. HOW LONG WILL IT TAKE - Pat Kelley
3. I LOVE YOU - Derrick Morgan 4. PUSH IT UP - The Termites
5. SOUL FOOD - Lynn Tait and the Jets
6. FIDDLESTICKS - Tommy McCook and his Orchestra
7. BANG BANG LULU - Lloyd Terrel

Side 2
1. WORRIES A YARD - The Versatiles 2. THE FIGHT - Clancy Eccles
3. THE HORSE - Eric Barnett 4. HEY BOY, HEY GIRL - Derrick & Patsy
5. RESCUE ME - The Reggae Girls 6. WHAT AM I TO DO - Tony Scott
7. JUST ONCE IN MY LIFE - Earnest Wilson and Freddy

Ska Ska Ska from Jamaica - So the title goes - although it's Boss Reggae
at its best. An unusual inclusion as it was issued in the Netherlands where
as the first track confirms Max Romeo's Wet Dream was known only as
Dream after censorship of early pressings.

The album came with a refreshingly informative list of musicians.

DERRICK HARRIOTT SINGS JAMAICA REGGAE   PAMA SECO 13 1969

ECONOMY   STEREO   ECO13

the sensational
DERRICK HARRIOTT
SINGS
JAMAICAN REGGAE

Side 1
1. SITTING ON TOP 2. BEEN SO LONG 3. CLOSE TO ME
4. LONG TIME 5. STANDING IN

Side 2
1. HAVE SOME MERCY 2. THE GIRL'S ALRIGHT 3. YOU REALLY GOT A HOLD ON ME
4. I'M NOT BEGGING 5. IT'S ALRIGHT

RHYTHM INSTRUMENTS
GUITARS - HUX BROWN, KEN LAZARUS, E SMITH
BASS - C JACKSON / ORGAN - WINSTON WRIGHT
PIANO - GLADY / DRUMS - TONY BENNETT
AFRO DRUMS - LES & HERMAN

OTHER INSTRUMENTS
TRUMPETS - BOBBY ELLIS, N BENNETT, S FRANCIS
TROMBONE - HANSEL SMITH / TENOR SAX - VAL BENNETT
ALTO SAX - KARL BRYAN
MUSICAL ARRANGEMENTS - BOBBY ELLIS & BORIS GARDINER

THE SENSATIONAL DERRICK HARRIOTT SINGS JAMAICA REGGAE, another great L.P. produced by singer - composer - DERRICK HARRIOTT.

Derrick who is still rated as one of Jamaica's top singers having been in the music industry for 12 years plus was bejewelled with four hit records for 1968 and is showing signs of greater achievements by the end of '70. Frankly '70 is expected to be the biggest year in Derrick's career, and if growing proof is needed - well just you take enough time and give a good lesson to his L.P. and you will end up agreeing with me one hundred per cent.

The artist has done a lot to enhance music and rightly deserves every credit he receives. In England the West Indian islands, and other parts of the world, fans of DERRICK HARRIOTT will be pleased to have another great production by the singer - THE SENSATIONAL DERRICK HARRIOTT SINGS JAMAICA REGGAE - and the best to date. - Jackie Estick

PRODUCTION AND SUPERVISION: DERRICK HARRIOTT
RECORDING ENGINEER: BUDDY DAVIDSON

 Distributed by:- PAMA RECORDS LIMITED 78 Craven Park Road London N.W.10 England

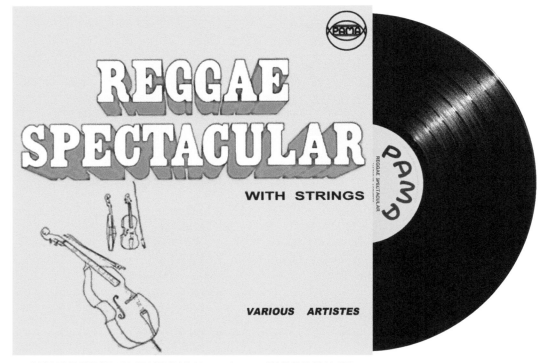

REGGAE SPECTACULAR WITH STRINGS Various Artistes PAMA PMP 2001 1971

Side 1	Side 2
1. MAY BE THE NEXT TIME - Pat Rhoden 2. I WISH I WAS AN APPLE - Derrick Morgan	1. SOMETHING ON MY MIND - Erol Dixon
3. SUGAR DUMPLING - Owen Gray 4. SWEETER THAN HONEY - Norman T. Washington	2. TAKE BACK YOUR NICKLET - Ferdinand And Dill
5. HERE IS MY HEART - Winston Groovy	3. I'LL NEVER LOVE ANOTHER - Laurel Aitken 4. I'LL DO IT - Derrick And Paulette
6. DON'T LET HER TAKE YOUR LOVE FROM ME - The Marvels	5. FIDDLESTICKS - Tommy McKenzie 6. FOR ONCE IN MY LIFE - Slim Smith

PAMA/MEDIUM   STEREO   PMP 2001

REGGAE SPECTACULAR
WITH STRINGS

VARIOUS ARTISTES

This is the very first album of its kind in the world, a full twelve track reggae album in full stereo with accompaniment of a full stringed orchestra.

Reggae has really come into its own this time, and if ever an album was bound for the charts, this is one with all those fine arrangements for violin and cello work by the finest string orchestra in the land.

Whilst singing the praises of the string work let's not forget to give praise also, where well due, to the Artistes on this Album, so beginning at track one, side one, we have one of the most beautiful of Reggae numbers ever performed. This is by a newcomer to the powerful world of Pama Studios, Mr Pat Rhoden. the song "May Be The Next Time" is penned by himself and performed to a tee, ably supported by the smoothest of Reggae backing I have heard. Derrick Morgan follows with one of his great hits "I Wish I Was An Apple". Again very well performed and musical backing fantastic. Owen Gray's "Sugar Dumpling" is as sweet as the title with Choral backing and a driving Reggae beat. "Sweeter Than Honey" is offered by great soul singer Norman T. Washington in his usual easy going style and Winston Groovy grooves with a Laurel Aitken production "Here Is My Heart". The Marvels sing one of their many Hits, "Don't Let Her Take Your Love From Me" to a Tamla type backing from Pama's "Mohawks".

Side two kicks off with Erol Dixon singing "Something On My Mind" followed by Ferdinand and Dill performing their Hit song "Take Back Your Nicklet", a great comedy duo, great fun and a great dancing beat. A stringed Reggae L.P. could not be complete without offering Laurel Aitken's "I'll Never Love Another" as this was the very first of the Reggae records with strings added. Derrick Morgan once again, this time with his girlie partner Paulette, singing "I'll Do It", next comes "Fiddlesticks", a brilliant piece of fiddle work, done to Reggae by Tommy McKenzie and his Orchestra. Last but not least, "For Once In My Life" with Slim Smith, a very good song, very well done and quite pleasing to the ear.

So all in all I am sure you are bound to agree that this is indeed a "REGGAE SPECTACULAR".

Rick Delano

A PAMA GROUP RECORD PRODUCTION

PAMA RECORDS 78 CRAVEN PARK ROAD LONDON NW10 ENGLAND

AFRICAN MELODY   Various Artistes   PAMA PMP 2004 1971

Side 1
1. AFRICAN MELODY - G.G. All Stars
2. MAN FROM CAROLINA - G.G. All Stars
3. STAND FOR YOUR RIGHT - Lloyd Tyrell
4. WARRIOR - The Sensations
5. GAMES PEOPLE PLAY - Winston Francis
6. OH ME OH MY - Lloyd Tyrell

Side 2
1. IMMIGRANT'S PLIGHT - Bim, Bam And Clover
2. FREEDOM STREET - Fitzroy Sterling
3. SALAAM - Charles Organaire
4. RETURN OF HERBERT SPLIFINGTON - Rupie & Sidy
5. LOOK WHO A BUST STYLE - The Mediators
6. BLESSED ARE THE MEEK - Slim Smith

PAMA RECORDS LIMITED 78 Craven Park Road London N.W.10 England

ESCORT
ERT-835 African Melody - GG Allstars 1970
C/W **Man From Carolina**
Produced by: Alvin Ranglin

SUCCESS
RE-910 Return Of Herbert Splifinton - Rupie And Sidy 1970
Produced by: Rupie Edwards

SUCCESS
RE-901 Look Who A Bust Style - The Mediators 1969
Produced by: Rupie Edwards

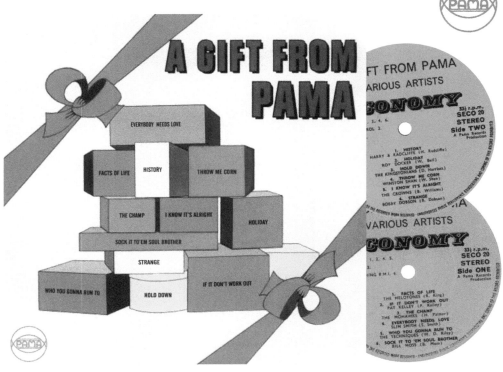

A GIFT FROM PAMA Various Artistes   PAMA SECO 20 1969

Side 1
1. FACTS OF LIFE - The Mellotones 2. IF IT DON'T WORK OUT - Pat Kelly
3. THE CHAMP - The Mohawks 4. EVERYBODY NEEDS LOVE - Slim Smith
5. WHO YOU GONNA RUN TO - The Techniques 6. SOCK IT TO'EM SOUL BROTHER - Bill Moss

Side 2
1. HISTORY - Harry & Radcliffe 2. HOLIDAY - Roy Docker
3. HOLD DOWN - The Kingstonians 4. THROW ME CORN - Winston Shan
5. I KNOW IT'S ALRIGHT - The Crowns 6. STRANGE - Dobby Dobson

A Gift from Pama was only 14/6 but came without the traditional Pama notes.

A Gift From Pama kicks off with **Facts Of Life** a boss sound issued on Camel CA-18 with a driving rhythm from The Mellotones and would guarantee to keep you on the dance - floor. Second up is another driving rhythm this time from the soulful Pat Kelly **If It Don't Work Out** released on the Gas label and featured on his 1969 album Pat Kelly Sings PMLP 12. The Mohawks come in with The Champ, the most sampled record of all time. The original version was released on the main Pama imprint - blue label - with the hint of early reggae version issued on Pama Supreme.

Passion and love fills Slim Smiths falsetto led vocal of **Everybody Needs Love**. The single was issued on Unity and the title of his 1970 Pama album ECO 9. Slim is back again this time with The Techniques asking the question **Where You Gonna Run To**, a true boss tune - you won't be able to keep your feet still - backed with melodic vocals. The single was issued on Camel CA-10 in 1969. A soul number is next from Bill Moss, **Sock It To' Em** another issued on the blue Pama label at the time when both reggae and Soul was being promoted by Pama.

The skinhead reggae is back with **History** from Harry And Radcliff, a driving beat backing a vocal cover of the classic Wonderful World. Roy Docker deliver another Pama soul number with **Holiday** issued on the Pama blue label. You can get your boots on again as The Kingstonians come in with their rocking vibrant reggae sound on **Hold Down** issued on Crab CRAB-19. Winston Shan's **Throw Me Corn** featured on Bullet Greatest Hits and Reggae '69 Volume 2 maintains the boss driving sound. The pace slows down a litttle with a soul number produced by Harry Palmer from The Crowns **I Know It's Alright**.

The Gift From Pama concludes with Dobby Dobson - a voice described as being as warm as the Caribbean sun - with **Strange** an up-tempo number issued on Punch and the title of his Pama album issued on SECO 33. The Gift From Pama was a mix of vibrant boss reggae and a few soul numbers, a rare combination but reflected the output from Pama at the time, after all it was a gift at 14/6.

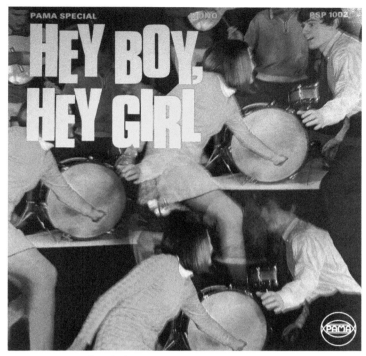

HEY BOY, HEY GIRL   Various Artistes   PAMA PSP 1002 1969

PAMA SPECIAL   MONO   PSP 1002

HEY BOY, HEY GIRL
VARIOUS ARTISTES

When it comes to Music, the half has not yet been told and when it comes to party music - well this album has a lot to say. HEY BOY, HEY GIRL get on the floor and let's have some fun. Just dig those cats on the front cover actually dancing to the tune entitled HEY BOY - HEY GIRL sung by our own Derrick & Patsy. See! they are enjoying themselves in no uncertain way, so why not join in and grab a piece of the action from this pleasure packed album. The title tune has been a HIT HIT HIT all over the world and here again it's HIT HIT HIT for HEY BOY, HEY GIRL, this time in album form. Apart from the title track, each of the other eleven tracks are designed to give the fullest amount of enjoyment to each and every proud owner and all who plays it. As one of the other Hit tracks says "If Music be the food of love" PLAY ON.

Harry Dee

Side 1
1. HEY BOY - HEY GIRL - Derrick & Patsy 2. YOU'VE LOST YOUR DATE - Flames
3. GIVE IT TO ME - Stranger Cole 4. ANOTHER HEARTACHE - Winston Sinclair
5. GIVE YOU MY HEART - Derrick & Patsy 6. BLOWING IN THE WIND - Max Romeo

A PAMA GROUP RECORD PRODUCTION

Side 2
1. I'LL DO IT - Derrick & Patsy 2. RING OF GOLD - Melodians
3. COME ON LITTLE GIRL - Winston Sinclair 4. SIMPLE SIMON - Monty Morris
5. MUSIC BE THE FOOD OF LOVE - Derrick Morgan 6. CHOO CHOO TRAIN - Soul Cats

Distributed by:- **PAMA RECORDS LIMITED**, 78 CRAVEN PARK ROAD LONDON NW10

The boss album gets under way with an early Nu-Beat tune from Derrick & Patsy coming in with the title track **Hey Boy, Hey Girl**. Derrick is of course Derrick Morgan and on this occasion Patsy is Patsy Todd. The Flames keep the party moving along with another Nu-Beat release boasting a driving beat on **You Have Lost Your Date**. Stranger Cole preferred performing as a duet but this time he comes up trumps on his own with **Give It To Me** issued on the Camel label. Next up is another Nu-Beat release this time a vibrant offering from Winston Sinclair with **Another Heartache**.

Derrick & Patsy are back this time he's singing with Paulette Williams. But whoever it is it's a boss tune asking to **Give Me Your Heart**. Max Romeo concludes side one with his inimitable style easily recognisable on his cover of **Blowing In The Wind**, another release on Nu- Beat and a cut of Lester Sterling's instrumental Reggie In The Wind.

Side two sees the return of Derrick & Patsy with **I'll Do It** issued as the B side to Give Me Your Heart which credits Paulette. No doubting it's Trevor McNaughton, Brent Dowe and Tony Brevett AKA The Melodians keeping the party mood going with their vocal led **Ring Of Gold** issued on Gas, a good boss sound. Winston Sinclair is back with **Come On Little Girl** issued as the B side to Another Heartache. The tracks were produced by Winston and Gregory Isaacs and some deem it's Gregory Isaacs on vocals. The nursery rhyme had been prevalent in Jamaican singles way before Judge Dread came up with his rude version and here Eric 'Monty' Morris talks us through some with a good early chugging reggae beat. One character he encounters along the way is **Simple Simon**. Derrick Morgan is back this time going solo on **Music Be The Food Of Love** from 1968. The album comes to an end with a chugging sound from Soul Cats with **Choo Choo Train**. The single Cho Cho Train was issued on Gas and featured on the Greatest Hits album. All in all a first rate early album for Pama.

REGGAE TO REGGAE   Various Artistes   PAMA PMP 2012 1972

PAMA/MEDIUM   STEREO   PMP 2012
                                    (Electronically Rebalanced)

REGGAE TO REGGAE
VARIOUS ARTISTES

Side 1
1. LIVELY UP YOURSELF - Bob Marley & The Wailers 2. JAMAICAN GIRL - Roy Shirley
3. SEND ME SOME LOVING - Slim Smith 4. YOU DON'T CARE FOR ME - Lloyd Sparkes
5. I WANT TO GO BACK HOME - The Groovers 6. THIS TROPICAL LAND - The Melodians
7. BEAT DOWN BABYLON - Junior Byles

Side 2
1. BLACK CINDERELLA - Errol Dunkley 2. BUTTER AND BREAD - Lloyd Young
3. SCREW FACE - Bob Marley & The Wailers 4. SOLID AS A ROCK - Rupie Edwards
5. MY ONLY LOVE - Gregory Isaacs 6. HIGH SCHOOL SERENADE - Lennox Brown
7. PUBLIC ENEMY NUMBER 1 - Max Romeo

A PAMA GROUP RECORD PRODUCTION

DISTRIBUTED BY
PAMA RECORDS LIMITED, 78 CRAVEN PARK ROAD LONDON NW10 4AE

Reggae To Reggae was issued in 1972 at a time when the boss sounds have eased but there are still a few gems in this release, some well known, others maybe underrated. **Butter And Bread** is probably in the latter, Lloyd Young toasting over Max Romeo's Ginal Ship rhythm, issued on Bullet in 1972, and it works well. The melodic Melodians deliver another first class Bullet issue with **This Tropical Land**. Lloyd Sparks - AKA Parks - falsetto voice negotiates a Pama release of **You Don't Care For Me**, originally recorded by The Techniques in 1967.

When Pat Kelly left The Techniques Lloyd took a stint with the group. Max Romeo's **Public Enemy Number 1** issued on Camel is a trade mark of his reinvented character. The Rasta theme runs through a vibrant offering from Junior Byles, a founding member of The Versatiles, on **Beat Down Babylon** issued on Bullet and credited to Junior in 1972.

REGGAE HIT THE TOWN   Various Artistes   PAMA PTP 1001 1975

PAMA MEDIUM

PTP 1001
COMPATIBLE STEREO

REGGAE HIT THE TOWN
VARIOUS ARTISTES

Side 1
1. SINNERS WHERE ARE YOU GOING TO HIDE - Justin Hinds
2. CAN'T YOU UNDERSTAND - Larry Marshall 3. DARLING IS YOU - Bill Gentles
4. IF IT'S LOVE YOU NEED - Justin Hinds
5. SING ABOUT LOVE - Pat Kelly
6. YOU LIE - Larry Marshall

Side 2
1. CAR POUND - Bill Gentles 2. JUST LIKE A WOMAN - Pat Kelly
3. NEVER STOP LOVING YOU - Derrick Morgan
4. BEAT THEM JAH JAH - The Twinkle Brothers
5. EDUCATION ROCK - Junior Byles
6. COME WHAT MAY - Fermena

A PAMA GROUP RECORD PRODUCTION

PAMA RECORDS LIMITED, 78 CRAVEN PARK ROAD LONDON NW10 4AE

THIS L.P. IS ALSO AVAILABLE IN CASSETTE AND CARTRIDGE.

Almost three years had elapsed since the last Pama album was released then Reggae Hit The Town came along, curiously missing The Ethiopians celebrated track from 1968. It was a short revival as this was the last issued under the Pama moniker. Things had moved on as the sleeve notes mention the L.P. is also available as a cassette. The opening track is from a veteran of the ska and rocksteady scene Justin Hinds with **Sinners Where Are You Going To Hide** issued on Pama second Series PM-4001 in 1975 and a trip back to the boss years with an overdub of strings. Track two comes from Larry Marshall the man who started the shift to reggae - Larry & Alvin - with their tune Nanny Goat way back in October '68 comes in with **Can't You Understand** issued on Ocean Second Series OC-004. Bill Gentles is up next with a sweetened strings medley version of Stranger Cole's Our High School Dance with his **Darling It's You** issued on Pama PM-4002. The boss sounds have returned with a cracking infectious beat and superb vocals from Justin Hinds with **If Its Love You Need** issued as the B side to Sinners. Pat Kelly comes next with a track **Sing About Love** and side one concludes with **You Lie** from Larry Marshall.

Side two kicks off with another B side this time **Car Pound** from Bill Gentles with a driving beat. Next up comes Pat Kelly with **Just Like A Woman** followed by Derrick Morgan with **Never Stop Loving You**, not the boss reggae we fell in love with from the man who was doing the Moon Hop, but it's now 1975. The Twinkle Brothers are next with a rootsy sound, **Beat Them Jah Jah**. The Penultimate offering comes from Junior Byles with **Education Rock,** a boss tune dating from 1973 issued on Pama PM-878. The final track comes from Fermena (Edwards) with **Come What May** a Ranny Williams production from 1972. The track is a cover of the English version of the Eurovision song Contest winner.

As there was little competition for reggae compilation albums at the time Reggae Hit The Town is said to have sold well.

The last two 45s issued on Pama in 1975 feature on the album.

SOUL ON PAMA

LITTLE BEVERLEY SIMMONS PAYS TRIBUTE TO OTIS REDDING   PAMA PMLP 1 1968

PAMA SPECIAL   STEREO   PMLP 9

REMEMBER OTIS

by Beverley Simmons

Side1	Side 2
1. MR.PITFUL 2. THESES ARMS OF MINE 3. RESPECT	1. DOWN IN THE VALLEY 2. THAT'S HOW STRONG MY LOVE IS
4. I'VE BEEN LOVING YOU TOO LONG (TO STOP NOW)	3. PAIN IN MY HEART 4. MY GIRL
5. OLE MAN TROUBLE 6. SATISFACTION	5. MY LOVERS PRAYER 6. FA FA FA (SAD SONG)

OTIS REDDING the Legendary Soul Singer who died in December 1967 has inspired countless numbers of people during his short lifetime and still today he goes on giving thrills to many and will do until the end of time. Therefore it seems only right as a Soul loving company that we (PAMA) should pay our tribute to the Great King of Soul by issuing the remembrance album in his honour.

As I said above, Otis will never be forgotten especially as people like the Emperor Rosko the great radio D.J. and many others has from time to time devoted as much as their hour long programme to this great Artistes songs and works.

It is only too sad that when we listen to his voice on the radio or on records that we have to reflect he died so tragically on that cold December morning, when his private aircraft plunged into deep icy waters affording only one survivor, which unfortunately for the soul-loving world was not the Great Master of Soul himself.

However do join with me in saying Rest in Peace dear Otis and thanks to people like MISS BEVERLEY SIMMONS who has done her part in the Remember Otis campaign, by recording this very fine album of some of the songs made famous by the late great Mr. Redding.

One would scarcely hope to find recordings of this high quality on a budget priced album. However as a gesture of respect to Otis we would not attempt to sell this album at the same price as his own recordings although the standard of this recording is in every way as good as Otis (the vocal work being performed by a delightful member of the opposite sex). So you are in luck - and for only a few shillings you can surely afford this luxury, in Remembrance of OTIS REDDING.

HARRY PALMER

Musical arrangements and production - by Palmer Brothers, London, England

Distributed by:- PAMA RECORDS LIMITED, 78 Craven Park Road, London N.W.10 England

There were two pressings of the album. PMLP 1 (shown above) and a black sleeve cover re-issued on PMLP 9 in 1969, Remember Otis. The sleeve notes on PMLP 9 were written by Harry Palmer and are appropriately included above.

Harry Palmer visited Jamaica to set up licensing deals with producers and came across Beverley Simmons. Otis Redding had passed in late '67 and Harry made arrangements for her to come to England to record an album of Otis Redding songs. The idea was that with a female singer it wouldn't be a straight cover of the great man's songs but as a tribute.

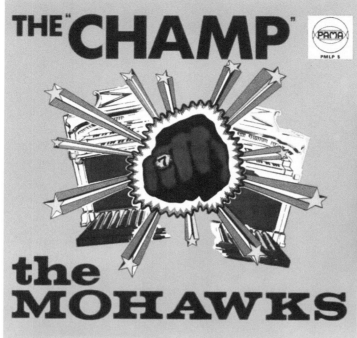

THE CHAMP THE MOHAWKS PAMA PMLP 5 1969

Side 1
1. THE CHAMP 2. HIP JIGGER 3. SWEET SOUL MUSIC
4. DR.JEKYLL & HYDE PARK 5. SENIOR THUMP 6. LANDSCAPE

Side 2
1. BABY HOLD ON 2. FUNKY BROADWAY 3. ROCKY MOUNTAIN ROUNDABOUT
4. SOUND OF THE WITCHDOCTORS 5. BEAT ME 'TILL I'M BLUE 6. CAN YOU HEAR ME

The Mohawks were the only soul group that tasted any real success from the many home grown talents Pama had produced. It was their first release The Champ that spurned the success with an album of the same title following. The track was an instrumental Hammond Organ led cover of Otis Redding's The Tramp. The group was fronted by Alan Hawkshaw who was already a veteran session player of the music scene going back to the mid 50's and played organ on several pop and soul hits during the 60's. He left the group in 1969. The group continued in various guises including recruiting Graham Hawke (Hesketh) a Jamaican keyboard player.

PM-719 The Champ - The Mohawks 1968 (Soul)
Produced by: Alan Hawkshaw - Jeff Palmer

Pama released over fifty soul records on the PM prefix issued on a blue label. The most relevant by far was The Champ from The Mohawks, who were a session group led by Alan Hawkshaw, issued on PM-719 in 1968, a record that has been sampled over 700 times.

At the time of launch it was described as the best ever soul instrumental, however despite the track selling well and receiving air-play it failed to enter the national chart. The song is based on a 1967 song Tramp with Champ sung rather than Tramp.

SOUL SAUCE   Various Artists   PAMA PMLP 8   1969

Side 1
1. JERKING THE DOG - The Crowns
2. FEEL GOOD ALL OVER - Betty Lovette
3. THE GOOD OL' DAYS - Bobby Patterson And The Mustangs
4. OH BABE - The Milwaukee Coasters
5. TIP TOE - Norman T. Wsahington
6. BABY HOLD ON - The Mohawks

Side 2
1. DR. GOLDGOOT AND HIS BIKINI MACHINE - The Beas
2. SAME THING ALL OVER - Norman T. Washington
3. SOUL MAN - Reco Rodriguez
4. I AM AN OUTCAST - Ray Docker
5. WHAT A GUY - Beverley Simmons
6. BROADWAY AIN'T FUNKY NO MORE - Bobby Patterson And The Mustangs

THE CROWNS   MADE OF GOLD   PAMA PMLP 6   1969

Side 1
1. MELLOW MOONLIGHT
2. I SURRENDER
3. LET'S GO BABY
4. MR. SUCCESS
5. MY BABY JUST CARES FOR ME
6. JERKING THE DOG

Side 2
1. SHE AIN'T GONNA DO RIGHT
2. I KNOW IT'S ALRIGHT
3. I'M SO PROUD
4. WOULD I LOVE YOU?
5. I NEED YOUR LOVING
6. KEEP ME GOING

A Palmer Brothers Production

CONCLUSION

Andy & Joey sang in 1964 You're Wondering Now What To Do. Well why not replace all those dubious quality Pama downloads from the past decade or so with high quality audio and enjoy them once again, or even maybe for the first time as Harry, Jeff and Carl had intended over half a century ago. At the time Trojan were repeatedly hitting the charts with strings and things but the raw sounds were still coming from a family company not far away issuing the authentic reggae coming from Jamaica, Pama never hit the same heights as its near neighbour but released an incredible output now among the most desirable and collectable vinyl from just a small window of time.

I was going to end with my favourite dozen Pama tunes but it's an impossible task as when you think you have it sorted another finds its way in, so as the man said there's only enough room for a dozen.

In case you're still wondering about SECO 1 and SECO 5 here they are.

INDEX

INDEX

INDEX

Lightning Source UK Ltd.
Milton Keynes UK
UKHW052346271022
411135UK00003B/135